Previous Years'

SOLVED PAPERS
(2007-2009, 2011, 2013-2018)

Computer Science

Includes
3 Practice Papers

G K Publications (P) Ltd

CL MEDIA (P) LTD.

Edition : 2018

© PUBLISHER

No part of this book may be reproduced in a retrieval system or transmitted, in any form or by any means, electronics, mechanical, photocopying, recording, scanning and or without the written permission of the publisher.

ISBN : **978-93-88426-0-84**

Typeset by : *CL Media DTP Unit*

Administrative and Production Offices

Published by : **CL Media (P) Ltd.**
A-41, Lower Ground Floor,
Espire Building,
Mohan Cooperative Industrial Area,
Main Mathura Road,
New Delhi - 110044

Marketed by : **G.K. Publications (P) Ltd.**
A-41, Lower Ground Floor,
Espire Building,
Mohan Cooperative Industrial Area,
Main Mathura Road,
New Delhi - 110044

For product information :
Visit *www.gkpublications.com* or email to *gkp@gkpublications.com*

PREFACE

Indian Space Research Organization (ISRO) is India's premier space agency for pursuing astronomy and planetary exploration while harnessing space technology for nation building. The esteemed organization recruits Computer Science professionals through online exam conducted annually in the Scientists and Engineers category. ISRO has always been preferred by computer science engineers for its highly rewarding and challenging job profile. For serious aspirants, practicing with previous year questions is essential to ace this prestigious exam.

In order to help students test their knowledge, GK Publications has come up with Solved Papers of last 9 years for Computer Science stream. The book covers all questions asked in the exams conducted from 2007-2009, 2011, 2013-2018. The book emphasizes on helping students get well-versed with exam pattern and managing their time while solving questions correctly.

The book also includes 3 practice paper sets based on previous year exam pattern and this year's syllabus. Moreover, students get access to a free online mock test for getting acquainted with the actual exam environment. The questions have been prepared by a team of experts with several years of experience in competition content development for various PSUs. With time bound practice, the students will be able to ace ISRO recruitment with flying colors. While due care has been taken to keep the book error-free, we look forward to receiving constructive feedback on how to make the subsequent editions more student-friendly.

All the Best
Team GKP

CONTENTS

Solved Papers

- Solved Paper 2007 — 1 – 10
- Solved Paper 2008 — 1 – 10
- Solved Paper 2009 — 1 – 12
- Solved Paper 2011 — 1 – 11
- Solved Paper 2013 — 1 – 12
- Solved Paper 2014 — 1 – 12
- Solved Paper 2015 — 1 – 12
- Solved Paper 2016 — 1 – 12
- Solved Paper 2017 (May) — 1 – 16
- Solved Paper 2017 (December) — 1 – 15
- Solved Paper 2018 — 1 – 20

Practice Papers

- **Practice Paper 1** — 1 – 6
- **Practice Paper 2** — 1 – 6
- **Practice Paper 3** — 1 – 6

SOLVED PAPER 2007
Computer Science

1. The Boolean expression $Y = (A + \bar{B} + \bar{A}B)\bar{C}$ is given by

(a) $A\bar{C}$

(b) $B\bar{C}$

(c) $\bar{C}$

(d) AB

2. The circuit shown in the following figure realizes the function.

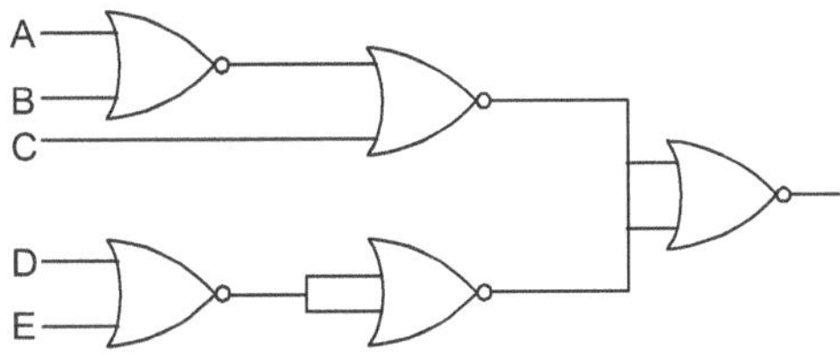

(a) $(\overline{A + B} + C)(\bar{D}\bar{E})$ (b) $(\overline{A + B} + C)(D\bar{E})$

(c) $(A + \overline{B + C})(\bar{D}E)$ (d) $(A + B + \bar{C})(\bar{D}\bar{E})$

3. The circuit shown in the given figure is a

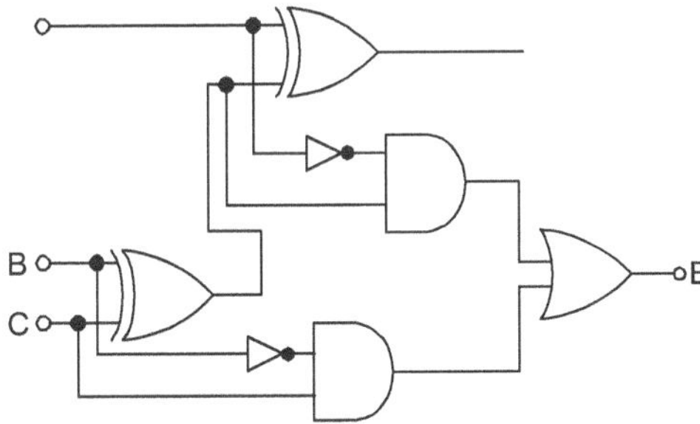

(a) full adder

(b) full subtracter

(c) shift register

(d) decade counter

4. When two numbers are added in excess-3 code and the sum is less than 9, then in order to get the correct answer it is necessary to

(a) subtract 0011 from the sum

(b) add 0011 to the sum

(c) subtract 0110 from the sum

(d) add 0110 to the sum

5. The characteristic equation of an SR flip-flop is given by

(a) $Q_{n+1} = S + RQ_n$

(b) $Q_{n+1} = R\bar{Q}_n + S\bar{Q}_n$

(c) $Q_{n+1} = \bar{S} + RQ_n$

(d) $Q_{n+1} = S + \bar{R}Q_n$

6. A graph with "n" vertices and $n - 1$ edges that is not a tree, is

(a) Connected

(b) Disconnected

(c) Euler

(d) A circuit

7. If a graph requires k different colours for its proper colouring, then the chromatic number of the graph is

(a) 1

(b) k

(c) $k - 1$

(d) $\dfrac{k}{2}$

8. A read bit can be read

(a) and written by CPU

(b) and written by peripheral

(c) by peripheral and written by CPU

(d) by CPU and written by the peripheral

9. Eigen Vectors of $\begin{bmatrix} 1 & \cos\theta \\ \cos\theta & 1 \end{bmatrix}$ are

(a) $\begin{bmatrix} a^R & 1 \\ 0 & a^n \end{bmatrix}$

(b) $\begin{bmatrix} a^n & n \\ 0 & a^n \end{bmatrix}$

(c) $\begin{bmatrix} a^n & na^{n-1} \\ 0 & a^n \end{bmatrix}$

(d) $\begin{bmatrix} a^n & na^{n-1} \\ -n & a^n \end{bmatrix}$

10. The term 'aging' refers to

(a) booting up the priority of a process in multi-level of queue without feedback.

(b) gradually increasing the priority of jobs that wait in the system for a long time to remedy infinite blocking

(c) keeping track of the following a page has been in memory for the purpose of LRU replacement

(d) letting job reside in memory for a certain amount of time so that the number of pages required can be estimated accurately.

11. Consider a set of n tasks with known runtimes $r_1, r_2, \ldots r_n$ to be run on a uniprocessor machine. Which of the following processor scheduling algorithms will result in the maximum throughput?

(a) Round Robin

(b) Shortest job first

(c) Highest response ratio next

(d) First cum first served

12. Consider a job scheduling problem with four jobs J_1, J_2, J_3 and J_4 with corresponding deadlines : $(d_1, d_2, d_3, d_4) = (4, 2, 4, 2)$.
Which of the following is not a feasible schedule without violating any job deadline?

(a) J_2, J_4, J_1, J_3

(b) J_4, J_1, J_2, J_3

(c) J_4, J_2, J_1, J_3

(d) J_4, J_2, J_3, J_1

13. By using an eight bit optical encoder the degree of resolution that can be obtained is (approximately)

(a) 1.8° (b) 3.4°

(c) 2.8° (d) 1.4°

14. The principal of the locality of reference justifies the use of

(a) virtual memory (b) interrupts

(c) main memory (d) cache memory

15. Consider the following pseudo-code

$x ; = 1;$

$i ; = 1;$

while $(x \leq 1000)$

begin

$x : = 2^x;$

$i; = i + 1;$

end;

What is the value of i at the end of the pseudo-code?

(a) 4 (b) 5

(c) 6 (d) 7

16. The five items : A, B, C, D, and E are pushed in a stack, one after other starting from A. The stack is popped four items and each element is inserted in a queue. The two elements are deleted from the queue and pushed back on the stack. Now one item is popped from the stack. The popped item is

(a) A (b) B

(c) C (d) D

17. Round Robin scheduling is essentially the pre-emptive version of

(a) FIFO

(b) Shortest job first

(c) Shortest remaining time

(d) Longest remaining time

18. The number of digit 1 present in the binary representation of $3 \times 512 + 7 \times 64 + 5 \times 8 + 3$ is

(a) 8 (b) 9

(c) 10 (d) 12

19. Assume that each character code consists of 8 bits. The number of characters that can be transmitted per second through an synchronous serial line at 2400 baud rate, and with two stop bits is

(a) 109 (b) 216

(c) 218 (d) 219

20. If the bandwidth of a signal is 5 kHz and the lowest frequency is 52 kHz, what is the highest frequency

(a) 5 kHz (b) 10 kHz

(c) 47 kHz (d) 57 kHZ

21. An Ethernet hub

(a) functions as a repeater

(b) connects to a digital PBX

(c) connects to a token-ring network

(d) functions as a gateway

22. Phase transition for each bit are used in

(a) Amplitude modulation

(b) Carrier modulation

(c) Manchester encoding

(d) NRZ encoding

23. Study the following programme

```
// precondition : x > = 0
public void demo (int x)
{
System. out.print(x% 10);
if ((x / 10) ! = 0)
{
demo (x / 10);
}
System.out.print (x % 10);
}
```

Which of the following is printed as a result of the call demo (1234)?

(a) 1441 (b) 3443

(c) 12344321 (d) 43211234

24. Bit stuffing refers to

(a) inserting a '0' in user stream to differentiate it with a flag

(b) Inserting a '0' in flag stream to avoid ambiguity

(c) appending a nipple to the flag sequence

(d) appending a nipple to the use data stream

25. What is the name of the technique in which the operating system of a computer executes several programs concurrently by switching back and forth between them?

(a) Partitioning (b) Multi-tasking

(c) Windowing (d) Paging

26. If there are five routers and six networks in intranet using link state routing, how many routing tables are there?

(a) 1 (b) 5

(c) 6 (d) 11

27. Virtual memory is

(a) Part of Main Memory only used for swapping

(b) A technique to allow a program, of size more than the size of main memory, to run

(c) Part of secondary storage used in program execution

(d) None of these

28. The level of aggregation of information required for operational control is
    (a) Detailed   (b) Aggregate
    (c) Qualitative   (d) None of these

29. The set of all Equivalence Classes of a set A of Cardinality C
    (a) is of cardinality 2^C
    (b) have the same cardinality as A
    (c) forms a partition of A
    (d) is of cardinality C^2

30. 0.75 in decimal system is equivalent to _________ in octal system
    (a) 0.60   (b) 0.52
    (c) 0.54   (d) 0.50

31. In an SR latch made by cross-coupling two NAND gates, if both S and R inputs are set to 0, then it will result in
    (a) $Q = 0, \bar{Q} = 1$ (b) $Q = 1, \bar{Q} = 0$
    (c) $Q = 1, \bar{Q} = 1$ (d) Indeterminate states

32. Identify the correct translation into logical notation of the following assertion. Some boys in the class are taller than all the girls
    Note: taller (x, y) is true if x is taller then y.
    (a) $(\exists \chi)(\text{boy}(\chi) \to (\forall \chi)(\text{girl}(\gamma) \wedge \text{taller}(\chi \gamma)))$
    (b) $(\exists \chi)(\text{boy}(\chi) \wedge (\forall \gamma)(\text{girl}(\gamma) \wedge \text{taller}(\chi \gamma)))$
    (c) $(\exists \chi)(\text{boy}(\chi) \to (\forall \chi)(\text{girl}(\gamma) \to (\text{taller}(\chi \gamma)))$
    (d) $(\exists \chi)(\text{boy}(\chi) \wedge (\forall \gamma)(\text{girl}(\gamma) \to \text{taller}(\chi \gamma)))$

33. Company X shipped 5 computer chips, 1 of which was defective, and company Y shipped 4 computer chips, 2 of which were defective. One computer chip is to be chosen uniformly at a random from the 9 chips shipped by the companies. If the chosen chip is found to be defective, what is the probability that the chip came from the company Y?
    (a) $\dfrac{2}{9}$ (b) $\dfrac{4}{9}$
    (c) $\dfrac{2}{3}$ (d) $\dfrac{1}{2}$

34. Ring counter is analogous to
    (a) Toggle Switch   (b) Latch
    (c) Stepping Switch   (d) S-R slip flop

35. The output 0 and 1 level for TTL logic family is approximately
    (a) 0.1 and 5V   (b) 0.6 and 3.5 V
    (c) 0.9 and 1.75 V   (d) −1.75 and 0.9 V

36. Consider a computer system that stores floating-point numbers with 16-bit mantissa and an 8-bit exponent, each in two's complement. The smallest and largest positive values which can be stored are
    (a) 1×10^{-128} and $2^{15} \times 10^{128}$
    (b) 1×10^{-256} and $2^{15} \times 10^{255}$
    (c) 1×10^{-128} and $2^{15} \times 10^{127}$
    (d) 1×10^{-128} and $(2^{15} - 1) \times 10^{127}$

37. In comparison with static RAM memory, the dynamic RAM memory has
    (a) lower bit density and higher power consumption
    (b) higher bit density and higher power consumption
    (c) lower bit density and lower power consumption
    (d) higher bit density and lower power consumption

38. The Hexadecimal equivalent of 01 1111 0 0 11 0 1 1 1 1 0 0 0 1 1 is
    (a) CD73E   (b) ABD3F
    (c) 7CDE3   (d) FA4CD

39. Disk requests are received by a disk drive for cylinder 5, 25,18, 3, 39, 8 and 35 in that order. A seek takes 5 msec per cylinder moved. How much seek time is needed to serve these requests for a Shortest Seek First (SSF) algorithm? Assume that the arm is at cylinder ?, 0 when the last of these requests is made with none of the requests yet served.
    (a) 125 msec   (b) 295 msec
    (c) 575 msec   (d) 750 msec

40. Consider a system having 'm' resources of the same type. The resources are shared by 3 processes A, B, C, which have peak time demands of 3, 4, 6 respectively. The minimum value of 'm' that ensures that deadlock will never occur is
    (a) 11   (b) 12
    (c) 13   (d) 14

41. A task in a blocked state
    (a) is executable
    (b) is running
    (c) must still be placed in the run queues
    (d) is waiting for some temporarily unavailable resources

42. Semaphores
    (a) synchronize critical resources to prevent deadlock
    (b) synchronize critical resources to prevent contention
    (c) are used to do input/output
    (d) are used for memory management

43. On a system using non-preemptive scheduling, processes with expected run times of 5, 18, 9 and 12 are in the ready queue. In what order should they be run to minimize wait time ?

   (a) 5,12, 9, 18   (b) 5, 9, 12, 18

   (c) 12, 18, 9, 5   (d) 9, 12, 18, 5

44. The number of page frames that must be allocated to a running process in a virtual memory environment is determined by

   (a) the instruction set architecture

   (b) page size

   (c) number of processes in memory

   (d) physical memory size

45. A program consists of two modules executed sequentially. Let $f_1(t)$ and $f_2(t)$ respectively denote the probability density functions of time taken to execute the two modules. The probability density function of the overall time taken to execute the program is given by

   (a) $f_1(t) + f_2(t)$ (b) $\int_0^1 f_1(x)f_2(x)dx$

   (c) $\int_0^t f_1(x)f_2(t-x)dx$ (d) $\max(f_1(t)+f_2(t))$

46. Consider a small 2-way set-associative cache memory, consisting of four blocks. For choosing the block to be replaced, use the least recently (LRU) scheme. The number of cache misses for the following sequence of block addresses is 8, 12, 0, 12, 8

   (a) 2   (b) 3

   (c) 4   (d) 5

47. Which commands are used to control access over objects in relational database?

   (a) CASCADE and MVD

   (b) GRANT and REVOKE

   (c) QUE and QUIST

   (d) None of these

48. Which of the following is aggregate function in SQL?

   (a) Avg   (b) Select

   (c) Ordered by   (d) distinct

49. One approach to handling fuzzy logic data might be to design a computer using ternary (base-3) logic so that data could be stored as "true", "false", and "unknown." If each ternary logic element is called a flit, how many flits are required to represent at least 256 different values?

   (a) 4   (b) 5

   (c) 6   (d) 7

50. A view of database that appears to an application program is known as

   (a) Schema   (b) Subschema

   (c) Virtual table   (d) None of these

51. Armstrong's inference rule does not determine

   (a) Reflexivity   (b) Augmentation

   (c) Transitivity   (d) Mutual dependency

52. Which operation is used to extract specified columns from a table?

   (a) Project   (b) Join

   (c) Extract   (d) Substitute

53. In the Big-Endian system, the computer stores

   (a) MSB of data in the lowest memory address of data unit

   (b) LSB of data in the lowest memory address of data unit

   (c) MSB of data in the highest memory address of data unit

   (d) LSB of data in the highest memory address of data unit

54. BCNF is not used for cases where a relation has

   (a) Two (or more) candidate keys

   (b) Two candidate keys and composite

   (c) The candidate key overlap

   (d) Two mutually exclusive foreign keys

55. Selection sort algorithm design technique is an example of

   (a) Greedy method

   (b) Divide-and-conquer

   (c) Dynamic Programming

   (d) Backtracking

56. Which of the following RAID level provides the highest Data Transfer Rate (Read /Write)

   (a) RAID 1   (b) RAID 3

   (c) RAID 4   (d) RAID 5

57. Which of the following programming languages (s) provides garbage collection automatically

   (a) Lisp   (b) C++

   (c) Fortan   (d) C

58. The average case and worst case complexities for Merge sort algorithm are

   (a) $O(n^2), O(n^2)$

   (b) $O(n^2), O(n\log_2 n)$

   (c) $O(n\log_2 n), O(n^2)$

   (d) $O(n\log_2 n), O(n\log_2 n)$

59. The time taken by binary search algorithm to search a key in a sorted array of n elements is

   (a) $O(\log_2 n)$ (b) $O(n)$

   (c) $O(n\log_2 n)$ (d) $O(n^2)$

60. Which of the following is correct with respect to Two phase commit protocol?

(a) Ensures serializability

(b) Prevents Deadlock

(c) Detects Deadlock

(d) Recover from Deadlock

61. The Fibonacci sequence is the sequence of integers

(a) 1, 3, 5, 7, 9, 11, 13

(b) 0, 1, 1, 2, 3, 5, 8, 13, 21, 54

(c) 0, 1, 3, 4, 7, 11, 18, 29, 47

(d) 0, 1, 3, 7, 15

62. Let X be the adjacency matrix of a graph G with no self loops. The entries along the principal diagonal of X are

(a) all zeros

(b) all ones

(c) both zeros and ones

(d) different

63. Which of these is not a feature of WAP 2.0

(a) Push and Pull Model

(b) Interface to a storage device

(c) Multimedia messaging

(d) Hashing

64. Feedback queues

(a) are very simple to implement

(b) dispatch tasks according to execution characteristics

(c) are used to favour real time tasks

(d) require manual intervention to implement properly

65. Which of the following is not a UML DIAGRAM?

(a) Use case

(b) Class diagram

(c) Analysis diagram

(d) Swimlane diagram

66. Silly Window Syndrome is related to

(a) Error during transmission

(b) File transfer protocol

(c) Degrade in TCP performance

(d) Interface problem

67. To execute all loops at their boundaries and within their operational bounds is an example of

(a) Black Box Testing

(b) Alpha Testing

(c) Recovery Testing

(d) White Box Testing

68. SSL is not responsible for

(a) Mutual authentication of client & server

(b) Secret communication

(c) Data integrity protection

(d) Error detection and correction

69. A rule in a limited entry decision table is a

(a) row of the table consisting of condition entries

(b) row of the table consisting of action entries

(c) column of the table consisting of condition entries and corresponding action entries

(d) columns of the table consisting of conditions of the stub

70. The standard for certificates used on internet is

(a) $X.25$　　　　(b) $X.301$

(c) $X.409$　　　　(d) $X.509$

71. Hashed message is signed by a sender using

(a) his public key

(b) his private key

(c) receiver's public key

(d) receiver's private key

72. An Email contains a texual birthday greeting, a picture of a cake and a song. The order is not important. What is the content-type?

(a) Multipart/mixed

(b) Multipart/parallel

(c) Multipart / digest

(d) Multipart/alternative

73. Range of IP Address from 224.0.0.0 to 239.255.255.255 are

(a) Reserved for loopback

(b) Reserved for broadcast

(c) Used for multicast packets

(d) Reserved for future addressing

74. IEEE 802.11 is standard for

(a) Ethernet

(b) Bluetooth

(c) Broadband Wireless

(d) Wireless LANs

75. When a host on network A sends a message to a host on network B, which address does the router look at?

(a) Port　　　　(b) IP

(c) Physical　　　　(d) Subnet mask

76. Which of the following is not an approach of Software Process Assessment?

(a) SPICE(ISO/IEC15504)

(b) Standard CMMI Assessment Method for process improvement

(c) ISO 9001 : 2000

(d) IEEE 2000 : 2001

77. A physical DFD specifies
   (*a*) what processes will be used
   (*b*) who generates data and who processes it
   (*c*) what each person in an organization does
   (*d*) which data will be generated

78. In UML diagram of a class
   (*a*) state of object cannot be represented
   (*b*) state is irrelevant
   (*c*) state is represented as an attribute
   (*d*) state is represented as a result of an operation

79. Which of the following models is used for software reliability
   (*a*) Waterfall
   (*b*) Musa
   (*c*) COCOMO
   (*d*) Rayleigh

80. Djikstra's algorithm is used to
   (*a*) Create LSAs
   (*b*) Flood an internet with information
   (*c*) Calculate the routing tables
   (*d*) Create a link state database

ANSWERS

1. (*c*)	**2.** (*a*)	**3.** (*b*)	**4.** (*a*)	**5.** (*d*)	**6.** (*b*)	**7.** (*b*)	**8.** (*d*)	**9.** (*)	**10.** (*b*)
11. (*b*)	**12.** (*b*)	**13.** (*d*)	**14.** (*d*)	**15.** (*b*)	**16.** (*d*)	**17.** (*a*)	**18.** (*b*)	**19.** (*c*)	**20.** (*d*)
21. (*a*)	**22.** (*c*)	**23.** (*d*)	**24.** (*a*)	**25.** (*b*)	**26.** (*b*)	**27.** (*b*)	**28.** (*a*)	**29.** (*c*)	**30.** (*a*)
31. (*d*)	**32.** (*d*)	**33.** (*c*)	**34.** (*c*)	**35.** (*b*)	**36.** (*d*)	**37.** (*b*)	**38.** (*c*)	**39.** (*b*)	**40.** (*a*)
41. (*d*)	**42.** (*b*)	**43.** (*b*)	**44.** (*a*)	**45.** (*c*)	**46.** (*c*)	**47.** (*b*)	**48.** (*a*)	**49.** (*c*)	**50.** (*b*)
51. (*d*)	**52.** (*a*)	**53.** (*a*)	**54.** (*b*)	**55.** (*a*)	**56.** (*a*)	**57.** (*a*)	**58.** (*d*)	**59.** (*a*)	**60.** (*a*)
61. (*)	**62.** (*a*)	**63.** (*d*)	**64.** (*b*)	**65.** (*c*)	**66.** (*c*)	**67.** (*d*)	**68.** (*d*)	**69.** (*c*)	**70.** (*d*)
71. (*b*)	**72.** (*b*)	**73.** (*c*)	**74.** (*d*)	**75.** (*b*)	**76.** (*d*)	**77.** (*b*)	**78.** (*c*)	**79.** (*d*)	**80.** (*c*)

Note: * None of the given option is correct. Question may contain insufficient data.

EXPLANATIONS

1. The Boolean expression

$$Y = (A + \bar{B} + \bar{A}B)\bar{C} = A\bar{C} + \bar{B}\bar{C} + \bar{A}B\bar{C}$$

$$= \bar{C}(A + \bar{A}B) + \bar{B}\bar{C}(X + YZ)$$
$$= (X + Y)(Y + Z)$$
$$= \bar{C}\big((A + \bar{A}) + (A + B)\big) + \bar{B}\bar{C}$$
$$= \bar{C}(A + B) + \bar{B}\bar{C} \qquad \{x + \bar{x} = 1,\ x \cdot 1 = x\}$$
$$= A\bar{C} + B\bar{C} + \bar{B}\bar{C}$$
$$= A\bar{C} + \bar{C}(B + \bar{B})$$
$$= \bar{C}(1 + A) = \bar{C}$$

2. Given circuit

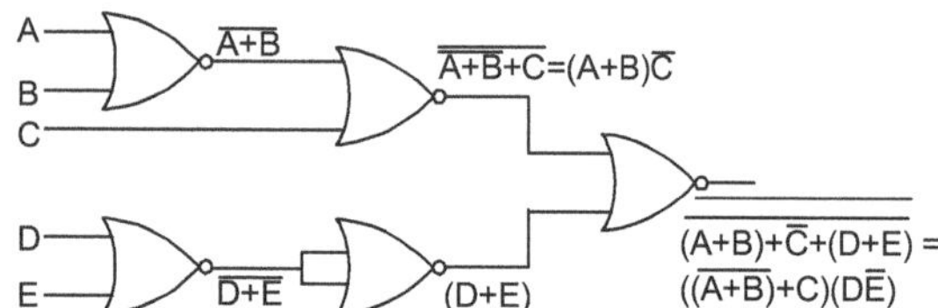

3. The circuit shown in the question is of a full subtracter which is constructed by the help of two half subtracters.

4. When two numbers are added in excess-3 code and the sum is less than 9, then in order to get the correct answer, we need to subtract 0011

5. Characteristic equation of SR flip-flop is,

$$Q_{n+1} = S + \bar{R}Q_n$$

The characteristic table for SR flip-flop is:

Q_n	S	R	Q_{n+1}
0	0	0	0
0	0	1	0
0	1	0	1
0	1	1	×
1	0	0	1
1	0	1	0
1	1	0	1
1	1	1	×

Drawing the k map:

Q_n \ SR	00	01	11	10
0			X	1
1	1		X	1

The characteristic equation will be

$$Q_{n+1} = S + \bar{R}Q_n$$

6. In a graph, if the number of vertices are 'n' and there are '$n-1$' edges and is not a tree. Considering the graph to be a simple graph, it can be said that the graph is disconnected.

7. Since to properly colour a graph, 'K' different colours are needed. Hence, the chromatic number of the graph is 'K'.

8. A read bit can be read by CPU and written by the peripheral.

10. **Aging :** Aging refers to gradually increasing the priority of jobs that wait in the system for a long time to remedy infinite blocking.

11. Given tasks = n and runtimes = $r_1, r_2 ..... r_n$

    Throughput refers to total number of tasks executed per unit time. Shortest job first scheduling algorithm will result in the maximum throughput because all the shortest jobs will be executed first hence many task will be completed.

12. Corresponding deadlines $(d_1, d_2, d_3, d_4) = (4, 2, 4, 2)$. Since the deadline of Jobs 'J_2' and 'J_4' is less as compared to the other two jobs, hence these two jobs must he executed first. So, completing J_1 after J_4 is will not be a feasible schedule of the four jobs.

13. Resolution $= \dfrac{360}{2^n}$

    By using an 8-bit optical encoder, the degree of resolution that can be obtained is

    $$n = 8$$

    $$\dfrac{360}{2^8} = 1.4 \text{ degree}$$

14. Locality of reference is a term which is used where the related storage locations are frequently accessed.

15. Considering the given pseudo code

    On execution of the program, initially 'i' = 1, 'x' = 1; while condition is true, so now; $x = 2$, $i = 2$, again condition satisfies, so now, $x = 4$, $i = 3$, again condition is satisfied, $x = 16$, $i = 4$; condition is satisfied so $x = 2^{16}$, $i = 5$. This time the condition will be false. So, the value of i will be 5 at the end.

16. Four items are pushed into stack A, B, C, D, where Top is pointing E. Now 4 elements are deleted and enqueue into queue. So queue contain E, D, C, B where Rear is pointing B and Front pointing E. Now two elements are deleted from the queue i.e. E and D respectively and pushed back on the stack i.e., e, d where stack Top pointing D now delete one element from stack gives D.

17. In round robin scheduling algorithm, the processes run for a fixed time quantum in the same schedule in which they have arrived and are then preempted after the time quantum expires. Later, they are inserted in the job queue and again get CPU for the fixed time quantum is required. So, it can be said that it's the pre-emptive version of FIFO.

18. Number of digit 1 in binary representation

    $$3 \times 512 + 7 \times 64 + 5 \times 8 + 3$$
    $$\Rightarrow (2 + 1)2^9 + (2^2 + 2 + 1)2^6 + (2^2 + 1)2^3 + (2 + 1)$$
    $$\Rightarrow 2^{10} + 2^9 + 2^8 + 2^7 + 2^6 + 2^5 + 2^3 + 2^1 + 2^0$$
    $$\Rightarrow 11111101011$$

    Therefore, total number of 1's are 9.

19. Given data

    each character code = 8 bit

    Baud rate = 2400

    Total number of bits = 8 + 1 start bit + 2 stop bits = 11 bits

    Number of characters transmitted / sec

    $$= \dfrac{2400}{11} = 218.18 \approx 218$$

    Hence, 218 characters can be transmitted per second.

20. Bandwidth of signal = 5 kHz

    Lowest frequency = 52 kHz

    Bandwidth = Highest frequency (x) – Lowest frequency

    $$\Rightarrow 5 = x - 52$$
    $$\Rightarrow x = 57 \text{ kHz}$$

    The highest frequency will be 57 kHz.

21. An ethernet hub functions as a repeater, a repeater is an electronic device that receives a signal and retransmits it at a higher level or a higher power.

22. Manchester encoding (also known as phase encoding) is a line code in which the encoding of each data bit is either low then high, or high then low.

23. Output of the program

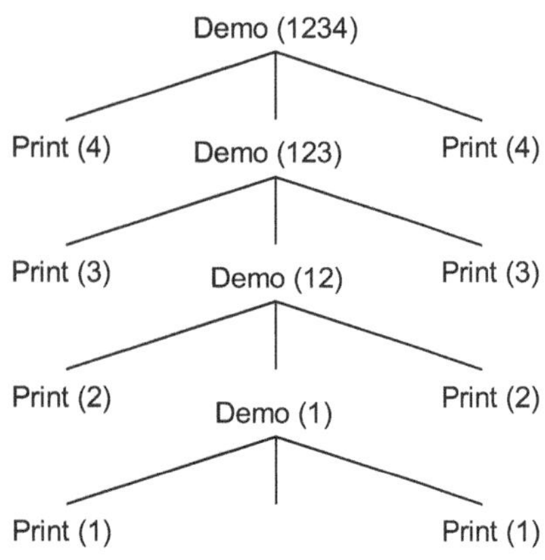

The result will be 43211234.

24. Bit stuffing refers to inserting 0 in user stream to differentiate it with a flag.

i.e., flag = 1111111

user stream = 1111111011110

So bit stuffing is 1111110011110

25. Name of the technique multitasking which is a concept of performing multiple tasks over a certain period of time by executing them concurrently. Now tasks start and interrupt already started ones before they have reached completion, instead of executing the task sequentially, so each started task needs to reach its end before a new one is started.

26. Since there are 5 routers, hence there will be 5 routing tables. Since every router has its own routing table.

27. Virtual memory is a memory management technique that is implemented using both hardware and software. It maps memory addresses used by a program, called virtual addresses, into physical addresses in computer memory.

28. The level of aggregation of information required for operational control is detailed.

29. The set of all equivalence class of a set A of cardinality C forms a partition of A.

31. In a SR latch, made by cross coupling two NAND gates, if both S and R inputs are set to 0, logic state is said to be in an indeterminate state or racing state. Race condition occurs and output becomes unstable.

32. From the given option we consider,

- There exist some x, such that if x is a boy then for every 'x' y is a girl and taller than y.
- There exist an 'x' such that 'x' is a boy and every 'y' is a girl and x is taller than 'y'.
- There exist an 'x' such that if 'x' is a boy then for every x, if 'y' is a girl then x is taller than y.
- Some boys in the class are taller than all the girls.

33. Considering the given conditions

Probability of chip shipped by $X = \dfrac{5}{9}$.

Probability of chip shipped by $Y = \dfrac{4}{9}$.

Probability of defect chip from $X = \dfrac{1}{5}$.

Probability of defect chip from $Y = \dfrac{2}{4}$.

Probability of defected chip from

$$Y = \frac{\dfrac{4}{9} \times \dfrac{2}{4}}{\left(\dfrac{4}{9} \times \dfrac{2}{4}\right) + \left(\dfrac{5}{9} \times \dfrac{1}{5}\right)} = \frac{2}{3}$$

34. Ring counter is analogous to stepping switch. A stepping switch is an electromechanical device which allows an input connection to be connected to one of a number of possible output connections, under the control of a series of electrical pulses.

35. 0 and 1 level for TTL logic is that the acceptable input signal voltage ranges from 0 volts to 0.8 volts for a low logic state, and 2 volts to 5 volts for a high logic state.

36. To store, 16 bit montissa, and 8 bit exponent the smallest and largest possible values that can be stored are 1×10^{-128} and $(2^{15} - 1) \times 10^{127}$.

37. In comparison with static RAM has lower density because there are 6 transistors while DRAM has one transistor and capacitor. Therefore density (SRAM) < Density of (DRAM). A DRAM has capacitor, therefore power consumption (DRAM) > (SRAM).

So, dynamic RAM memory has higher bit density and higher power consumption.

38. The hexadecimal equivalent of

$$\underset{7}{\underline{0111}}\,\underset{C}{\underline{1100}}\,\underset{D}{\underline{1101}}\,\underset{E}{\underline{1110}}\,\underset{3}{\underline{0011}} = (7CDE3)_{16}$$

39. Disk drive requests

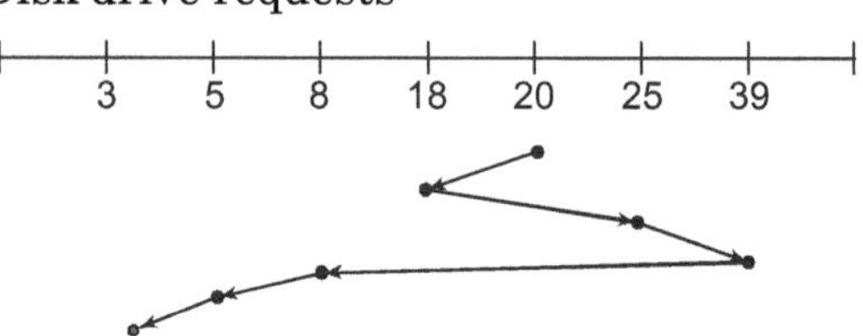

Total number of seeks

$= (20 - 18) + (25 - 18) + (39 - 25) + (39 - 8)$

$+ (8 - 5) + (5 - 3) = 59$

Each take 5 ms per cylinder.

Total time = $59 \times 5 = 295$ ms.

40. All the resources are some type so minimum value of 'm' can be obtained by taking (peak demands) –1 from each process and adding 1 to it.

$$= (3 - 1) + (4 - 1) + (6 - 1) + 1$$
$$= 11$$

41. A task in a blocked state is waiting for some temporarily unavailable resources. A process that is blocked is one that is waiting for some event.

42. Semaphores are used for synchronization. Semaphores ensure that only one process is in its critical section at a time. They synchronize critical resources to prevent contention.

43. Run time = 5, 18, 19 and 12

In order to reduce wait time, shorted job first is the scheduling policy that can be used. So, the execution manner of the processes should be 5, 9, 12 and 18.

44. The number of page frames that must be allocated to a running process in a virtual memory environment is determined by instruction set architectures. The frames will be allocated as per the instruction sets that are allowed.

45. Since the two modules execute sequentially. The total runtime of the program is the sum of runtime of the two module. Probability density function of overall time taken

$$= \int_0^t f_1(x) f_2(t - x) dx$$

46. Lets condering a small 2-way set associative cache memory

Sequence of block addresses:

8, 12,0, 12,8

8, 12, 0, 12, 8

0	Set 0
8	
	Set 1

Total number of cache misses are 4.

47. GRANT, REVOKE and DENY are the three commands that are used to control access over objects in relational database.

48. 'Avg' is an aggregate function is SQL. It take the average of the input set provided to the query.

49. Number of values to be represented = 256 If take flit = 5, $3^5 = 243$, which is insufficient to hold 256. So, answer will be, since $3^6 = 729$, which is sufficient to hold 256 values.

50. A view of database that appears to an application program is the external level is the user's view of the database end is closest to the users. A subschema expresses the external view.

51. Armstrong's inference rule satisfies:

(i) Reflexivity, $Y \subseteq X$ then $X \to Y$

(ii) Augmentation if $X \to Y$ then $XT \to YT$

(iii)Transitivity, if $X \to Y$, $Y \to Z$ then $X \to Z$

It does not determine mutual dependency.

52. To extract a specified column from a table projection operation is used. To extract a specified row in a table, selection operation is used.

53. In the computer stones two system are used for mapping (i) Big endian system (ii) Little endian system. In big endian system, MSB of the data is in lowest memory address of data unit and LSB of the data is in higher memory address of data unit.

54. From the given options BCNF is not used for cases where a relation has two candidate keys and composite.

55. Selection sort algorithm design technique is an example of greedy method.

56. RAID level 1 provides the highest data transfer rate (read /write). Where RAID levels 2, 3 and 4 are theoretically defined but not used in practice.

57. LISP language provide garbage collection automatically, whereas Fortan, C++ and C don't provide automatic garbage collection.

58. Merge sort algorithm has complexity of $O(n \log_2 n)$ in both average case as well as worst case.

59. The time taken by binary search algorithm to search a key in a sorted array of n-elements is $O(\log_2 n)$.

60. Two phase commit protocol ensures serializability. It does not prevent deadlock. —Neither it detects deadlock nor it recover from deadlock.

62. X be the adjacency matrix of a graph G has no self loops, hence there is no edge from a vertex to itself. Hence, the corresponding entry will be 0. So, the entries along the principal diagonal of X are all zeros.

63. WAP 2.0 is a push and pull model. It provides interface to a storage device and also, it provides multimedia messaging.

So, hashing is not a feature of WAP 2.0.

64. Feedback queries dispatch task according to execution characteristics. It allows a process to move between queries.

65. An analysis diagram is not a UML diagram. It is simplified activity diagram, which is used to capture high level business processes and early models of system behaviour and elements.

66. Silly Window Syndrome is a problem in computer networking caused by poorly implemented TCP flow control. The problem that can arise in the silly window operation when the sending application program creates data slowly, the receiving application program consumes data slowly, or both.

67. Black box testing checks incorrect functions, interface errors, performance errors etc. Alpha testing is a kind of system testing that is performed at developer's end. Recovery testing forces the system to fail and then verifies that the recovery is properly performed.

68. Secure socket layer (SSL) is the standard security technology for establishing an encrypted link between a web server and a browser.

    This link ensures that all data is passed between the web server and browsers remain private and integral. It is not responsible for error detection and correction.

69. A rule in a limited entry decision table is a column of the table consisting of the condition entries and the corresponding action entries. A decision table is a tool to use in both testing and requirements management.

70. X.509 is an important standard for a public key infrastructure (PKI) to manage digital certificates and public-key encryption and a key part of the important layer security protocol used to secure web and E-mail communi-cation.

71. A hashed message is signed by a sender using his private key and is verified by the verifier using the sender's public key.

72. An email contains the data is defines the parallel subtype of the multipart context type. It is syntactically identical to multipart / mixed type but not semantically. In a parallel entity, all of the parts are intended to be presented in parallel i.e., simultaneously on hardware and software that are capable of doing it.

73. Range of IP address from 224.0.0.0 to 239.255.255.255 are used for multicast packets.

74. IEEE-802.11 is a standard for wireless LANs.

75. When a host network send a message, IP addresses are used for the routing purposes. With the help of IP address, routers decide to which interface the packet should be forwarded.

76. SPICE, standard CMI assessment method for process improvement and ISO 90001:2000 are approaches to software process assessment but not IEEE 2000 : 2001.

77. A physical DFD specifies the Data flow diagrams are categorized as either physical or logical. A logical DFD captures the data flows that are necessary for a systems to operate. On the other hand, a physical DFD shows how the system is actually implemented, either at the moment (current physical DFD) or how the designer intends it to be in future (required physical DFD).

78. Unified modelling language (UML) is a type of static structure diagram that describes the structure of a system by showing the system's classes, their attributes, operations (or methods) and relationship among objects.

79. Software reliability is the process of the software components of producing incorrect output. Software should not wear out and continue to operate after a bad result. Rayleigh, Jelinski-Moranda, Weibull are some of the models that are used for software reliability.

80. Dijkstra's algorithm is used to calculate the routing table. The algorithm is generally used in link state routing protocol.

1. Which of the following is an illegal array definition?

   (a) type COLONGE : (LIME, PINE, MUSK, MENTHOL); var a : array [COLONGE] of REAL;

   (b) var a : array [REAL] of REAL;

   (c) var a : array ['A'... 'Z] of REAL ;

   (d) var a : array [BOOLEAN] of REAL;

2. The term Phong is associated with

   (a) Ray tracing

   (b) Shading

   (c) Hiddenline removal

   (d) a game

3. The subnet mask 255.255.255.192

   (a) extends the network portion to 16 bits

   (b) extends the network portion to 26 bits

   (c) extends the network portion to 36 bits

   (d) has no effect on the network portion of an IP address

4. On a LAN, where are IP datagrams transported?

   (a) In the LAN header

   (b) In the application field

   (c) In the information field of the LAN frame

   (d) After the TCP header

5. In Ethernet, the source address field in the MAC frame is the _________ address.

   (a) original sender's physical

   (b) previous station's physical

   (c) next destination's physical

   (d) original sender's service port

6. Which of the following transmission media is not readily suitable to CSMA operation?

   (a) Radio (b) Optical fibers

   (c) Coaxial cable (d) Twisted pair

7. Consider the grammar

   S → ABCc | bc

   BA → AB

   Bb → bb

   Ab → ab

   Aa → aa

   Which of the following sentences can be derived by this grammar?

   (a) abc (b) aab

   (c) abcc (d) abbe

8. The TCP sliding window

   (a) can be used to control the flow of information

   (b) always occurs when the field value is 0

   (c) always occurs when the field value is 1

   (d) occurs horizontally

9. What is the bandwidth of the signal that ranges from 40 kHz 4 MHz

   (a) 36 MHz (b) 360 kHz

   (c) 3.96 MHz (d) 396 MHz

10. Which Project 802 standard provides for a collision-free protocol?

    (a) 802.2 (b) 802.3

    (c) 802.5 (d) 802.6

11. The Boolean theorem $AB + \bar{A}C + BC = AB + \bar{A}C$ corresponds to

    (a) $(A + B) \cdot (\bar{A} + C) \cdot (B + C) = (A + B) \cdot (\bar{A} + C)$

    (b) $AB + \bar{A}C + BC = AB + BC$

    (c) $AB + \bar{A}C + BC = (A + B) \cdot (\bar{A} + C) \cdot (B + C)$

    (d) $(A + B) \cdot (\bar{A} + C) \cdot (B + C) = AB + \bar{A}C$

12. In the given network of AND and OR gates f can be written as

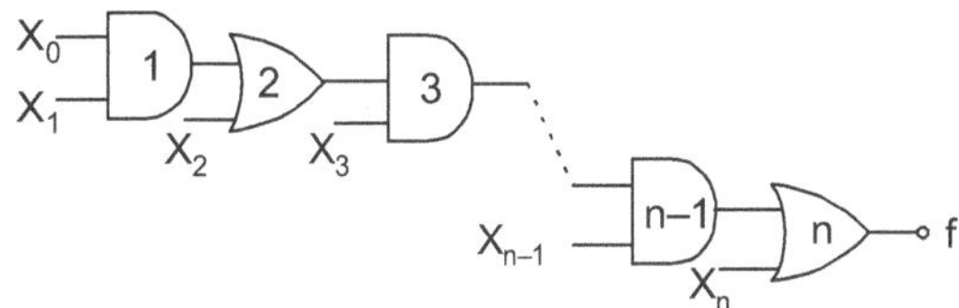

    (a) $X_0 X_1 X_2 ... X_n + X_1 X_2 ... X_n + X_2 X_3 ... X_n^+ + ... + X_n$

    (b) $X_0 X_1 + X_2 X_3 + ... + X_{n-1} X_n$

    (c) $X_0 + X_1 + X_2 + ... + X_n$

    (d) $X_0 X_1 + X_3 ... X_{n-1} + X_2 X_3 + X_5 ... X_{n-1} + ... + X_{n-2} X_{n-1} + X_n$

13. If $N^2 = (7601)_g$ where N is a positive integer, then the value of N is

    (a) $(241)_5$

    (b) $(143)_6$

    (c) $(165)_7$

    (d) $(39)_{16}$

14. Assume that each character code consists of 8 bits. The number of characters that can be transmitted per second through an synchronous serial line at 2400 baud rate, and with two stop bits, is :

   (*a*) 109   (*b*) 216

   (*c*) 218   (*d*) 219

15. Four jobs to be executed on a single processor system arrive at time 0 in the order A, B, C, D. There burst CPU time requirements are 4, 1, 8, 1 time units respectively. The completion time of A under robin round scheduling with time slice of one time unit is

   (*a*) 10   (*b*) 4

   (*c*) 8   (*d*) 9

16. Which one of the following algorithm design techniques is used in finding all pairs of shortest distances in a graph?

   (*a*) Dynamic programming

   (*b*) Backtracking

   (*c*) Greedy

   (*d*) Divide and Conquer

17. The address space of 8086 CPU is

   (*a*) 1 Megabyte   (*b*) 256 Kilobytes

   (*c*) 1 K Megabytes (*d*) 64 Kilobytes

18. More than one word are put in one cache block to

   (*a*) exploit the temporal locality of reference in a program

   (*b*) exploit the spatial locality of reference in a program

   (*c*) reduce the miss penalty

   (*d*) None of these

19. The performance of a pipelined processor suffers if

   (*a*) the pipeline stages have different delays

   (*b*) consecutive instructions are dependent on each other

   (*c*) the pipeline stages share hardware resources

   (*d*) All of the above

20. If $(12x)_3 = (123)_x$, then the value of x is

   (*a*) 3   (*b*) 3 or 4

   (*c*) 2   (*d*) None of these

21. The advantage of MOS devices over bipolar devices is that

   (*a*) it allows higher bit densities and also cost effective

   (*b*) it is easy to fabricate

   (*c*) it is higher-impedance and operational speed

   (*d*) all of these

22. How many 2-input multiplexers are required to construct a 2^{10}-input multiplexer?

   (*a*) 1023   (*b*) 31

   (*c*) 10   (*d*) 127

23. A computer uses 8 digit mantissa and 2 digit exponent. If $a = 0.052$ and $b = 28E + 11$ then $b + a - b$ will

   (*a*) result in an overflow error

   (*b*) result in an underflow error

   (*c*) be 0

   (*d*) be 5.28E + 11

24. The Boolean expression $(A + \bar{C})(\bar{B} + \bar{C})$ simplifies to

   (*a*) $\bar{C} + A\bar{B}$ (*b*) $\bar{C}(\bar{A} + B)$

   (*c*) $\bar{B}\bar{C} + A\bar{B}$ (*d*) None of these

25. In the expression $\bar{A}(\bar{A} + \bar{B})$ by writing the first term A as $A + 0$, the expression is best simplified as

   (*a*) $A + AB$ (*b*) AB

   (*c*) A (*d*) $A + B$

26. The logic operations of two combinational circuits given in Figure-I and Figure-II are

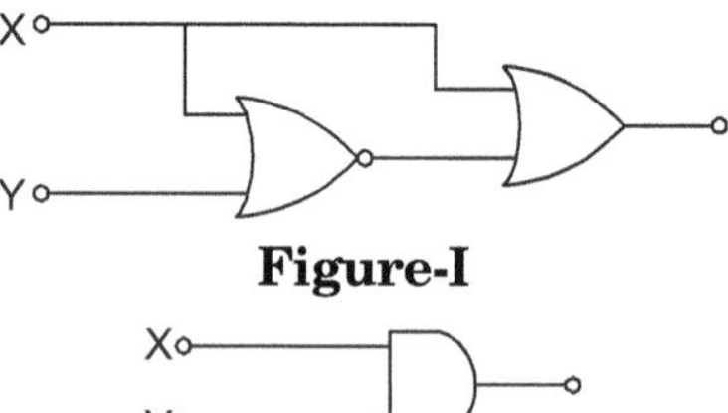

Figure-I

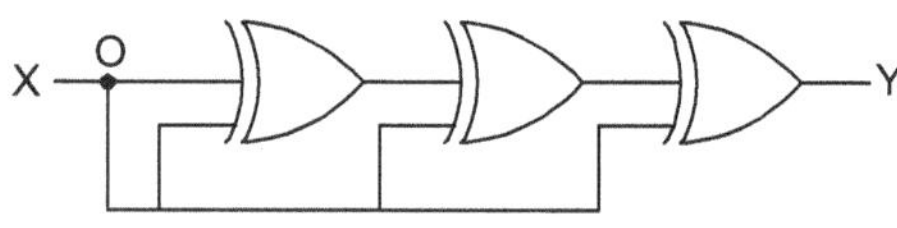

Figure-II

   (*a*) entirely different (*b*) identical

   (*c*) complementary (*d*) dual

27. The output Y of the given circuit

   (*a*) 1   (*b*) 0

   (*c*) X   (*d*) X′

28. Which of the following is not a valid rule of XOR?

   (*a*) 0 XOR 0 = 0   (*b*) 1 XOR 1 = 1

   (*c*) 1 XOR 0=1   (*d*) B XOR B = 0

29. The number of distinct simple graphs with up to three nodes is

   (*a*) 15

   (*b*) 10

   (*c*) 7

   (*d*) 9

30. The maximum number of edges in a n-node undirected graph without self loops is

(a) n^2

(b) $\dfrac{n(n-1)}{2}$

(c) $n-1$

(d) $\dfrac{n(n+1)}{2}$

31. If the two matrices $\begin{bmatrix} 1 & 0 & x \\ 0 & x & 1 \\ 0 & 1 & x \end{bmatrix}$ and $\begin{bmatrix} x & 1 & 0 \\ x & 0 & 1 \\ 0 & x & 1 \end{bmatrix}$ have the same determinant, then the value of x is

(a) $\dfrac{1}{2}$

(b) $\sqrt{2}$

(c) $\pm\dfrac{1}{2}$

(d) $\pm\dfrac{1}{\sqrt{2}}$

32. A network 198.78.41.0 is a

(a) Class A network (b) Class B network

(c) Class C network (d) Class D network

33. The join operation can be defined as

(a) a cartesian product of two relations followed by a selection

(b) a cartesian product of two relations

(c) a union of two relations followed by cartesian product of the two relations

(d) a union of two relations

34. If a square matrix A satisfies $A^T A = I$, then the matrix A is

(a) Idempotent (b) Symmetric

(c) Orthogonal (d) Hermitian

35. Embedded pointer provides

(a) An inverted index

(b) A secondary access path

(c) A physical record key

(d) A primary key

36. An interrupt in which the external device supplies its address as well as the interrupt requests is known as

(a) vectored interrupt

(b) maskable interrupt

(c) non maskable interrupt

(d) designated interrupt

37. The ability to temporarily halt the CPU and use this time to send information on buses is called

(a) direct memory access

(b) vectoring the interrupt

(c) polling

(d) cycle stealing

38. Relative to the program translated by a complier, the same program when interpreted runs

(a) Faster

(b) Slower

(c) At the same speed

(d) May be faster or slower

39. Consider the following Assembly language program

MVIA	30 H
ACI	30 H
XRA	A
POP	H

After the execution of the above program, the contents of the accumulator will be

(a) 30 H (b) 60 H

(c) 00 H (d) contents of stack

40. Consider the following C function :

```
int f(int n)
{static int i = 1;
if (n >= 5) return n;
n = n + i;
i++;
return f(n)
}
```

The value returned by $f(1)$ is

(a) 5 (b) 6

(c) 7 (d) 8

41. In a resident-OS computer, which of the following systems must reside in the main memory under all situations?

(a) Assembler (b) Linker

(c) Loader (d) Compiler

42. Which of the following architecture is/are not suitable for realising SIMD?

(a) Vector processor (b) Array processor

(c) Von Neumann (d) All of the above

43. Consider the following code segment:

```
for (int k = 0; k < 20; k = k + 2)
{
    if(k % 3 == 1)
       system.out.print (k + " ");
}
```

What is printed as a result of executing the code segment?

(a) 4 16 (b) 4 10 16

(c) 0 6 12 18 (d) 1 4 7 10 13 16 19

44. The device which is used to connect a peripheral to bus is known as

(a) control register

(b) interface

(c) communication protocol

(d) none of these

45. The TRAP is one of the interrupts available in INTEL 8085. Which one of the following statements is true of TRAP?

(a) it is level triggered

(b) it is negative edge triggered

(c) it is +ve edge triggered

(d) it is both +ve and -ve edges triggered

46. Raid configurations of disks are used to provide

(a) Fault-tolerance

(b) High speed

(c) High data density

(d) None of these

47. Which of the following need not necessarily be saved on a context switch between processes?

(a) General purpose registers

(b) Translation lookaside buffer

(c) Program counter

(d) All of the above

48. Which of the following is termed as minimum error code

(a) Binary code   (b) Gray code

(c) Excess 3 code   (d) Octal code

49. The total time to prepare a disk drive mechanism for a block of data to be read from it is

(a) seek time

(b) latency

(c) latency plus seek time

(d) transmission time

50. Feedback queues

(a) are very simple to implement

(b) dispatch tasks according to execution characteristics

(c) are used to favour real time tasks

(d) require manual intervention to implement properly

51. With Round-Robin CPU scheduling in a time shared system

(a) using very large time slices (quantas) degenerates into First-Come First Served (FCFS) algorithm.

(b) using extremely small time slices improves performance

(c) using very small time slices degenerates into Last-in First-Out (LIFO) algorithm.

(d) using medium sized time slices leads to shortest Request time First (SRTF) algorithm

52. Dynamic address translation

(a) is part of the operating system paging algorithm

(b) is useless when swapping is used

(c) is the hardware necessary to implement paging

(d) storage pages at a specific location on disk

53. Thrashing

(a) always occurs on large computers

(b) is a natural consequence of virtual memory systems

(c) can always be avoided by swapping

(d) can be caused by poor paging algorithms

54. What is the name of the operating system that reads and reacts in terms of actual time ?

(a) Batch system   (b) Quick response time

(c) Real time system (d) Time sharing system

55. The Memory Address Register

(a) is a hardware memory device which denotes the location of the current instruction being executed.

(b) is a group of electrical circuit, that performs the intent of instructions fetched from memory

(c) contains the address of the memory location that is to be read from or stored into

(d) contains a copy of the designated memory location specified by the MAR after a "read" or the new contents of the memory prior to a "write"

56. An example of spooled device is a

(a) line printer used to print the output of a number of jobs.

(b) terminal used to enter input data to a running program.

(c) secondary storage device in a virtual memory system.

(d) graphic display device.

57. Dirty bit for a page in a page table

(a) helps avoid unnecessary writes on a paging device

(b) helps maintain LRU information

(c) allows only read on a page

(d) None of the above

58. Check pointing a job

(*a*) allows it to be completed successfully

(*b*) allows it to continue executing later

(*c*) prepares it for finishing

(*d*) occurs only when there is an error in it

59. A public key encryption system

(*a*) allows anyone to decode the transmissions

(*b*) allows only the correct sender to decode the data

(*c*) allows only the correct receiver to decode the data

(*d*) does not encode the data before transmitting it

60. Overlaying

(*a*) requires use of a loader

(*b*) allows larger programs, but requires more effort

(*c*) is most used on large computers

(*d*) is transparent to the user

61. A critical section is a program segment

(*a*) which should run in a certain specified amount of time.

(*b*) which avoids deadlock.

(*c*) where shared resources are accessed.

(*d*) which must be endorsed by a pair of semaphore operations, P and U.

62. In which of the following four necessary conditions for deadlock processes claim exclusive control of the resources they require?

(*a*) no preemption   (*b*) mutual exclusion

(*c*) circular wait   (*d*) hold and wait

63. Fork is

(*a*) the creation of a new job

(*b*) the dispatching of a task

(*c*) increasing the priority of a task

(*d*) the creation of a new process

64. Which of the following need not necessarily be saved on a Context Switch between processes?

(*a*) General purpose register

(*b*) Translation look-aside buffer

(*c*) Program counter

(*d*) Stack pointer

65. Consider a logical address space of 8 pages of 1024 words mapped into memory of 32 frames. How many bits are there in the logical address?

(*a*) 13 bits   (*b*) 15 bits

(*c*) 14 bits   (*d*) 12 bits

66. The performance of Round Robin algorithm depends heavily on

(*a*) size of the process

(*b*) the I/O bursts of the process

(*c*) the CPU bursts of the process

(*d*) the size of the time quantum

67. The page replacement algorithm which gives the lowest page fault rate is

(*a*) LRU

(*b*) FIFO

(*c*) Optional page replacement

(*d*) Second chance algorithm

68. Which of the following class of statement usually produces no executable code when compiled?

(*a*) declaration

(*b*) assignment statements

(*c*) input and output statements

(*d*) structural statements

69. What is the value of F(4) using the following procedure :

Function F(K: integer)

integer;

begin

if ($k<3$) then $F := k$ else $F := F(k-1) * F(k-2) + F(k-3)$

end

(*a*) 5   (*b*) 6

(*c*) 7   (*d*) 8

70. Stack A has the entries a, b, c (with a on top). Stack B is empty. An entry popped out of stack A can be printed immediately or pushed to stack B. An entry popped out of the stack B can only be printed. In this arrangement, which of the following permutations of a, b, c are not possible?

(*a*) b a c   (*b*) b c a

(*c*) c a b   (*d*) a b c

71. The time required to search an element in a linked list of length n is

(*a*) $O(\log_2 n)$ (*b*) $O(n)$

(*c*) $O(1)$ (*d*) $O(n^2)$

72. Which of the following operations is performed more efficiently by doubly linked list then by linear linked list?

(*a*) Deleting a node whose location is given

(*b*) Searching an unsorted list for a given item

(*c*) Inserting a node after the node with a given location

(*d*) Traversing the list to process each node

73. We can make a class abstract by

(a) Declaring it abstract using the virtual keyword

(b) Making at least one member function as virtual function

(c) Making at least one member function as pure virtual function

(d) Making all member function const.

74. A Steiner patch is

(a) Biquadratic Bezier patch

(b) Bicubic patch

(c) Circular patch only

(d) Bilinear Bezier patch

75. A complete binary tree with the property that the value at each node is at least as large as the values at its children is known as

(a) binary search tree

(b) AVL tree

(c) completely balanced tree

(d) Heap

76. The minimum number of fields with each node of doubly linked lists is

(a) 1   (b) 2

(c) 3   (d) 4

77. How many comparisons are needed to sort an array of length 5 if a straight selection sort is used and array is already in the opposite order?

(a) 1   (b) 10

(c) 15   (d) 20

78. Consider the graph shown in the figure below:

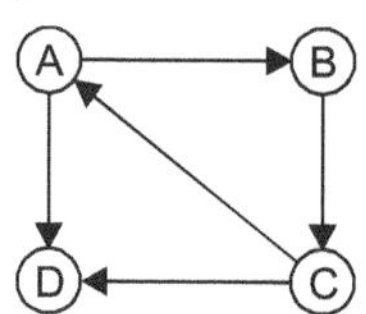

Which of the following is a valid strong component?

(a) a, c, d   (b) a, b, d

(c) b, c, d   (d) a, b, c

79. Repeated execution of simple computation may cause compounding of

(a) round-off errors   (b) syntax errors

(c) run-time errors   (d) logic errors

80. In C, what is the effect of a negative number in a field width specifier?

(a) the values are displayed right justified

(b) the values are displayed centered

(c) the values are displayed left justified

(d) the values are displayed as negative numbers

ANSWERS

1. (b)	**2.** (b)	**3.** (b)	**4.** (c)	**5.** (b)	**6.** (a)	**7.** (*)	**8.** (a)	**9.** (c)	**10.** (c)
11. (a)	**12.** (*)	**13.** (b)	**14.** (c)	**15.** (d)	**16.** (a)	**17.** (a)	**18.** (b)	**19.** (d)	**20.** (d)
21. (d)	**22.** (a)	**23.** (c)	**24.** (a)	**25.** (*)	**26.** (a)	**27.** (b)	**28.** (b)	**29.** (c)	**30.** (b)
31. (a)	**32.** (c)	**33.** (a)	**34.** (c)	**35.** (a)	**36.** (a)	**37.** (d)	**38.** (b)	**39.** (c)	**40.** (c)
41. (c)	**42.** (c)	**43.** (b)	**44.** (b)	**45.** (d)	**46.** (d)	**47.** (b)	**48.** (b)	**49.** (c)	**50.** (b)
51. (a)	**52.** (c)	**53.** (d)	**54.** (c)	**55.** (c)	**56.** (a)	**57.** (a)	**58.** (b)	**59.** (c)	**60.** (d)
61. (c)	**62.** (b)	**63.** (d)	**64.** (b)	**65.** (a)	**66.** (d)	**67.** (c)	**68.** (a)	**69.** (a)	**70.** (c)
71. (b)	**72.** (a)	**73.** (c)	**74.** (a)	**75.** (d)	**76.** (c)	**77.** (b)	**78.** (d)	**79.** (a)	**80.** (c)

Note: * None of the given option is correct. Question may contain insufficient data.

EXPLANATIONS

1. The correct definition to an array is, Array index must be integers. Enumerators, characters and boolean can be used in place of an integer but not real.

2. The term 'Phong' is associated with shading. Phong shading refers to surface shading in 3D computer graphics. It is also known as Phong interpolation or normal-vector interpolation shading.

3. The subnet mask 255.255.255.192 has total 26 bits. 192 is written as 11000000 which has 2 subnet id bits and rest are host id bits.

4. On a LAN, the IP datagrams are transported in the information field of ethernet frame.

5. In ethernet, the source address field in the MAC frame is the previous stations physical address. Source and destination's physical address changes multiple time throughout the route may times.

6. In CSMA operation Radio is not suitable to the collision may remain undetected if CSMA operation is used.

8. TCP sliding window can be used to control the flow of information. A sliding window protocol allows an unlimited number of packets to be communicated using fixed-size sequence numbers.

9. Highest frequency = 4 MHz

   Lowest frequency = 40 kHz

   Bandwidth = Highest frequency – Lowest frequency

   $\quad\quad$ = 4 MHz-0.04 MHz

   Bandwidth = 3.96 MHz

10. In IEEE 802.5, the token passing scheme is used. The token passing is a channel access method providing fair access for all stations, and eliminating the collision of contention-based access methods.

11. **Boolean theorem:**

   $AB + \bar{A} C + BC = AB + \bar{A} C$

   Boolean theorem in which '.' is replaced by '+' and '+' is replaced by '.', we get

   $(A + B)(\bar{A} + C)(B + C) = (A + B)(\bar{A} + C)$

13. Given Integer,

   $$N^2 = (7601)_8$$
   $$\Rightarrow \quad N^2 = 7 \times 8^3 + 6 \times 8^2 + 0 \times 8^1 + 1 \times 8°$$
   $$\Rightarrow \quad N^2 = 3969 = (63)^2$$
   $$\Rightarrow \quad N = 63$$

i.e., $(143)_6$, it can be written as

   $$= 1 \times 6^2 + 4 \times 6^1 + 3 \times 6°$$
   $$= 36 + 24 + 3 = 63$$

14. Given baud rate is 2400, hence a maximum of 2400 bits are transferred per second. Total data is of 11 bits, since there are 8 bits of character code, 1 start bit and 2 stop bits.

   Hence, number of characters transmitted per second

   $$= \frac{2400}{11} = [218.18] = 218.$$

15. Process will execute in the following manner,

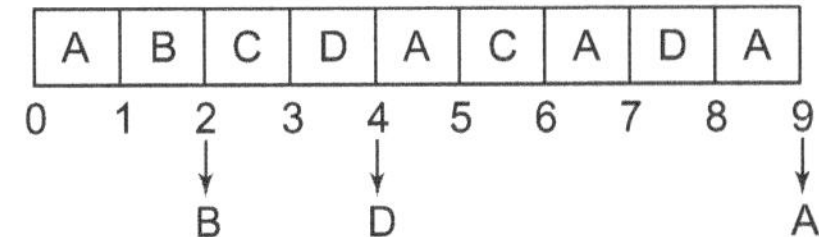

   Hence, the completion times of process 'A' is 9 time units using round robin scheduling with time slice of 1 time unit.

16. To find all pair shortest distance in a graph using floydd Warshal's algorithm which works on dynamic programming approach.

17. 8086 is a 16 bit microprocessor, that means data lines are of 16 bit and address lines are of 20 bit which constitutes the address space of 2^{20} bytes.

18. When more than one word are put in one cache block to exploit the spatial locality of reference in a program.

19. When pipeline stages have different delay, then the maximum of all the delays is taken for every stage.

   Hence all the condition will lead to an impact on the performance of pipelined processor.

20. Given number $(12x)_3 = (123)_x$ from condition, if the radix of a number is 'x' the any number of that radix can contain digits from 0 to $x – 1$. So, as per the question the radix of LHS is 3 so there can only be digits from 0 to 2. Since, 2 is in the option, hence considering 2 as the radix of RHS will make 123 invalid, since only 0 and 1 digits will be allowed.

   All the condition of MoS satisfied over bipolar device.

22. When we design MUX for 2^{10} input then. At the first, there will be 512 MUX, at second level, there will be 256 MUX, at third level 128 MUX will be there continuous so at last level 1 MUX is required.

   Total required = 512 + 256 + 128 + 64 + 64

   $\quad\quad\quad\quad\quad$ + 32 + 16 + 8 + 4 + 2 + 1

   $\quad\quad$ = 1023

23. Given 'a' is 0.052, hence Mantissa will be '0.52' and exponent will be '–1'.

Since 'b' is '28E + 11', hence Mantissa will be '0.28' and exponent will be '13'.

'$b + a$' will be 280000000000000. 52E-1 = 28 E + 11.

So, now '$b - b$' will be 0.

24. Given expression

$$= (A + \bar{C})(\bar{B} + \bar{C})$$
$$= A\bar{B} + A\bar{C} + \bar{B}\bar{C} + \bar{C}$$
$$= A\bar{B} + \bar{B}\bar{C} + \bar{C}(1 + A) \quad [\because 1 + A = 1]$$
$$= A\bar{B} + \bar{B}\bar{C} + \bar{C}$$
$$= A\bar{B} + \bar{C}(1 + \bar{B}) \quad \left[\because 1 + \bar{B} = 1\right]$$
$$= A\bar{B} + \bar{C}$$

26. From figure-1 output of first OR GATE is, $\overline{X + \bar{Y}}$

and second will give $\overline{X + \bar{X}Y}$, which can be written as $\bar{X}(X + \bar{Y})$ which is $\overline{X}\overline{Y}$.

Figure-2 output of $X\bar{Y}$.

Hence, both are entirely different.

27. All the gate are XOR gate in the circuit so, first XOR gate, input 0 is provide which will result in 0, again for the second and third XOR gate, input 0 will be there, hence the final output will be 0.

28. From the truth table of XOR gate when 'A' and 'B' are set of inputs and 'X' is the output.

A	B	X
0	0	0
0	1	1
1	0	1
1	1	0

All the condition are true except (b).

29. Maximum number of edges in a simple graph can be $\dfrac{n(n-1)}{2}$ where 'n' is the number of vertices.

Since, maximum 3 edges are possible in the graph with three nodes. So total 4 cases are possible, there can be a graph with 0 edge, 1 edge. 2 edges or 3 edges.

30. The maximum number of edges in a n-node undirected graph without self loops is $\dfrac{n(n-1)}{2}$ i.e., n nodes each having degree $(n-1)$ then divide by 2. Because we are calculating each degree 2 times.

31. Magnitude of 1st matrix = x² – 1

Magnitude of 2nd matrix = $-x^2 - x$

So, Magnitude of 1st matrix
$$= \text{Magnitude of } 2^{nd} \text{ matrix}$$
$$x^2 - 1 = -x^2 - x$$
$$2x^2 + x - 1 = 0$$

Hence, the value of x is $\dfrac{1}{2}$.

32. Class 'C' network has the range between is 192.0.0.0 to 223.255.255.0. So, 198.78.41.0 lies this network, hence it is a class 'C' network.

33. The join operation can be defined as a combination of Cartesian product followed by a selection processes. The join operation can be defined as a Cartesian product of two relations followed by a selection.

34. An orthogonal matrix is a square matrix with real entries whose columns and rows are orthogonal unit vectors (i.e., orthogonal vectors), i.e.,

$$A^T A = A A^T = I$$

where I is the identity matrix.

35. Embedded pointer are pointer set in a data record. So it provides a secondary access path.

36. A vectored interrupt is an input/output interrupt that tells part of the computer that handless input/output interrupts at the hardware level that a request for attention from an input/output device has been received.

37. Cycle stealing is a method of accessing RAM without interfering with the CPU. Most systems halt the CPU during the steal and use this time to send information on buses.

38. An interpreter will interpret program every-time, the program is made to execute unlike compiler which will run the source code. Hence, relative to the program translated by a compiler run fast the same program when interpreted runs.

39.

Instruction	Meaning	Execution
MVI A 30 H	Move 30H to accumulator	[A] = 30H = 0011 0000
ACI 30 H	Add 30H to accumulator with carry	[A] = 60H = 01100000
XRA A	XOR between the content of 'A' and accumulator	A ⊕ A = 0000 0000

Hence, after the execution of the above program, the content of accumulator will be 00H.

40. From the given C function

Consider, $f(1) \rightarrow n = 2, i = 2$

$\qquad f(2) \rightarrow n = 4, i = 3$

$\qquad f(4) \rightarrow n = 7, i = 4$

$\qquad f(7) \rightarrow$ return 7

The value returned by $f(1)$ is 7.

41. In resident OS computer, Loader is a program that loads machines codes of a program into the system memory.

42. For releasing SIMD, Von Neumann architecture is a computer architecture that describes a design ' architec-ture for an electronic digital computer with parts consisting of a processing unit containing an arithmetic logic unit and processor registers, a control unit containing an instruction register and program counter, a memory to store both data and instructions, external mass storage, and input and output mechanism.

43. After considering the following code, the value of 'k' is incremented by 2, so at the value of 'k' = '4, 10' and '16' if condition will return true, hence the output will be 4 10 16.

44. By using interface we can correct peripheral to computer.

45. There are 6 pins available in 8085 for interrupt that are TRAP, RST 7.5, RST 6.5, RST 5.5, INTR and INTA. Interrupt TRAP' is both positive and negative edge triggered.

46. RAID configurations of disks are used to provide both fault tolerance as well as high speed.

47. On a context switch between the process, translation look-aside buffers need not necessarily be saved. But program counter, stack and registers must be saved, otherwise program can not resume.

48. Gray code is a binary numeral system where two successive values differ in only one bit. Gray codes are widely used to facilitate error correction in digital communication.

49. The total time to prepare a disk drive mechanism for a block of data to be read from it is latency plus seek time.

50. Feedback queries dispatch task according to execution characteristics. It allows a process to move between queries.

51. In round robin CPU scheduling algorithm in a time shared system.

52. In computer science dynamic address translation is the process of translating a virtual address into the corres-ponding physical address which is done by a hardware called memory management unit.

53. Thrashing occurs when a computer's virtual memory subsystem is in a constant state of paging, rapidly exchanging data in memory for data on disk, to the exclusion of most application level processing.

54. Operating system that reads and reacts in terms of actual time is called real time system. A real time system is an operating system intended to serve real time application process data as it comes in, typically without buffering delays.

55. The memory address register is a register in CPU that contains the address of the memory location that is to be read from or stored into.

57. Dirty bit for a page in a page table helps avoid unnecessary writes on a paging device.

58. Checkpointing is a method of periodically saving the state of a job so that, if for some reason, the job could not be completed, it can be resumed later from the same stage.

59. Public key cryptosystem is a cryptographic system that uses pairs of keys: Public keys that may be disseminated widely paired with private keys which are known only to the owner. The encryption system ensures that only the correct receiver decodes the data.

60. Overlaying means the process of transferring a block of program code or other data into internal memory, replacing what is already stored. It is a programming method that allows programs to be larger than the computer's main memory.

61. A critical section is a part of multi-threaded program that may not be concurrently executed by more than one of the program's processes.

62. Mutual exclusion condition is a property of concurrency control, which is instituted for the purpose of preventing race conditions.

63. Fork ( ) is a system call that is used for the creation of a new process.

64. Translation look-aside buffer need not necessarily be saved on a context switch between processes. In a process content switch, the state of the first process must be saved somehow.

So, that when the scheduler gets back to the execution of the first process, it can restore this state and continue.

65. Logical address space

$\qquad$ = Number of pages × Number of words

$\qquad$ = 8 × 1024W

$\qquad$ = 2^{13} W

Required address bit are 13.

66. The performance of Round Robin algorithm depends heavily on the size of the time quantum, size of the process and the CPU bursts of the process.

67. In optimal page replacement algorithm; at the moment when a page fault has occurred, some set of pages are in the memory. One of those pages will be referenced on the very next instruction. Other pages may not be referenced.

68. Declaration statements usually produces no executable code when compiled.

69. $F(4)^{(5)}$

$|$

$F(3)^{(2)} \times F(2)^{(2)} + F(1)^{(1)}$

$|$

$F(2)^{(2)} \times F(1)^{(1)} + F(0)^{(0)}$

The value returned by $F(4)$ will be 5,

70. Let if element 'c' is printed then it can be said that the contentof the stack before printing was,

c
b
a

which after printing 'c' becomes

b
a

So, since stack is a first-in first-out kind of data structure, hence 'b' will be printed before element'a'.

71. The time required to search an element in a linked list of length 'n' is $O(n)$.

72. Deleting a new node whose location is given is the operation that is performed more efficiently by doubly linked list than by linear list because we have both the pointers i.e., the pointer to the previous as well as to the next node, since there two pointers need to be edited. But in case of linear list, we don't have pointer to the previous node.

73. We can make a class abstracted by making at least one member function as pure virtual function. A pure virtual is a virtual function which does not have any sort of implementation, they just can be declared.

74. A steiner patch is biquadratic bezier patch. Bezier surface are a species of mathematical spline used in the computer.

75. Heap is a complete binary tree which has the property that the value at each node is at least as large as the values at its children.

76. Every node of a doubly linked list has three fields namely data section, pointer to the next node pointer to the previous node. For example,

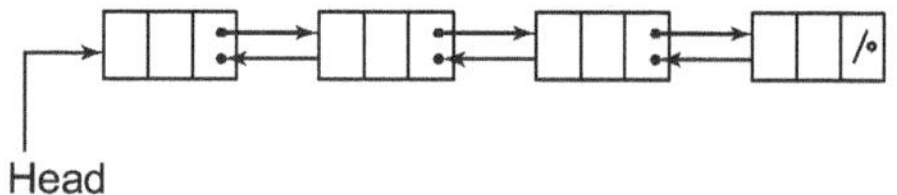

77. At 1st iteration, there will be 4 comparisons. At 2nd iteration, there will be 3 comparisons, followed by 2 and 1 comparisons at 3rd and 4th iteration.

So, total comparisons will be 4 + 3 + 2 + 1 = 10 comparisons.

78. A valide strong component is the subgraph of the graph where every node has a path to every other node of the subgraph.

In the given graph, considering the subgraph 'abc'. Hence every vertex has a path to every other vertex. Hence, this is a valid strong component.

79. The difference between the calculated approximation of a number and its exact mathematical value due to rounding. Repeated execution of simple computation may cause compounding of round-off errors.

80. In C the effect of a negative number in a field width specifier is that the values are displayed left justified.

■■

SOLVED PAPER 2009
Computer Science

1. The subnet mask for a particular network is 255. 255.31.0. Which of the following pairs of IP addresses could belong to this network?

   (*a*) 172.57.88.62 and 172.56.87.23

   (*b*) 10.35.28.2 and 10.35.29.4

   (*c*) 191.203.31.87 and 191.234. 31.88

   (*d*) 128.8.129.43 and 128.8.161.55

2. In networking, UTP stands for

   (*a*) Unshielded T-connector port

   (*b*) Unshielded twisted pair

   (*c*) Unshielded terminating pair

   (*d*) Unshielded transmission process

3. The address resolution protocol (ARP) is used for

   (*a*) Finding the IP address from the DNS

   (*b*) Finding the IP address of the default gateway

   (*c*) Finding the IP address that corresponds to a MAC address

   (*d*) Finding the MAC address that corresponds to an IP address

4. Which of the following is a MAC address?

   (*a*) 192.166.200.50

   (*b*) 00056A:01A01A5CCA7FF60

   (*c*) 568, Airport Road

   (*d*) 01 : A5 : BB : A7 : FF : 60

5. What is the primary purpose of a VLAN?

   (*a*) Demonstrating the proper layout for a network

   (*b*) Simulating a network

   (*c*) To create a virtual private network

   (*d*) Segmenting a network inside a switch or device

6. SHA-1 is a

   (*a*) Encryption algorithm

   (*b*) Decryption algorithm

   (*c*) Key exchange algorithm

   (*d*) Message digest function

7. Advanced Encryption Standard (AES) is based on

   (*a*) Asymmetric key algorithm

   (*b*) Symmetric key algorithm

   (*c*) Public key algorithm

   (*d*) Key exchange

8. The primary purpose of an operating system is

   (*a*) To make the most efficient use of the computer hardware

   (*b*) To allow people to use the computer

   (*c*) To keep systems programmers employed

   (*d*) To make computers easier to use

9. Which is the correct definition of a valid process transition in an operating system?

   (*a*) Wake up : ready → running

   (*b*) Dispatch : ready → running

   (*c*) Block: ready → running

   (*d*) Timer runout: → ready → blocked

10. The correct matching of the following pairs is

List-I	List-II
A. Disk check	1. Round robin
B. Batch processing	2. Scan
C. Time sharing	3. LIFO
D. Stack operation	4. FIFO

Codes :

	A	B	C	D
(*a*)	3	4	2	1
(*b*)	4	3	2	1
(*c*)	3	4	1	2
(*d*)	2	4	1	3

11. A page fault

   (*a*) Occurs when a program accesses an available page of memory

   (*b*) is an error in a specific page

   (*c*) is a reference to a page belonging to another program

   (*d*) occurs when a program accesses a page not currently in memory

12. Using a larger block size in a fixed block size file system leads to

   (*a*) better disk throughput but poorer disk space utilization

   (*b*) better disk throughput and better disk space utilization

   (*c*) poorer disk throughput but better disk space utilization

   (*d*) poorer disk throughput and poorer disk space utilization

13. Which of the following statements about synchronous and asynchronous I/O is NOT true?

(a) An ISR is invoked on completion of I/O in synchronous I/O but not in asynchronous I/O

(b) In both synchronous and asynchronous I/O an ISR (Interrupt Service Routine) is invoked after completion of the I/O

(c) A process making a synchronous I/O call waits until I/O is complete, but a process making an asynchronous I/O call does not wait for completion of the I/O

(d) In the case of synchronous I/O, the process waiting for the completion of I/O is woken up by the ISR that is invoked after the completion of I/O

14. Consider three CPU-intensive processes, which require 10, 20 and 30 time units and arrive at times 0, 2 and 6, respectively. How many context switches are needed if the operating system implements a shortest remaining time first scheduling algorithm? Do not count the context switches at time zero and at the end.

(a) 1   (b) 2

(c) 3   (d) 4

15. The performance of Round Robin algorithm depends heavily on

(a) size of the process

(b) the I/O bursts of the process

(c) the CPU bursts of the process

(d) the size of the time quantum

16. Consider a system having "n" resources of same type. These resources are shared by 3 processes, A, B, C. These have peak demands of 3, 4, and 6 respectively. For what value of "n" deadlock won't occur

(a) 15   (b) 9

(c) 10   (d) 13

17. Consider a set of 5 processes whose arrival time, CPU time needed and the priority are given below:

Process Priority	Arrival Time (in ms)	CPU Time needed (in ms)	Priority
P_1	0	10	5
P_2	0	5	2
P_3	2	3	1
P_4	5	20	4
P_5	10	2	3

(Smaller the number, higher the priority).

If the CPU scheduling policy is priority scheduling without pre-emption, the average waiting time will be

(a) 12.8 ms   (b) 11.8 ms

(c) 10.8 ms   (d) 09.8 ms

18. The range of integers that can be represented by an n-bit 2's complement number system is

(a) -2^{n-1} to $(2^{n-1}-1)$

(b) $-(2^{n-1} - 1)$ to $(2^{n-1} - 1)$

(c) -2^{n-1} to 2^{n-1}

(b) $-(2^{n-1} + 1)$ to $(2^{n-1} - 1)$

19. The switching expression corresponding to $f(A, B, C, D) = \Sigma(1, 4, 5, 9, 11, 12)$ is

(a) $BC'D' + A'C'D + AB'D$

(b) $ABC' + ACD + B'C'D$

(c) $ACD' + A'BC' + AC'D'$

(d) $A'BD + ACD' + BCD'$

20. Consider the following boolean function of four variables $f(w, x, y, z) = \Sigma(1, 3, 4, 6, 9, 11, 12, 14)$, the function is

(a) Independent of one variable

(b) Independent of two variables

(c) Independent of three variables

(d) Dependent on all the variables

21. In which addressing mode, the effectives address of the operand is generated by adding a constant value to the content of a register?

(a) Absolute mode

(b) Indirect mode

(c) Immediate mode

(d) Index mode

22. A certain microprocessor requires 4.5 microseconds to respond to an interrupt. Assuming that the three interrupts l_1, l_2 and l_3 require the following execution time after the interrupt is recognized :

1. l_1 requires 25 microseconds

2. l_2 requires 35 microseconds

3. l_3 requires 20 microseconds

l_1 has the highest priority and l_3 has the lowest. What is the possible range of time for l_3 to be executed assuming that it may or may not occur simultaneously with other interrupts?

(a) 24.5 microseconds to 39.5 microseconds

(b) 24.5 microseconds to 93.5 microseconds

(c) 4.5 microseconds to 24.5 microseconds

(d) 29.5 microseconds to 93.5 microseconds

23. The process of organizing the memory into two banks to allow 8 and 16 bit data operation is called

(a) Bank switching

(b) Indexed mapping

(c) Two-way memory interleaving

(d) Memory segmentation

24. Suppose the numbers 7, 5, 1, 8, 3, 6, 0, 9, 4, 2 are inserted in that order into an initially empty binary search tree. The binary search tree uses the usual ordering on natural numbers. What is the in-order traversal sequence of the resultant tree?

(a) 7 5 1 0 3 2 4 6 8 9

(b) 0 2 4 3 1 6 5 9 8 7

(c) 0 1 2 3 4 5 6 7 8 9

(d) 9 8 6 4 2 3 0 1 5 7

25. A data structure is required for storing a set of integers such that each of the following operations can be done in (log n) time, where n is the number of elements in the set.

1. Deletion of the smallest element

2. Insertion of an element if it is not already present in the set

Which of the following data structures can be used for this purpose?

(a) A heap can be used but not a balanced binary search tree

(b) A balanced binary search tree can be used but not a heap

(c) Both balanced binary search tree and heap can be used

(d) Neither balanced search tree nor heap can be used

26. The following numbers are inserted into an empty binary search tree in the given order: 10, 1, 3, 5, 15, 12,16. What is the height of the binary search tree (the height is the maximum distance of a leaf node from the root)?

(a) 2   (b) 3

(c) 4   (d) 6

27. Assume that the operators +, −, × are left associative and ^ is right associative. The order of precedence (from highest to lowest) is ^, ×, +, −. The postfix expression corresponding to the infix expression $a + b \times c - d \wedge e \wedge f$ is

(a) $abc \times + def \wedge\wedge -$

(b) $abc \times + de \wedge f \wedge$

(c) $ab + c \times d - e \wedge f \wedge$

(d) $- + a \times bc \wedge\wedge def$

28. The infix expression $A + (B - C) * D$ is correctly represented in prefix notation as

(a) $A + B - C * D$ (b) $+ A * - BCD$

(c) $ABC - D*+$ (d) $A + BC - D*$

29. A one dimensional array A has indices 1... 75. Each element is a string and takes up three memory words. The array is stored location 1120 decimal. The starting address of A[49] is

(a) 1267   (b) 1164

(c) 1264   (d) 1169

30. The five items : A, B, C, D, and E are pushed in a stack, one after the other starting from A. The stack is popped four times and each element is inserted in a queue. Then two elements are deleted from the queue and pushed back on the stack. Now one item is popped from the stack. The popped item is

(a) A   (b) B

(c) C   (d) D

31. A full binary tree with n leaves contains

(a) n nodes   (b) $\log_2 n$ nodes

(c) $2n - 1$ (d) 2^n nodes

32. The expression $1 * 2 \wedge 3 * 4 \wedge 5 * 6$ will be evaluated as

(a) 32^{30} (b) 162^{30}

(c) 49152   (d) 173458

33. The feature in object-oriented programming that allows the same operation to be carried out differently, depending on the object, is

(a) Inheritance   (b) Polymorphism

(c) Over functioning (d) Overriding

34. The microinstructions stored in the control memory of a processor have a width of 26 bits. Each microinstruction is divided into three fields : a micro operation field of 13 bits, a next address field (X), and a MUX select field (Y). There are 8 status bits in the inputs of the MUX. How many bits are there in the X and Y fields, and what is the size of the control memory in number of words?

(a) 10, 3, 1024   (b) 8, 5, 256

(c) 5, 8, 2048   (d) 10, 3, 512

35. A CPU has 24-bit instructions. A program starts at address 300 (in decimal). Which one of the following is a legal program, counter (all values in decimal)?

(a) 400   (b) 500

(c) 600   (d) 700

36. Consider a disk pack with 16 surfaces, 128 tracks per surface and 256 sectors per track. 512 bytes of data are stores in a bit serial manner in a sector. The capacity of the disk pack and the number of bits required to specify a particular sector in the disk are respectively.

(a) 256 Mbyte, 19 bits

(b) 256 Mbyte, 28 bits

(c) 512 Mbyte, 20 bits

(d) 64 Gbyte, 28 bits

37. Consider a pipelined processor with the following four stages:

- IF : Instruction Fetch
- ID : Instruction Decode and Operand Fetch
- EX: Execute
- WB : Write Back

The IF, ID and WB stages take one clock cycle each to complete the operation. The ADD and SUB instructions need 1 clock cycle and the MUL instruction need 3 clock cycles in the EX stage. Operand forwarding is used in the pipelined processor. What is the number of clock cycles taken to complete the following sequence of instructions?

ADD   R2, R1, R0   R2 ← R1 + R0

MUL   R4, R3, R2   R4 ← R3 * R2

SUB   R6, R5, R4   R6 ← R5 − R4

(a) 7   (b) 8

(c) 10   (d) 14

38. The use of multiple register windows with overlap causes a reduction in the number of memory accesses for

1. Function locals and parameters
2. Register saves and restores
3. Instruction fetches

(a) 1 only   (b) 2 only

(c) 3 only   (d) 1, 2 and 3

39. A processor that has carry, overflow and sign flag bits as part of its program status word (PSW) performs addition of the following two 2's complement numbers 01001101 and 11101001. After the execution of this addition operation, the status of the carry, overflow and sign flags, respectively will be

(a) 1, 1, 0

(b) 1, 0, 0

(c) 0, 1, 0

(d) 1, 0, 1

40. The two numbers given below are multiplied using the Booth's algorithm

Multiplicand : 0101 1010 1110 1110

Multiplier : 0111 0111 1011 1101

How many additions/subtraction, are required for the multiplication of the above two numbers?

(a) 6   (b) 8

(c) 10   (d) 12

41. The addition of 4-bit, two's complement, binary numbers 1101 and 0100 results in

(a) 0001 and an overflow

(b) 1001 and no overflow '

(c) 0001 and no overflow

(d) 1001 and an overflow

42. Which of the following statements about relative addressing mode is FALSE?

(a) It enables reduced instruction size

(b) It allows indexing of array element with same instruction

(c) It enables easy relocation of data

(d) It enables faster address calculation than absolute addressing

43. Substitution of values for names (whose values are constants) is done in

(a) Local optimization

(b) Loop optimization

(c) Constant folding

(d) Strength reduction

44. A root α of equation $f(x) = 0$ can be computed to any degree of accuracy if a 'good' initial approximation x_0 is chosen for which

(a) $f(x_0) > 0$ (b) $f(x_0) f''(x_0) > 0$

(c) $f(x_0) f''(x_0) < 0$ (d) $f''(x_0) > 0$

45. Which of the following statement is correct

(a) $\Delta(u_k v_k) = u_k \Delta v_k + v_k \Delta u_k$

(b) $\Delta(u_k v_k) = v_{k+1} \Delta v_k + v_{k+1} \Delta u_k$

(c) $\Delta(u_k v_k) = v_{k+1} \Delta u_k + u_k \Delta v_k$

(d) $\Delta(u_k v_k) = u_{k+1} \Delta v_k + v_k \Delta u_k$

46. The shift operator E is defined as $E[f(x_i)] = f(x_i + h)$ and $E^{-1}[f(x_i)] = f(x_i - h)$. Then Δ (forward difference) in terms of E is

(a) $E - 1$

(b) E

(c) $1 - E^{-1}$

(d) $1 - E$

47. The formula

$$\int_{x0}^{xn} y(n)dx \simeq \frac{h}{2}(y_0 + 2y_1 + \dots + 2y_{n-1} + y_n)$$

$$-\frac{h}{12}(\nabla y_n - \Delta y_0) - \frac{h}{24}(\nabla^2 y_n + \Delta^2 y_0)\frac{-19h}{720}$$

$(\nabla^3 y_n - \Delta^3 y_0)\dots$ is called

(a) Simpson rule   (b) Trapezoidal rule

(c) Romberg's rule   (d) Gregory's formula

48. The cubic polynomial $y(x)$ which takes the following values : $y(0) = 1$, $y(1) = 0$, $y(2) = 1$ and $y(3) = 10$ is

(a) $x^3 + 2x^2 + 1$ (b) $x^3 + 3x^2 - 1$

(c) $x^3 + 1$ (d) $x^3 - 2x^2 + 1$

49. $x = a\cos(t)$, $y = b\sin(t)$ is the parametric form of

(a) Ellipse   (b) Hyperbola

(c) Circle   (d) Parabola

50. The value of x at which y is minimum for $y = x^2 - 3x + 1$ is

(a) $-3/2$ (b) $3/2$

(c) 0 (d) $-5/4$

51. The formula

$$P_k = y_0 + k\nabla y_0 + \frac{k(k+1)}{2}\nabla^2 y_0 + \dots + k\dots$$

$$\frac{(k+n-1)}{n!}\nabla^n y_0 \text{ is}$$

(a) Newton's backward formula

(b) Gauss forward formula

(c) Gauss backward formula

(d) Stirling's formula

52. If G is a graph with e edges and n vertices the sum of the degrees of all vertices in G is

(a) e (b) $e/2$

(c) e^2 (d) $2e$

53. Let G be an arbitrary graph with n nodes and k components. If a vertex is removed from G, the number of components in the resultant graph must necessarily lie between

(a) k and n (b) $k - 1$ and $k + 1$

(c) $k - 1$ and $n - 1$ (d) $k + 1$ and $n - k$

54. A graph in which all nodes are of equal degree, is known as

(a) Multigraph   (b) Non regular graph

(c) Regular graph   (d) Complete graph

55. If in a graph G there is one and only one path between every pair of vertices then G is a

(a) Path   (b) Walk

(c) Tree   (d) Circuit

56. A simple graph (a graph without parallel edge or loops) with n vertices and k components can have at most

(a) n edges

(b) $(n - k)$ edges

(c) $(n - k)(n - k + 1)$

(d) $(n - k)(n - k + 1)/2$ edges

57. Consider the polynomial $p(x) = a_0 + a_1 x + a_2 x^2 + a_3 x^3$, where $a_i \neq 0$, $\forall i$. The minimum number of multiplications needed to evaluate p on an input is

(a) 3   (b) 4

(c) 6   (d) 9

58. Consider the following code written in a pass-by-reference language like FORTRAN subroutine swap (ix, iy)

    $it = ix$

L1: $ix = iy$

L2: $iy = it$

    end

    $ia = 3$

    $ib = 8$

    call swap $(ia, ib + 5)$

    print*, ia, ib end

S_1: The compiler will generate code to allocate a temporary nameless cell, initialize it to 13, and pass the address of the cell to swap

S_2: On execution the code will generate a runtime error on line L1.

S_3: On execution the code will generate a runtime error on line L2.

S_4: The program will print 13 and 8.

S_5: The program will print 13 and –2.

Exactly the following set of statement(s) is correct

(a) S_1 and S_2 (b) S_1 and S_4

(c) S_3 only   (d) S_1 and S_5

59. A square matrix A is called orthogonal if $A'A =$

(a) I (b) A

(c) $-A$ (d) $-I$

60. If two adjacent rows of a determinant are interchanged, the value of the determinant

(a) becomes zero

(b) remains unaltered

(c) becomes infinite

(d) becomes negative of its original value

61. If $\begin{vmatrix} 3 & 3 \\ x & 5 \end{vmatrix} = 3$, then the value of x is

(a) 2   (b) 3

(c) 4   (d) 5

62. If A, B, C are any three matrices, then $A' + B' + C'$ is equal to

(a) a null matrix   (b) $A + B + C$

(c) $(A + B + C)'$ (d) $-(A + B + C)$

63. $\begin{vmatrix} 265 & 240 & 219 \\ 240 & 225 & 198 \\ 219 & 198 & 181 \end{vmatrix} =$

(a) 779   (b) 679

(c) 0   (d) 256

64. Let $f(x)$ be the continuous probability density function of a random variable x, the probability that $a < x \leq b$, is

(a) $f(b - a)$ (b) $f(b) - f(a)$

(c) $\int_a^b f(x)dx$ (d) $\int_a^b xf(x)dx$

65. If the mean of a normal frequency distribution of 1000 items is 25 and its standard deviation is 2.5, then its maximum ordinate is

(a) $\dfrac{1000}{\sqrt{2\pi}}e^{-25}$ (b) $\dfrac{1000}{\sqrt{2\pi}}$

(c) $\dfrac{1000}{\sqrt{2\pi}}e^{-2.5}$ (d) $\dfrac{400}{\sqrt{2\pi}}$

66. If the pdf of a Poisson distribution is given by $f(x) = \dfrac{e^{-2}2^x}{x!}$ then its mean is

(a) 2^x (b) 2

(c) -2 (d) 1

67. Activities which ensure that the software that has been built, is traceable to customer requirement is covered as part of

(a) Verification   (b) Validation

(c) Maintenance   (d) Modeling

68. A testing method which is normally used as the acceptance test for a software system, is

(a) Regression Testing

(b) Integration Testing

(c) Unit Testing

(d) System Testing

69. The 'command' used to change contents of one database using the contents of another database by linking them on a common key field is called

(a) Replace   (b) Join

(c) Change   (d) Update

70. A locked database file can be

(a) Accessed by only one user

(b) Modified by users with the correct password

(c) Used to hide sensitive information

(d) Updated by more than one user

71. Which of the following contains complete record of all activity that affected the contents of a database during a certain period of time?

(a) Transaction log

(b) Query language

(c) Report writer

(d) Data manipulation language

72. Purpose of 'Foreign Key' in a table is to ensure

(a) Null Integrity

(b) Referential Integrity

(c) Domain Integrity

(d) Null and Domain Integrity

73. Which of the following scenarios may lead to an irrecoverable error in a database system?

(a) A transaction writes a data item after it is read by an uncommitted transaction

(b) A transaction reads a data item after it is read by an uncommitted transaction

(c) A transaction reads a data item after it is written by a committed transaction

(d) A transaction reads a data item after it is written by an uncommitted transaction

74. Use of IPSEC in tunnel mode results in

(a) IP packet with same header

(b) IP packet with new header

(c) IP packet without header

(d) No changes in IP packet

75. Special software to create a job queue is called a

(a) Driver   (b) Spooler

(c) Interpreter   (d) Linkage editor

76. Process is

(a) A program in high level language kept on disk

(b) Contents of main memory

(c) A program in execution

(d) A job in secondary memory

77. When a process is rolled back as a result of deadlock the difficulty which arises is

(a) Starvation

(b) System throughput

(c) Low device utilization

(d) Cycle stealing

78. On receiving an interrupt from an I/O device, the CPU

(a) Halts for a predetermined time

(b) Branches off to the interrupt service routine after completion of the current instruction

(c) Branches off to the interrupt service routine immediately

(d) Hands over control of address bus and data bus to the interrupting device

79. Compared to CISC processors, RISC processors contain

(a) More register and smaller instruction set

(b) larger instruction set and less registers

(c) less registers and smaller instruction set

(d) more transistor elements

80. Which of the following is/are true of the auto-increment addressing mode?

1. It is useful in creating self-relocating code

2. If it is included in an Instruction Set Architecture, then an additional ALU is required for effective address calculation

3. The amount of increment depends on the size of the data item accessed

(a) 1 only

(b) 2 only

(c) 3 only

(d) 2 and 3 only

ANSWERS

1. (d)	**2.** (b)	**3.** (d)	**4.** (d)	**5.** (d)	**6.** (d)	**7.** (b)	**8.** (a)	**9.** (b)	**10.** (d)
11. (d)	**12.** (a)	**13.** (b)	**14.** (b)	**15.** (d)	**16.** (d)	**17.** (c)	**18.** (a)	**19.** (a)	**20.** (b)
21. (d)	**22.** (b)	**23.** (c)	**24.** (b)	**25.** (b)	**26.** (a)	**27.** (a)	**28.** (b)	**29.** (c)	**30.** (d)
31. (c)	**32.** (b)	**33.** (a)	**34.** (a)	**35.** (c)	**36.** (b)	**37.** (b)	**38.** (b)	**39.** (b)	**40.** (b)
41. (a)	**42.** (b)	**43.** (c)	**44.** (b)	**45.** (b)	**46.** (b)	**47.** (d)	**48.** (a)	**49.** (b)	**50.** (a)
51. (d)	**52.** (c)	**53.** (c)	**54.** (c)	**55.** (d)	**56.** (a)	**57.** (b)	**58.** (a)	**59.** (d)	**60.** (c)
61. (c)	**62.** (c)	**63.** (c)	**64.** (c)	**65.** (b)	**66.** (b)	**67.** (d)	**68.** (b)	**69.** (a)	**70.** (a)
71. (b)	**72.** (d)	**73.** (d)	**74.** (b)	**75.** (c)	**76.** (a)	**77.** (b)	**78.** (a)	**79.** (c)	**80.** (c)

Note: * None of the given option is correct. Question may contain insufficient data.

EXPLANATIONS

1. Given network, 255.255.31.0

   For belong on same network, pair of IP will give same network address after anding with subnet mask.

   (i) 128.8.129.43   (ii) 128.8.161.55
        255.255.31.0   255.255.31.0
   ______________   ______________
        128.8.1.0   128.8.1.0

   So, both IP are belong to same address 128.8.1.0.

2. In networking UTP stands for unshielded twisted pair which is made up by twisting two unshielded wires on each other.

3. Address resalution protocol ARP stands for address resolution protocol used for finding mac address for the corresponding IP address.

4. The standard format of MAC contain 48 bit. Where each 4 bit represented in hexa decimal formal i.e., 12 hexadecimal numbers in group, each contain 2 hexadecimal number, each separated by:

   or – or;

   So, .01 : A5 : BB : A7 : FF : .60.

5. The primary purpose of VLAN is to segmenting a network inside a switch or device.

6. SHA-1 stands for secure hashing algorithm used in cryptograph to create message digest.

7. Advance encryption standard (AES) is used in symmetric key algorithm.

8. The primary purpose of operating system is to make efficient use of computer hardware i.e., easy to use and time efficient.

9. Correct difinition of a valid process is given

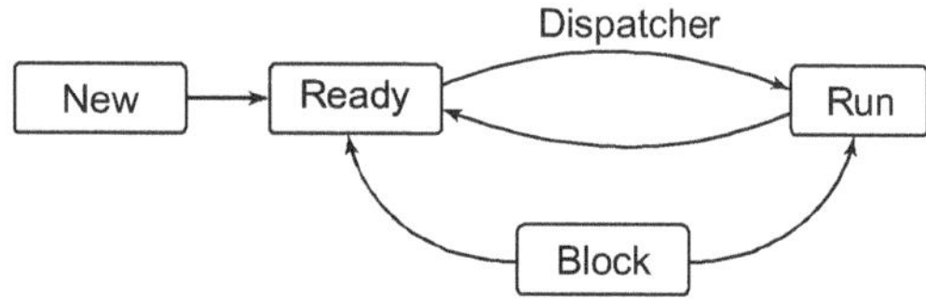

   So, ready to running is done by dispatching process.

10. Disk check is done by scan algorithm. Batch processing processes jobs is first-in first-out. Time sharing is done via round robin based on time quantum.

    Stack operations is based on last is first out order.

11. A Page fault occur when OS refer some page in memory but it is not present. So a trap is generated and page is brought into main memory from hard disk.

12. Using larger block size in fixed block size file system leads to better disk throughput i.e., large amount of data will be transfer in given time but at same time which small block request is come than more space is wasted. So poorer disk utilization.

13. The statement in synchronous I/O ISR is used to place process from block state to ready state but in asynchronous I/O in place ISR, an handler function is used and during I/O operation process will be in active state.

14. Considering three-CPU Process

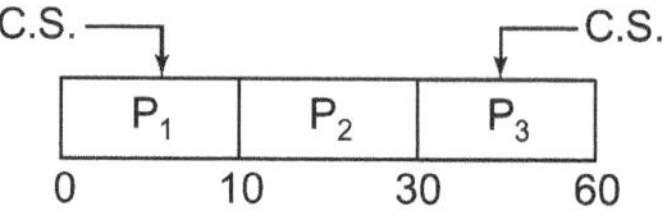

    2 context switching is needed.

15. The performance of round robin is depends on time quantum size. When time quantum size greater the time needed to run of all process then it behaves as FCFS.

16. Resources = n,   Three processes A, B, C

A	B	C
2	3	5

    if we give one more resource to any one of the process will ensure, their is no deadlock.

    i.e., $2 + 3 + 5 + 1 = 11$

    Since 11 is not present, so we go for next higher value i.e., 13.

17.

Process	Arrival Time (In ms)	Burst time	Completion time	Turn around time	Waiting time
P_1	0	10	40	40	30
P_2	0	5	5	5	0
P_3	2	3	8	6	3
P_4	5	20	28	23	3
P_4	10	2	30	20	18
					54/5 = 10.8

Gantt chart:

18. For n-bit range of 2's bit representation of integer is (-2^{n-1}) to $(2^{n-1} - 1)$.

19. expression $= f(A, B, C, D) = \Sigma(1, 4, 5, 9, 11, 12)$

    By using K-map :

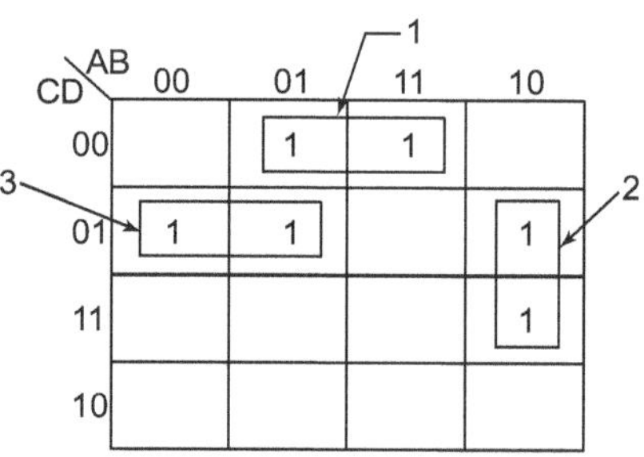

$f(A, B, C, D) = BC'D' + AB'D + A'C'D$

20. $f(w, x, y, z) = \Sigma(1, 3, 4, 6, 9, 11, 12, 14)$

By using K-map :

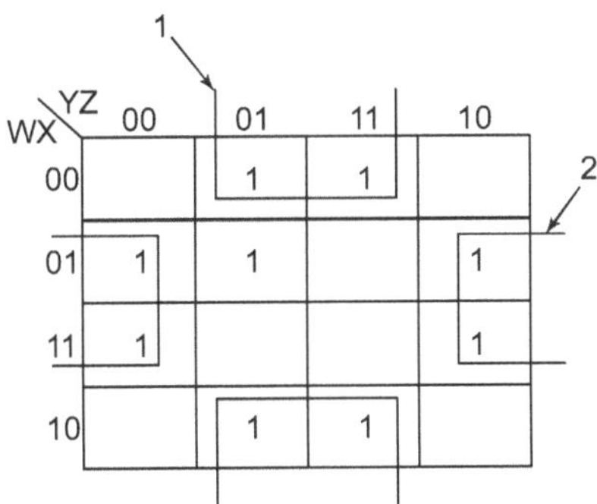

$f(w, x, y, z) = X'Z + XZ$

Since function is not depending on variable y. So independent of one variable.

21. Index addressing mode:

Effective address = [Base address + Displacement]

22. In a microprocessor minimum time required without simultaneous occurrence is = Execution time of I_3 + Response time

$$= 4.5 + 20 = 24.5 \text{ µsec}$$

Maximum time require when all work simultaneously.

$= I_1 + I_2 + I_3$ [Since I_1 and I_2 have high priority]

$= (4.5 + 25) + (4.5 + 35) + (4.5 + 20) = 93.5 \text{ µsec}$

23. The process or organizing the memory into two banks to allow 8 and 16 bits data operation is called two way memory interleaving.

24. The in-order traversal of binary search tree is increasing sorted order.

i.e., 0, 1, 2, 3, 4, 5, 6, 7, 8, 9

25. Given condition,

In heap deletion max element in min heap will take $O(n)$ so heap cannot be used in balanced binary search tree insertion and deletion will take $O(\log n)$.

26. Given numbers in the orders (10, 1, 3, 5, 15, 12, 16)

Binary search tree will represented as:

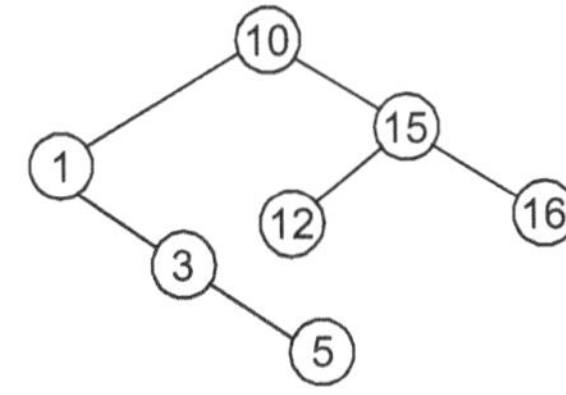

So, height is 3.

27. Given infix expression: $a + b \times c - d \wedge e \wedge f$

$a + b \times c - d \wedge e \wedge f$ (since $\wedge$ is right associative)

$a + b \times c - \text{def} \wedge\wedge$

$abc \times + - \text{def} \wedge\wedge$

$abc \times + \text{def} \wedge\wedge -$

28. Given infix expression :

So correctly represent in prefix notation

$A + (B - C) \times D$

$A + - BC \times D$

$A + \times - BCD$

$+ A \times - BCD$

29. Base address = 1120

Total element = 75

So, $A[49]$ = Base address + [(Location)] × 3

$$= 1120 + (48 \times 3)$$
$$= 1120 + 144 = 1264$$

30. Four item are pushed into stack A, B, C, D, E where Top is pointing E. Now 4 elements are deleted and enqueue into queue. So queue contain E, D, C, B where Rear is pointing B and Front pointing E.

Now two elements are deleted from the queue i.e. E and D respectively and pushed back on the stack i.e., e, d where stack Top pointing D now delete one element from stack gives D.

31. Full binary tree with n leaves contains (i.e., every node contain 2 child except leaf node)

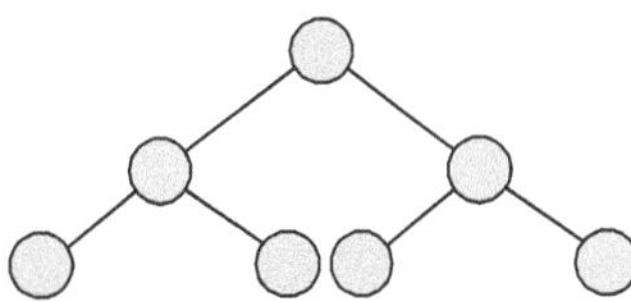

If leaf = n then total node = $2n - 1$.

32. Expression

$= 1 \times 2^3 \times 4^5 \times 6$ will evaluated as

$= 1 \times 8 \times 4^5 \times 6$

$= 1 \times 8 \times 1024 \times 6$

$= 49152$

In original question '5' is missing.

33. Polymorphism allow same operation to carried different meaning at different place.

34. Microinstruction width = 26 bits

	26	
Y	µ-operation	Address

log (8)=3   log (13)   26–(13+3)=10

So control memory size = 2^{10} = 1024

Number of bits for X = 10

Number of bits for Y = 3

35. Instruction size = 24 bits

Starting address of the program = 300. The size of instruction = 3 byte long.

So the address is always the multiple of 3 byte next address is 600 it is also the next instruction of the program.

36. Given data

Number of surfaces = 16

Number of tracks / sector = 128

Number of sector / track = 256

Total size of disk = $16 \times 128 \times 256 \times 512$ bytes

$\quad = 2^4 \times 2^7 \times 2^8 \times 2^9$ bytes

$\quad = 2^8 \times 2^{20}$ bytes

$\quad = 2^8$ Mega bytes

$\quad = 256$ MB

Total Number of Sector in the disk

$\quad = 16 \times 128 \times 256$ bytes

$\quad = 2^4 \times 2^7 \times 2^8$ bytes

$\quad = 2^{19}$ bytes

So 19 bits are needed

37. Pipelined processor has 4 stages IF, ID, EX, WB

Clock Cycles	Instruction
1	ADD
1	SUB
3	MUL

Consider the following diagram:

Clock Cycles	1	2	3	4	5	6	7	8
$R_2 \leftarrow R_1 + R_0$	IF	ID	EX	WB				
$R_4 \leftarrow R_3 * R_2$		IF	ID	EX	EX	EX	WB	
$R_6 \leftarrow R_5 - R_4$			IF	ID			EX	WB

So total required clocks cycle is 8.

38. The use of multiple register window with overlap cause a reduction in number of memory access for function. Locals and parameters because overlapped register eliminates the need of memory register.

39. Overflow and sign flag bits are given in 2's complement form.

01001101 is equivalent to decimal 77

11101001 is equivalent to decimal (−23)

addition operation: $77 + (-23) = 54$

11101001 + 01001101 = 00110110 (overflow flag set to 1). Carry flag = 0, Overflow flag = 1, and Sign flag = 0.

40. Apply booth's algorithm;

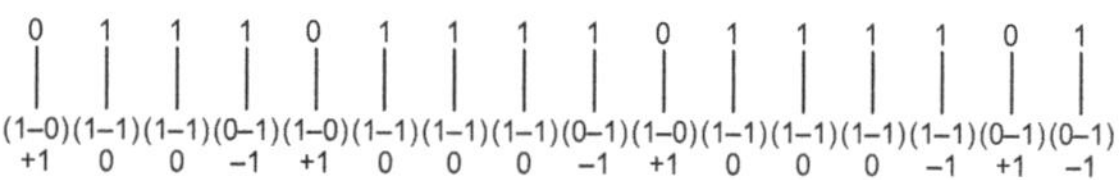

4 additions and 4 subtractions total 8 operations.

41. Given numbers 1101 and 0100

Addition of their two's complements

$$
\begin{array}{r}
\text{Overflow} \quad 1\ 1\ 0\ 1 \\
0\ 1\ 0\ 0 \\
\hline
1\ 0\ 0\ 0\ 1 \\
\hline
\end{array}
$$

42. Relative addressing cannot be faster than absolute addressing as absolute address must be calculated from relative address.

- is true as instead of absolute address we can use a much smaller relative address in instructions which results in smaller instruction size.

- by using the base address of array we can index array elements using relative addressing.

43. Substitution of values for name whose values are constant is done in constant folding.

46. For shift operator E is,

$\quad E[f(\alpha_i)] = f(x_i + h)$ and $E^{-1}[f(x_i)] = f(\alpha_i - h)$

Forward difference operator = Δ

$\Delta(f(x)) = f(x + h) - f(x)$ [we know that]

$Ef(x) = f(x + h) - f(x) + f(x)$ [add or subtract $f(x)$]

$\quad = (1 + \Delta) f(x)$

So comparing $E(f(x)) = (1 + \Delta) f(x)$

$\quad E = 1 + \Delta$

$\quad \Delta = E + 1$

47. Given formula is of Trapezodial rule.

48. Given conditions,

$\quad y(0) = 1, y(1) = 0, y(2) = 1, y(3) = 10$

By simple put value of x is given option will give answer to this problem.

$\quad y = x^3 - 2x^2 + 1$

$\quad y(0) = 0 - 0 + 1 = 1$

$\quad y(1) = 1 - 2 + 1 = 0$

$\quad y(2) = 8 - 8 + 1 = 1$

$\quad y(3) = 27 - 18 + 1$

$\quad\quad = 9 + 1 = 10$

49. Given $x = a \cos(t)$ and $y = b \sin(t)$

squaring both side

$\quad x^2 = a^2 \cos^2(t)$ and $y^2 = b^2 \sin^2(t)$

$\quad \dfrac{x^2}{a^2} = \cos^2(t)$ and $\dfrac{y^2}{b^2} = \sin^2(t)$

by adding both equation we get

$$\frac{x^2}{a^2} + \frac{y^2}{b^2} = \sin^2(t) + \cos^2(t)$$

$$\frac{x^2}{a^2} + \frac{y^2}{b^2} = 1$$

50. Value of x at which y is minimum

$$y = x^2 - 3x + 1$$

$$\frac{dy}{dx} = 2x - 3$$

$$\left(\frac{d^2 y}{dx\,dx}\right) = 2$$

So y has minimum value

So, $2x - 3 = 0$

$$x = 3/2$$

51. Given formula is Newton's backward formula.

52. Sum of all degree of vertices = 2e

53. Maximum components will result after removal of a node if graph G is a star graph as shown below.

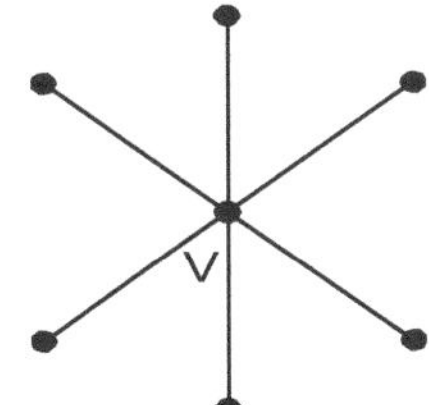

or a null graph of n vertices as shown below;

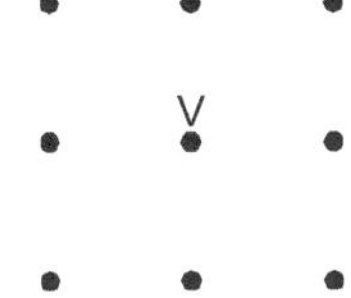

In either case, if node v is removed, the number of components will be $n - 1$, where n is the total number of nodes in the star graph.

$\therefore$ $n - 1$ is the maximum number of components possible. Minimum components will result if the node being removed is a lone vertex in which case, the number of components will be $k - 1$.

$\therefore$ The number of components must necessarily lie between $k - 1$ and $n - 1$.

54. A graph in which all vertices have same degree is called regular graph.

55. In graph if is only path between any two vertices then it is called tree or vice versa.

56. A simple graph with n-edges (without loop and parallel edges) and K components can have

$$e \le \frac{(n - K)\,(n - K + 1)}{2}$$

for $K = 1$, $e \le \dfrac{n(n - 1)}{2}$

57. By using Horner's rules, consider the polynomial

$$P(x) = a_0 + x(a_1 + x(a_2 + a_3 x))$$

So, only 3 multiplication required.

50. There is no error in code and it produce output as 13 and 8 and the given code allocate a temporary nameless cells, initialize it to 13, and pass the address of cell to swap.

59. A square matrix is orthogonal if $AA^T = I$.

60. If two adjacent rows or column of a determinants are exchanged, then the value of determinant becomes negative of its original value.

61.

$$\begin{vmatrix} 3 & 3 \\ x & 5 \end{vmatrix} = 3$$

Determinant of the matrix

$$15 - 3x = 3$$

$$-3x = -15 + 3$$

$$3x = 12$$

$$x = 4$$

62. We know that transpose with respect to additional $A' + B' + C' = (A + B + C)'$

63. Determinant of the matrix

Determinant of given matrix is 0.

64. If $f(x)$ is the continuous probability density function of a random variable X then,

$$p(a < x \le b) = p(a \le x \le b)$$

$$= \int_a^b f(x)\,dx$$

65. Probability density function

$$f(x) = e\,\frac{(x - \mu)^2}{2\sigma^2} \bigg/ \sigma(2\pi)^{1/2}$$

When $x = \mu$ then $f(x)$ get maximum value.

i.e., $\dfrac{1}{\sigma(2\pi)^{1/2}}$

So, maximum value $= \dfrac{1000}{2.5(2\pi)^{1/2}} = \dfrac{400}{\sqrt{2\pi}}$

66. Poisson distribution is given by

Probability density function

$$f(x) = \frac{e^{-\lambda}\lambda^x}{x!} \qquad \text{...(1)}$$

Given that

$$f(x) = \frac{e^{-2}2^x}{x!} \qquad \ldots(2)$$

Comparing both (1) and (2)

We get, $\lambda = 2$

In poisson distribution mean $(\mu) = \lambda$

So, $\mu = 2$

67. In testing validation, we test software after completing build, whether software product is according to customer requirement or not.

68. Acceptance test for a software is done under system testing.

69. The join command is used to change contents of one database using the contents of another database by linking them on a common field.

70. Locking database file can be accessed by only one user.

71. 'Transaction log' is a file stored on disk, which contain all set of activity applied on database with some problem happen during transaction is abort to make database in previous consistence state.

72. The main purpose of 'foreign key' in table is to ensure referential integrity i.e., the foreign key of one table can have only the values that are in some primary key of referenced table.

$$R_1(\underline{A}, B, C)\ R_2(\underline{A, B}, C)$$

So, A in R_2 is foreign key.

73. A transaction reads a data item after it is written then we can't recover the errors in this situation by an uncommitted transaction.

74. IPSEC in tunnel mode is used to provide security to IP packet with new header.

75. Spooler is a special software to create job queue.

76. The program under execution is called process.

77. When process is rolled back as a result of deadlock then there is possible of starvation.

78. On receiving an interrupt from I/O device, CPU branch to the interrupt service routine.

79. RISC processor has more register and smaller instruction in comparison to CISC processor.

80. The amount of increment depends upon the size of data item accessed.

■■

1. The encoding technique used to transmit the signal in giga ethernet technology over fiber optic medium is
   - (a) Differential manchester encoding
   - (b) Non Return to zero
   - (c) 4 B/5 B encoding
   - (d) 8 B/10 B encoding

2. Which of the following is an unsupervised neural network
   - (a) RBS
   - (b) Hopfield
   - (c) Back propagation
   - (d) Kohonen

3. In compiler terminology, reduction in strength means
   - (a) Replacing run time computation by compile time computation
   - (b) Removing loop invariant computation
   - (c) Removing common subexpressions
   - (d) Replacing a costly operation by a relatively cheaper one

4. The following table shows the processes in the ready queue and time required for each process for completing its job.

Process	Time (ms)
P_1	10
P_2	5
P_3	20
P_4	8
P_5	15

   If round robin scheduling with 5 ms is used what is the average waiting time of the processes in the queue?
   - (a) 27 ms
   - (b) 26.2 ms
   - (c) 27.5 ms
   - (d) 27.2 ms

5. MOV [BX], AL type of data addressing is called
   - (a) Register addressing
   - (b) Immediate addressing
   - (c) Register indirect addressing
   - (d) Register relative

6. Evaluate $(X\,X\,\text{OR}\,Y)\,X\,\text{OR}\,Y$
   - (a) All 1's
   - (b) All 0's
   - (c) X
   - (d) Y

7. Which of the following is true about the z-buffer algorithm?
   - (a) It is a depth sort algorithm
   - (b) No limitation on total number of objects in the scene
   - (c) Comparison of objects is done
   - (d) z-buffer is initialized to background colour at start of algorithm

8. What is the decimal value of the floating-point number C1D00000 (hexadecimal notation)? (Assume 32-bit, single precision floating point IEEE representation)
   - (a) 28
   - (b) −15
   - (c) −26
   - (d) −28

9. What is the raw throughput of USB 2.0 technology?
   - (a) 480 Mbps
   - (b) 400 Mbps
   - (c) 200 Mbps
   - (d) 12 Mbps

10. Below is the precedence graph for a set of tasks to be executed on a parallel processing system S.

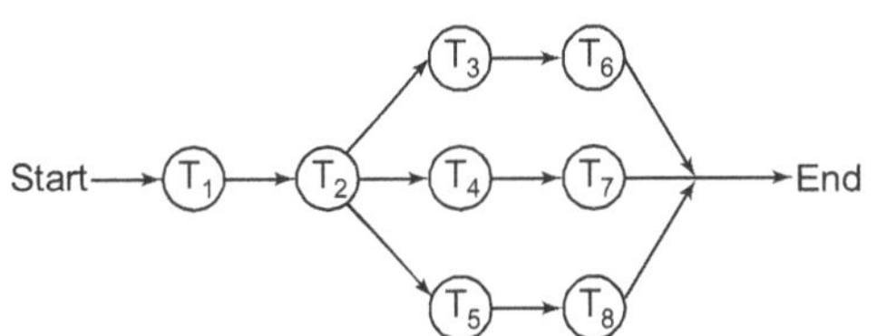

   What is the efficiency of this precedence graph on S if each of the tasks $T_1, ..., T_8$ takes the same time and the system S has five processors?
   - (a) 25%
   - (b) 40%
   - (c) 50%
   - (d) 90%

11. How many distinct binary search trees can be created out of 4 distinct keys?
   - (a) 5
   - (b) 14
   - (c) 24
   - (d) 35

12. The network protocol which is used to get MAC address of a node by providing IP address is
   - (a) SMTP
   - (b) ARP
   - (c) RIP
   - (d) BOOTP

13. Which of the following statements about peephole optimizations is False?

    (a) It is applied to a small part of the code

    (b) It can be used to optimize intermediate code

    (c) To get the best out of this, it has to be applied repeatedly

    (d) It can be applied to a portion of the code that is not contiguous

14. Which one of the following in place sorting algorithms needs the minimum number of swaps?

    (a) Quick-sort   (b) Insertion sort

    (c) Selection sort   (d) Heap sort

15. What is the equivalent serial schedule for the following transactions?

T_1	T_2	T_3
		$R(Y)$
		$R(Z)$
$R(X)$		
$W(X)$		
		$W(Y)$
		$W(Z)$
	$W(Z)$	
$R(Y)$		
$W(Y)$		
	$R(Y)$	
	$W(Y)$	
	$R(X)$	
	$W(X)$	

    (a) $T_1 - T_2 - T_3$ (b) $T_3 - T_1 - T_2$

    (c) $T_2 - T_1 - T_3$ (d) $T_1 - T_3 - T_2$

16. Consider a direct mapped cache with 64 blocks and a block size of 16 bytes. To what block number dooc the byte address 1206 map to?

    (a) Does not map   (b) 6

    (c) 11   (d) 54

17. A context model of a software system can be shown by drawing a

    (a) LEVEL-0 DFD   (b) LEVEL-1 DFD

    (c) LEVEL-2 DFD   (d) LEVEL-3 DFD

18. An example of poly-alphabetic substitution is

    (a) P-box   (b) S-box

    (c) Caesar cipher   (d) Vigenere cipher

19. If node A has three siblings and B is parent of A, what is the degree of A?

    (a) 0   (b) 3

    (c) 4   (d) 5

20. The IEEE standard for WiMax technology is

    (a) IEEE 802.16   (b) IEEE 802.36

    (c) IEEE 812.16   (d) IEEE 806.16

21. Which type of DBMS provides support for maintaining several versions of the same entity?

    (a) Relational Data Base Management Systems

    (b) Hierarchical

    (c) Object Oriented Data Base Management Systems

    (d) Network

22. A system is having 8 M bytes of video memory for bit-mapped graphics with 64-bit colour. What is the maximum resolution it can support?

    (a) 800×600 (b) 1024×768

    (c) 1280×1024 (d) 1920×1440

23. What is the meaning of $\overline{RD}$ signal in Intel 8151A?

    (a) Read (when it is low)

    (b) Read (when it is high)

    (c) Write (when it is low)

    (d) Read and Write (when it is high)

24. If the page size in a 32-bit machine is 4K bytes then the size of page table is

    (a) 1 M bytes   (b) 2 M bytes

    (c) 4 M bytes   (d) 4 K bytes

25. A processor takes 12 cycles to complete an instruction I. The corresponding pipelined processor uses 6 stages with the execution times of 3, 2, 5,4, 6 and 2 cycles respectively. What is the asymptotic speedup assuming that a very large number speedup assuming that a very large number of instructions are to be executed?

    (a) 1.83   (b) 2

    (c) 3   (d) 6

26. The in-order traversal of a tree resulted in FBGADCE. Then the pre-order traversal of that tree would result in

    (a) FGBDECA

    (b) ABFGCDE

    (c) BFGCDEA

    (d) AFGBDEC

27. Which one of the following is 'true'?

    (a) $R \cap S = (R \cup S) - [(R - S) \cup (S - R)]$

    (b) $R \cup S = (R \cap S) - [(R - S) \cup (S - R)]$

    (c) $R \cap S = (R \cup S) - [(R - S) \cap (S - R)]$

    (d) $R \cap S = (R \cup S) \cup (R - S)$

28. The below figure represents which one of the following UML diagram for a single send session of an online chat system,

●──→ Login ─→ Send ─→ Logout ─→ ◉

(a) Package Diagram

(b) Activity Diagram

(c) Class Diagram

(d) Sequence Diagram

29. Which 'Normal Form' is based on the concept of 'full functional dependency' is

(a) First Normal Form

(b) Second Normal Form

(c) Third Normal Form

(d) Fourth Normal Form

30. In Boolean algebra, rule $(X + Y)(X + Z) =$ _______

(a) $Y + XZ$ (b) $X + YZ$

(c) $XY + Z$ (d) $XZ + Y$

31. How many 3-to-8 line decoders with a chip having enable pin are needed to construct a 6-to-64 line decoder without using any other logic gates?

(a) 7   (b) 8

(c) 9   (d) 10

32. In which layer of network architecture, the secured socket layer (SSL) is used?

(a) physical layer   (b) session layer

(c) application layer   (d) presentation layer

33. What is the bit rate of a video terminal unit with 80 character/line, 8 bits/character and horizontal sweep time of 100 μs (including 20 μs of retrace time)?

(a) 8 Mbps   (b) 6.4 Mbps

(c) 0.8 Mbps   (d) 0.64 Mbps

34. Black Box software testing method focuses on the

(a) Boundary condition of the software

(b) Control structure of the software

(c) Functional requirement of the software

(d) Independent paths of the software

35. How many edges are there in a forest with v vertices and k components?

(a) $(v + 1) - k$ (b) $(v + 1)/2 - k$

(c) $v - k$ (d) $v + k$

36. If A and B are square matrices of the same order and A is symmetric, then $B^T A B$ is

(a) Skew symmetric   (b) Symmetric

(c) Orthogonal   (d) Idempotent

37. Find the memory address of the next instruction executed by the microprocessor (8086), when operated in real mode for CS = 1000 and IP = E000

(a) 10E00   (b) 1E000

(c) F000   (d) 1000E

38. A fast wide SCSI-II disk drive spins at 7200 RPM, has a sector size of 512 bytes, and holds 160 sectors per track. Estimate the sustained transfer rate of this drive.

(a) 576000 Kilobytes / sec

(b) 9600 Kilobytes / sec

(c) 4800 Kilobytes / sec

(d) 19200 Kilobytes/sec

39. Two control signals in microprocessor which are related to Direct Memory Access (DMA) are

(a) INTR and INTA   (b) RD and WR

(c) S0 and S1   (d) HOLD and HLDA

40. Consider the following pseudocode.

$x := 1;$

$i := 1;$

while $(x \leq 500)$

begin

$\quad x := 2^x;$

$\quad i := i + 1;$

end;

What is the value of i at the end of the pseudo-code?

(a) 4   (b) 5

(c) 6   (d) 7

41. If a microcomputer operates at 5 MHz with an 8-bit bus and a newer version operates at 20 MHz with a 32-bit bus, the maximum speed-up possible approximately will be

(a) 2   (b) 4

(c) 8   (d) 16

42. The search concept used in associative memory is

(a) Parallel search   (b) Sequential search

(c) Binary search   (d) Selection search

43. Which variable does not drive a terminal string in the grammar

$S \rightarrow AB$

$A \rightarrow a$

$B \rightarrow b$

$B \rightarrow C$

(a) A   (b) B

(c) C   (d) S

44. In Java, after executing the following code what are the values of x, y and z?

> int x, $y = 10$, $z = 12$;
>
> $x = y$++ + z++;

(a) $x = 22$, $y = 10$, $z = 12$

(b) $x = 24$, $y = 10$, $z = 12$

(c) $x = 24$, $y = 11$, $z = 13$

(d) $x = 22$, $y = 11$, $z = 13$

45. The broadcast address for IP network 172.16.0.0 with subnet mask 255.255.0.0 is

(a) 172.16.0.255   (b) 172.16.255.255

(c) 255.255.255.255   (d) 172.255.255.255

46. Which RAID level gives block level striping with double distributed parity

(a) RAID 10   (b) RAID 2

(c) RAID 6   (d) RAID 5

47. The output expression of the following gate network is

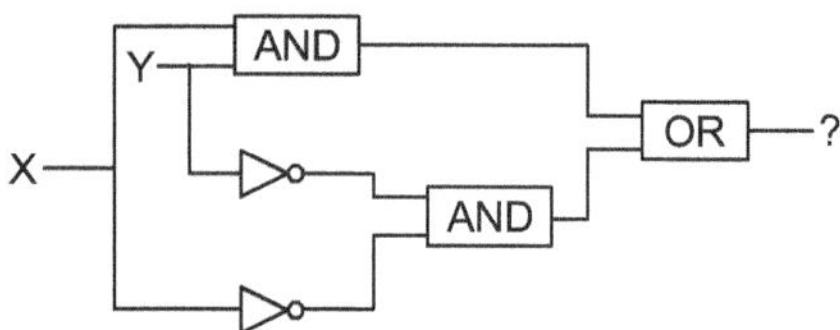

(a) $X.Y + \bar{X}.\bar{Y}$ (b) $X.Y + X.Y$

(c) $X.Y$ (d) $X + Y$

48. The Hamming distance between the octets of $0 \times AA$ and 0×55 is

(a) 7   (b) 5

(c) 8   (d) 6

49. Consider a 32-bit machine where four-level paging scheme is used. If the hit ratio to TLB is 98%, and it takes 20 nanoseconds to search the TLB and 100 nanoseconds to access the main memory what is effective memory access time in nanoseconds?

(a) 126   (b) 128

(c) 122   (d) 120

50. Data is transmitted continuously at 2.048 Mbps rate for 10 hours and received 512 bit errors. What is the bit error rate?

(a) $6.9\,e\text{-}9$ (b) $6.9\,e\text{-}6$

(c) $69\,e\text{-}9$ (d) $4\,e\text{-}9$

51. Warnier Diagram enables the analyst to represent

(a) Class Structure   (b) Information Hierarchy

(c) Data Flow   (d) State Transition

52. Given

> X : 0 10 16
>
> Y : 6 16 28

The interpolated value at $X = 4$ using piecewise linear interpolation is

(a) 11   (b) 4

(c) 22   (d) 10

53. In functional dependency, Armstrong's inference rules refers to

(a) Reflexive, Augmentation and Decomposition

(b) Transitive, Augmentation and Reflexive

(c) Augmentation, Transitive, Reflexive and Decomposition

(d) Reflexive, Transitive and Decomposition

54. Number of chips (128×8 RAM) needed to provide a memory capacity of 2048 bytes

(a) 2   (b) 4

(c) 8   (d) 16

55. There are three processes in the ready queue. When the currently running process requests for I/O how many process switches take place?

(a) 1   (b) 2

(c) 3   (d) 4

56. Let $T(n)$ be defined by $T(1) = 10$ and $T(n + 1) = 2n + T(n)$ for all integers $n \geq 1$. Which of the following represents the order of growth of $T(n)$ as a function of n?

(a) $O(n)$ (b) $O(n \log n)$

(c) $O(n^2)$ (d) $O(n^3)$

57. Which of the following UNIX command allows scheduling a program to be executed at the specified time?

(a) cron   (b) nice

(c) date and time   (d) schedule

58. In DMA transfer scheme, the transfer scheme other than burst mode is

(a) cycle technique

(b) stealing technique

(c) cycle stealing technique

(d) cycle bypass technique

59. n^{th} derivative of x^n is

(a) nx^{n-1}

(b) $nx^n!$

(c) $n^n.n!$

(d) $n!$

60. A total of 9 units of a resource type are available, and given the safe state shown below, which of the following sequence will be a safe state?

Process	Used	Max
P_1	2	7
P_2	1	6
P_3	2	5
P_4	1	4

(a) $<P_4, P_1, P_3, P_2>$

(b) $<P_4, P_2, P_1, P_3>$

(c) $<P_4, P_2, P_3, P_1>$

(d) $<P_3, P_1, P_2, P_4>$

61. Three coins are tossed simultaneously. The probability that they will fall two heads and one tail is

(a) 5/8   (b) 1/8

(c) 2/3   (d) 3/8

62. The average depth of a binary search tree is

(a) $O(n^{0.5})$ (b) $O(n)$

(c) $O(\log n)$ (d) $O(n \log n)$

63. What is the output of the following C code?

```c
#include <stdio.h>
#include<conio.h>
void main()
{
    int index;
    for (index = 1; index <= 5; z++)
    {
        printf("%d", index);
        if(i == 3)
            continue;
    }
}
```

(a) 1245

(b) 12345

(c) 12245

(d) 12354

64. When n-type semiconductor is heated?

(a) number of electrons increases while that of holes decreases

(b) number of holes increases while that of electrons decreases

(c) number of electrons and holes remain same

(d) number of electron and holes increases equally

65. The Cyclomatic Complexity metric $V(G)$ of the following control flow graph is

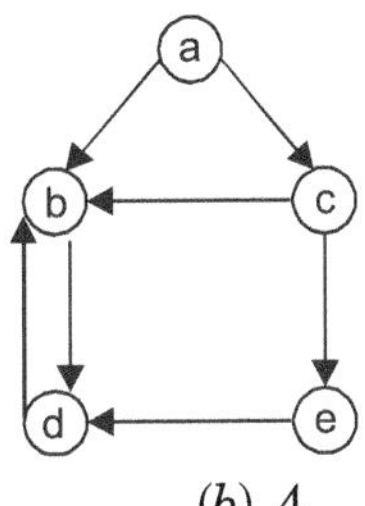

(a) 3   (b) 4

(c) 5   (d) 6

66. Which of the following algorithm design techniques is used in merge sort?

(a) Greedy method

(b) Backtracking

(c) Dynamic programming

(d) Divide and Conquer

67. The arithmetic mean of attendance of 49 students of class A is 40% and that of 53 students of class B is 35%. Then the % of arithmetic mean of attendance of class A and B is

(a) 27.2%   (b) 50.25%

(c) 51.13%   (d) 37.4%

68. Which of the following sentences can be generated by

$$S \to aS \mid bA$$
$$A \to d \mid cA$$

(a) $bccdd$ (b) $abbcca$

(c) $abcabc$ (d) $abcd$

69. Lightweight Directory Access Protocol is used for

(a) Routing the packets

(b) Authentication

(c) Obtaining IP address

(d) Domain name resolving

70. Number of comparisons required for an unsuccessful search of an element in a sequential search organized, fixed length, symbol table of length L is

(a) L (b) $L/2$

(c) $(L + 1)/2$ (d) $2L$

71. One SAN switch has 24 ports. All 24 port supports 8 Gbps Fiber Channel technology. What is the aggregate bandwidth of that SAN switch?

(a) 96 Gbps

(b) 192 Mbps

(c) 51 2 Gbps

(d) 192 Gbps

72. Find the output of the following Java code line System.out.println(math.floor (–7. 4))

(a) –7   (b) –8

(c) –7.4   (d) –7.0

73. Belady's anomaly means

(a) Page fault rate is constant even on increasing the number of allocated frames

(b) Pages fault rate may increase on increasing the number of allocated frames

(c) Pages fault rate may increase on decreasing the number of allocated frames

(d) Pages fault rate may decrease on increasing the number of allocated frames

74. In an RS flip-flop, if the S line (Set line) is set high (1) and the R line (Reset line) is set low (0), then the state of the flip flop is

(a) Set to 1

(b) Set to 0

(c) No change in state

(d) Forbidden

75. In HTML, which of the following can be considered a container?

(a) <SELECT>

(b) <Value>

(c) <INPUT>

(d) <BODY>

76. What is the matrix that represents rotation of an object by θ° about the origin in 2D?

(a) $\begin{bmatrix} \cos\theta & -\sin\theta \\ \sin\theta & \cos\theta \end{bmatrix}$ (b) $\begin{bmatrix} \sin\theta & -\cos\theta \\ \cos\theta & \sin\theta \end{bmatrix}$

(c) $\begin{bmatrix} \cos\theta & -\sin\theta \\ \cos\theta & \sin\theta \end{bmatrix}$ (d) $\begin{bmatrix} \sin\theta & -\cos\theta \\ \cos\theta & \sin\theta \end{bmatrix}$

77. In a system having a single processor, a new process arrives at the rate of six processes per minute and each such process requires seven seconds of service time. What is the CPU utilization?

(a) 70%   (b) 30%

(c) 60%   (d) 64%

78. A symbol table of length 152 is possessing 25 entries at any instant. What is occupation density?

(a) 0.164   (b) 127

(c) 8.06   (d) 6.08

79. A problem whose language is recursion is called?

(a) Unified problem

(b) Boolean function

(c) Recursive problem

(d) Decidable

80. Logic family popular for low power dissipation

(a) CMOS   (b) ECL

(c) TTL   (d) DTL

ANSWERS

1. (d)	**2.** (d)	**3.** (d)	**4.** (b)	**5.** (c)	**6.** (c)	**7.** (a)	**8.** (c)	**9.** (a)	**10.** (b)
11. (b)	**12.** (b)	**13.** (d)	**14.** (c)	**15.** (b)	**16.** (c)	**17.** (a)	**18.** (d)	**19.** (c)	**20.** (a)
21. (c)	**22.** (b)	**23.** (a)	**24.** (c)	**25.** (b)	**26.** (*)	**27.** (a)	**28.** (b)	**29.** (b)	**30.** (b)
31. (c)	**32.** (d)	**33.** (b)	**34.** (c)	**35.** (c)	**36.** (b)	**37.** (*)	**38.** (b)	**39.** (d)	**40.** (b)
41. (b)	**42.** (a)	**43.** (c)	**44.** (d)	**45.** (b)	**46.** (c)	**47.** (a)	**48.** (c)	**49.** (b)	**50.** (a)
51. (b)	**52.** (d)	**53.** (b)	**54.** (d)	**55.** (b)	**56.** (c)	**57.** (a)	**58.** (c)	**59.** (d)	**60.** (d)
61. (d)	**62.** (c)	**63.** (b)	**64.** (b)	**65.** (b)	**66.** (d)	**67.** (d)	**68.** (d)	**69.** (b)	**70.** (a)
71. (b)	**72.** (b)	**73.** (b)	**74.** (a)	**75.** (d)	**76.** (a)	**77.** (a)	**78.** (a)	**79.** (d)	**80.** (a)

Note: * None of the given option is correct. Question may contain insufficient data.

EXPLANATIONS

1. 8 B/10 B encoding is the encoding technique which is used to transmit the signal in giga ethernet technology over fiber optic medium.

2. Kohonen is an unsupervised neural network. It is a self organizing map which is a type of artificial neural network.

3. In compiler terminology, reduction in strength means replacing a costly operation by a relatively cheaper one.

4. Given table

Process	Time (ms)
P_1	10
P_2	5
P_3	20
P_4	8
P_5	15

Preparing the Gantt chart:

P_1	P_2	P_3	P_4	P_5	P_1	P_3	P_4	P_5	P_3	P_5	P_3

0   5   10   15   20   25   30   35   38   43   48   53   58

P_2 P_1 P_4 P_5 P_3

Calculating the turn-around time:

$P_1 \to 30$ ms

$P_2 \to 10$ ms

$P_3 \to 58$ ms

$P_4 \to 38$ ms

$P_5 \to 53$ ms

Calculating waiting time:

$P_1 \to 30 - 10 = 20$ ms

$P_2 \to 10 - 5 = 5$ ms

$P_3 \to 58 - 20 = 38$ ms

$P_4 \to 38 - 8 = 30$ ms

$P_5 \to 53 - 15 = 38$ ms

Average waiting time

$$= \frac{20 + 5 + 38 + 30 + 38}{5}$$

$$= \frac{131}{5} = 26.2 \text{ ms}$$

5. MOV[BX], AL is register Indirect addressing mode.

   [BX] refers to the memory location which is written in the content of BX.

6. [X(XOR)Y] XORY that means

   $[X \oplus Y] \oplus Y$

   $[X\bar{Y} + \bar{X}Y] \oplus Y = [X\bar{Y} + \bar{X}Y]\bar{Y} + [XY + \bar{X}\bar{Y}]Y$

   $= X\bar{Y} + XY \quad [Y.\bar{Y} = 0, A + 0 = A]$

   $= X(Y + \bar{Y}) = X$

7. z-buffer algorithm is a depth sort algorithm. This algorithm is used for hidden surface elimination.

8. First bit is for sign next 8 bits are for exponent and last 23 bits are for mantissa which excludes the implicit '1' before '0' unless the number is not normalized. In IEEE representation for single precision floating point numbers.

   Given C1D00000

   First bit = 1 so, number is negative

   Exponent = 131 − 127 = 4

   Significant = $1.10\underbrace{100...0}_{200's}$

   $= (1)2^0 + (1)2^{-1} + (0)2^{-2} + (1)2^{-3}$

   $= 1 + \dfrac{1}{2} + 0 + \dfrac{1}{8} = \dfrac{13}{8}$

   Final value = Sign $\times 2^{\text{exponent}} \times$ Significant

   $= -26$

9. USB 2.0 technology operates at 480 Mbps (high speed), 12 Mbps (full speed) or 1.5 Mbps (low speed).

10. First we consider the as task T_1 executes on processor 1. At that time rest other processors are idle. Similarly again, task T_2 executes on processor 1 and other processors are idle. Now, as per the precedence graph tasks T_3, T_4 and T_5 can work in parallel even on different processors, so this time 3 processors will be busy and the other two are idle. After that T_6, T_7 and T_8 will operate in the same manner.

    Now, at every level of the graph, we have 5 processors, so considering each level, there are total 20 instance of the processor. As per the utilization, at each level 1 + 1 + 3 + 3, 8 are utilized.

    $$\text{Efficiency} = \frac{8}{20} \times 100 = 8 \times 5 = 40\%$$

11. Given $n = 4$

    Number of distinct Binary Search Tree = $\dfrac{^{2n}C_n}{n+1}$.

    So, $= \dfrac{^8C_4}{5} = \dfrac{\lfloor 8}{\lfloor 4 \times 5 \times \lfloor 4} = 14$

12. (ARP) Address Resolution Protocol is the protocol which is used to get MAC addresses of a node by providing IP address.

13. Peephole optimization is applied over a very small set of instructions in a segment of generated code. So statement (d) is false.

14. In selection sort, the minimum element is find out in the unsorted array and is swapped with the element at 0th index. Similarly, the second minimum element is find out and is swapped with the element at index 1.

15. Preparing the dependency graph, we get

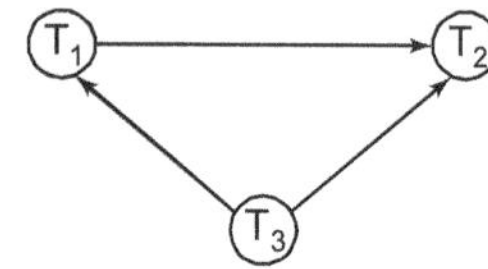

By observing the dependency graph, it can be concluded that T_3, should be executed before T_1, and T_2. Since T_3 has a dependency edge over both T_1 and T_2. Similarly, T_1 must be executed before T_2. Since T_1 has a dependency edge over T_2. So, the correct order is $T_3 - T_1 - T_2$.

16. In direct mapped cache,

Cache block number = (Memory block number) mod (Total number of blocks in cache)

$\Rightarrow$ Total number of blocks in cache = 64

Since, block size = 16 B

$$\text{Memory block number} = \frac{\text{Byte address}}{\text{Block size}}$$
$$= \frac{1206}{16} = 75$$

Cache block number = 75 mod 64 = 11.

17. A context model of a software system can be shown by drawing a level-0 DFD.

18. Vigenere cipher is a method of encrypting alphabetic text by using a series of different Caesar cipher based on the letters of a keyword.

19. According to given condition, we draw,

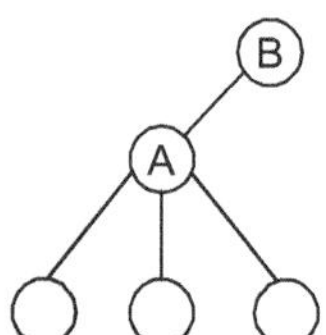

So, degree of A is 4.

20. According to IEEE standard for WiFi Max technology is IEE802.16.

21. Database Management System provide support for maintaining several versions of same entity. An old version of an object that represents a tested and verified design should be retained until a new version is tested and verified.

22. The size of video memory is 8 MB, which is equal to 83, 88, 608 byte. Considering option (b), the resolution is 1024 × 768 with a 64 bit (8 B) colour so, 1024 × 768 × 8 = 62,91,456, which is less than maximum file size and also provide maximum resolution.

23. $\overline{RD}$ signal in Intel 8151A means read, when it is low.

24.
$$\text{Page size} = 4 \text{ kbyte}$$
$$\text{Machine size} = 32 \text{ bit}$$

No. of entries in page table $= \dfrac{2^{32}}{2^{12}} = 2^{20}$

Size of page table $= 2^{20} \times 20$ bits = 4 MB.

25. **Non-pipelined processor:** An instruction takes 12 cycles, so if there are 'n' instructions, total 12n cycles.

Pipelined processor: Here, each stage will take 6 ns. So, first instruction out of 'n' instructions will take 36 ns and $(n - 1)$ instructions will take 6ns each.

$$\text{Speed-up} = \frac{12n}{36 + 6(n - 1)} = 2$$

27. From the given option

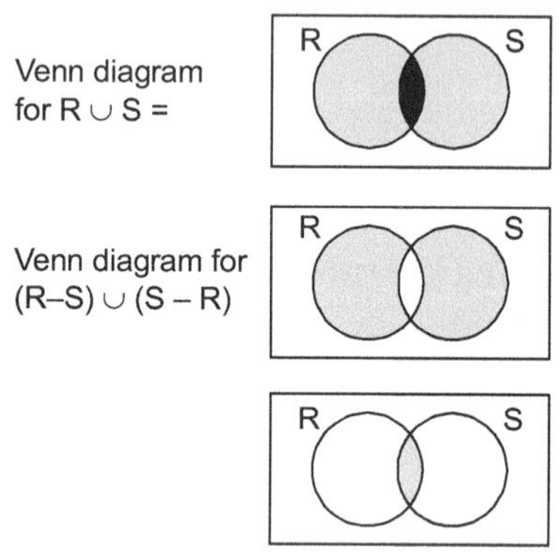

So, R $\cap$ S = (R $\cup$ S) + [(R – S) $\cup$ (S – R)]

28. An activity diagram is a flow chart to represent the flow from one activity to another activity. This flow can be sequential, branched or concurrent.

29. A functional dependency $X \rightarrow Y$ is a full functional dependency if removal of any attribute from X will conclude that, the dependency does not hold any more. Second normal form is based on concept of full functional dependency.

30. Boolean Expression,
$$(X + Y)(X + Z) = X + XZ + XY + YZ$$
$$= X(1 + Z) + XY + YZ$$
$$= X + XY + YZ \quad [\because 1 + Z = 1]$$
$$= X(1 + Y) + YZ \quad [\because 1 + Y = 1]$$
$$= X + YZ$$

31. Construction of a 6 × 64 decoder by using 3 × 8 line decoder.

$$\frac{64}{8} = 8 + 1 \rightarrow \text{extra decoder for combining output}$$

result 6 × 64 $\xrightarrow{8+1}$ 3 × 8.

32. Secured socket layer is defined as 'operating over some reliable transport layer' which places it as application layer protocol in the TCP/IP reference model and as presentation layer protocol in the OSI model.

33. Given,

Horizontal sweep time $t = 100$ μs

Number of character per line $N = 80$

Number of bits per character $n = 8$

Bit rate of video terminal unit

$$= \frac{80 \times 8 \text{ bits}}{100 \text{ μs}} = 6.4 \text{ Mbps}$$

34. This type of testing is a method of software testing that examines the functionality of an application without peering into its internal structures or workings. This method of test can be applied to virtually every level of software testing.

35. Number of edges in 'k components of 'v' vertices

$$= \sum_{i=1}^{k} v_i - 1$$

Where v_i is the number of vertices in i^{th} component,

Since, $$\sum_{i=1}^{k} v_i = v$$

so, $$\sum_{i=1}^{k} v_i - 1 = v - k$$

So, there are '$v - k$' edges in a forest with 'v' vertices and 'k' components.

36. Given A is symmetric matrix, hence $A = A^T$.

So, the transpose of B^TAB,

$$(B^TAB)^T = B^TA^T.B$$
$$= B^TAB$$

$\because$ Since, $(B^TAB)^T = B^TAB$.

So, B^TAB is symmetric.

38. Given

$$\text{Size of track} = 160 \times 512 \text{ B}$$

Rotation per minute $= 7200$

$$1 \text{ revolution time} = \frac{1}{120} \text{sec.}$$

$$\text{In 1 sec, it will read} = \frac{160 \times 512}{1 / 120} \text{ byte}$$
$$= 160 \times 512 \times 120$$
$$= 9600 \times 10^3 \text{ byte}$$
$$= 9600 \text{ KBps}$$

39. The DMA controller sends a 'hold' request line to the CPU and waits for the CPU to assert the HLDA.

40. On execution of the program, initially put 'i' = 1, 'x' =1; while condition is true, so now $x = 2$, $i = 2$, again condition satisfies, if, $x = 4$, $i = 3$, again condition is satisfied, now $x = 2^{16}$, $i = 5$. This time the condition will be false. So, the value of i will be 5 at the end.

41. Increasing the bandwidth will help in achieving speed-up. Hence, the maximum speed-up possible should be,

$$\max\left(\frac{20}{5}, \frac{32}{8}\right) = 4$$

42. Parallel search is the search concept used in associative memory.

43. $B \to C$ is a production and there is no production in which variable 'C' derive some terminal string.

44. 'y' and 'z' have post increment operator, so the value of 'x' will be calculated first, then their value will be incremented.

Hence x becomes 22 and y and z becomes 11 and 13 respectively.

45. Broadcast address is 172.16.0.0 and subnet mask is 255.255.0.0, Adding both will result in Subnet ID 172.16.0.0.

So, the broadcast address will be 172.16.255.255.

46. RAID 6 gives block level striping with double distributed parity. Considering other options, RAID 10 is the combination for mirroring and striping. RAID 1 is for mirroring and RAID 5 is for striping with parity.

47. XY is obtained from first AND gate and $\overline{X}\overline{Y}$ from the second AND gate. Both output are apply to the input of OR gate.

48. The hamming distance between 0×AA and 0×55

0×AA can be written as 1010 1010

0×55 can be written as 0101 0101

Performing XOR between the two will give the hamming distance 8.

49. Given

Hit ratio $(h) = 98\%$

search time $(C) = 20$ ns

Main memory access time $(M) = 100$ ns

Number of levels of paging $(n) = 4$

$$\text{EMAT} = h(C + M) + (1 - h)(C + (n + 1)M)$$
$$= 0.98 (20 + 100) + 0.02 (20 + 500)$$
$$= 0.98 (120) + 0.02 (520) = 128 \text{ ns}$$

51. Warnier diagram is a graphic charting technique used in software engineering for system analysis and design.

52. Piecewise linear interpolation is a simple way of connecting points through straight lines. So, equation of line joining the point ($x = 0$, $y = 6$), $y - x = 6$. So $x = 4$ the interpolated value will be 10.

53. Armstrong's inference rules refers to transitive, augmentation and reflexive.

These 3 rules are :

Reflexivity: If, Y is a subset of X, then $X \to Y$.

Augmentation: If $X \to Y$, then $XZ \to YZ$

Transitivity: If $X \to Y$, and $Y \to Z$ then $X \to Z$

54. Given data

$$\text{Memory size} = 2048 \text{ B}$$
$$\text{Chip size} = 128 \times 8$$
$$\text{Number of chips} = 2048/128 = 16$$

16 chips are needed to provide a memory capacity of 2048 bytes.

55. When the three process in the ready queue. There will be two process switches. A process to be switched will be swapped out and the next scheduled process will be swapped in.

Hence 2 process switch will take place.

56.
$$T(n + 1) = T(n) + 2n$$
$$= T(n - 1) + 2(n - 1) + 2n$$
$$= T(n - 2) + 2(n - 2) + 2(n - 1) + 2n$$
$$\vdots$$
$$= T(1) + 2[n + (n - 1) + (n - 2) + \dots 1]$$
$$= 10 + 2\frac{n(n + 1)}{2} = O(n^2)$$

57. Cron is the Unix command that allows scheduling a program to be executed at the specified time.

58. Cycle stealing mode is another transfer scheme that is used by DMA other than burst mode. In this mode, the DMA steals cycle from the processor in order to transfer the byte.

59.
$$f(x) = x^n$$
$$f'(x) = n.x^{(n-1)}$$
$$f''(x) = n(n - 1) x^{n-2}$$
$$f''(x) = n(n - 1)(n - 2) x^{n-3}$$
$$f^n(x) = n! \, x^{(n-n)}$$
$$= n! \, x^0$$
$$= n!$$
$$f^n(x) = n \, !$$

60. Total available resources are 9 unit type. The available resources are $(9 - 6) = 3$. Need of each process is 5, 5, 3, 3 respectively.

From the option (d). Satisfying the need of P_3, available resources are 5, now satisfying the need of P_1, available resources are 7. Now, satisfying P_2's demand available resources are 9, now P4 can be executed.

61. When three coins are tossed simultaneously, there will be 3 ways to arrange 2 heads and 1 tail that are {HTH} {HHT} {THH}. Hence out of total 2^3 i.e., 8 possible combinations, there are 3 ways.

$$\text{Probability} = \frac{3}{8}.$$

62. A binary search tree is a tree in which that the key of left child is less than equal to the key of parent and the key of right child is greater than the parent key. The average depth over all nodes is $\log_2 n$.

63. At every iteration of the for loop, the value of 'i' will be printed. Since, 'continue' is the , last line of the code, hence it will not skip any number.

64. In a semiconductor device, when the number of holes increases while that of electrons decreases, then n-type semi-conductor is heated.

65. Cyclomatic Complexity $= E - V + 2(P)$
$$= 7 - 5 + 2(1) = 4$$

66. In merge sort, the array is divided into 2 subarrays recursively and then the merge procedure is applied. It uses divide and conquer technique.

67. Arithmetic mean of attendance of 49 students of class A = 40%

Arithmetic means of attendance of 53 students of class B = 35%

Arithmetic mean of attendance of class A and B
$$= \frac{49 \times 40 + 35 \times 53}{49 + 53}$$
$$= \frac{3818}{102} = 37.43\%$$

68.

S $\to$ aS	[S $\to$ aS]
abA	[S $\to$ bA]
abcA	[A $\to$ cA]
abcd	[A $\to$ d]

69. LDAP is used for authentication. The main idea of LDAP is to keep in one place all the information of a user so that it is easier to maintain network administration.

70. Symbol table is implemented as a sequential search table. So, every the time the entire table need to be searched.

71. Given data, SAN switch has

Number of ports = 24

Bandwidth = 8 Gbps

Aggregate bandwidth = 24 × 8 = 192 Gbps

72. Floor indicates the lower limits, since, $-8 < -7.4 < -7$. Hence, -8 will be the output.

73. Belady's anomaly is commonly experienced in FIFO page replacement algorithm, which indicates that page fault rate may increase on increasing the number of allocated frames.

74. In RS flip-flop, if S is 1 (high) and R is 0 (low), then state of flip-flop is set to 1.

75. In HTML <BODY> can be considered as a container.

76. The matrix that represents rotation of an object by $\theta°$ about the origin in 2D is

$$\begin{bmatrix} \cos\theta & -\sin\theta \\ \sin\theta & \cos\theta \end{bmatrix}$$

77. Given data

Number of processes = 6

Time required by each process = 7 sec

Useful time = 6 × 7

$$\text{CPU utilization} = \frac{\text{Useful time}}{\text{Total time}}$$

$$= \frac{42}{60} \times 100 = 70\%$$

78. Given data, $n = 25$, $l = 152$

$$\text{Occupation density} = \frac{\text{Number of entries}}{\text{Length of symbol table}}$$

$$= \frac{25}{152} = 0.164$$

79. If the problem and its complement are both semidecidable then the problem is decidable (recursive).

80. CMOS belong from logical family which is popular for low power dissipation and fast responce.

■■

SOLVED PAPER 2013
Computer Science

1. Let $A\,(1:8, -5:5, -10:5)$ be a three dimensional array. How many elements are there in the array A?
   (a) 1200   (b) 1408
   (c) 33   (d) 1050

2. The number of rotations required to insert a sequence of elements 9, 6, 5, 8, 7,10 into an empty AVL tree is ?
   (a) 0   (b) 1
   (c) 2   (d) 3

3. Opportunistic reasoning is addressed by which of the following knowledge representation?
   (a) Script
   (b) Blackboard
   (c) Production Rules
   (d) Fuzzy Logic

4. The following steps in a linked list
   $p =$ getnode () info $(p) = 10$
   next $(p) =$ list   list $= p$
   result in which type of operation?
   (a) Pop operation in stack.
   (b) Removal of a node.
   (c) Inserting a node.
   (d) Modifying an existing node.

5. Shift reduce parsing belongs to a class of
   (a) Bottom up parsing.
   (b) Top down parsing.
   (c) Recursive parsing.
   (d) Predictive parsing.

6. Which of the following productions eliminate left recursion in the production given below:
   $S \rightarrow Aa \mid b$
   $S \rightarrow Ac \mid Sd \mid \varepsilon$
   (a) $S \rightarrow Aa \mid b, A \rightarrow bdA', A' \rightarrow A'c \mid A'ba \mid A \mid \varepsilon$
   (b) $S \rightarrow Aa \mid b, A \rightarrow A' \mid bdA', A' \rightarrow cA \mid adA' \mid \varepsilon$
   (c) $S \rightarrow Aa \mid b, A \rightarrow A'c, \mid A'd, A' \rightarrow bdA' \mid cA' \mid \varepsilon$
   (d) $S \rightarrow Aa \mid b, A \rightarrow cA' \mid adA' \mid bdA', A' \rightarrow \mid A \mid \varepsilon$

7. Consider the following psuedocode :
   $x :$ integer $: = 1$
   $y :$ integer $: = 2$

procedure add
   $x : = x + y$
procedure second $(P$: procedure)
   $x :$ integer $: = 2$
   $P()$
procedure first
   $y :$ integer $: = 3$
second (add)
   first ( )
   write_integer(x)

What does it print if the language uses dynamic scoping with deep binding?
   (a) 2   (b) 3
   (c) 4   (d) 5

8. Which logic gate is used to detect overflow in 2's compliment arithmetic?
   (a) OR gate   (b) AND gate
   (c) NAND gate   (d) XOR gate

9. In an array of $2N$ elements that is both 2-ordered and 3-ordered, what is the maximum number of positions that an element can be from its position if the array were 1-ordered?
   (a) 1   (b) 2
   (c) $N/2$ (d) $2N - 1$

10. If the frame buffer has 8 bits per pixel and 8 bits are allocated for each of the R, G, B components, what would be the size of the lookup table?
    (a) 24 bytes   (b) 1024 bytes
    (c) 768 bytes   (d) 256 bytes

11. When two BCD numbers 0×14 and 0×08 are added what is the binary representation of the resultant number?
    (a) 0×22 (b) $0 \times 1c$
    (c) 0×16 (d) Results in overflow

12. Which of the following sorting algorithms has the minimum running time complexity in the best and average case?
    (a) Insertion sort, Quick sort
    (b) Quick sort, Quick sort
    (c) Quick sort, Insertion sort
    (d) Insertion sort, Insertion sort

13. The number 1102 in base 3 is equivalent to 123 in which base system?

   (a) 4   (b) 5

   (c) 6   (d) 8

14. A processor is fetching instructions at the rate of 1 MIPS. A DMA module is used to transfer characters to RAM from a device transmitting at 9600 bps. How much time will the processor be slowed down due to DMA activity?

   (a) 9.6 ms   (b) 4.8 ms

   (c) 2.4 ms   (d) 1.2 ms

15. A pipeline P operating at 400 MHz has a speedup factor of 6 and operating at 70% efficiency. How many stages are there in pipeline?

   (a) 5   (b) 6

   (c) 8   (d) 9

16. How much speed do we gain by using the cache, when cache is used 80% of the time? Assume cache is faster than main memory.

   (a) 5.27   (b) 2.00

   (c) 4.16   (d) 6.09

17. Two eight bit bytes 11000011 and 01001100 are added. What are the values of the overflow, carry and zero flags respectively, if the arithmetic unit of the CPU uses 2's complement form?

   (a) 0, 1, 1   (b) 1, 1, 0

   (c) 1, 0, 1   (d) 0, 1, 0

18. How many check bits are required for 16 bit data word to detect 2 bit errors and single bit correction using hamming code?

   (a) 5   (b) 6

   (c) 7   (d) 8

19. What is the maximum number of characters (7 bits + parity) that can be transmitted in a second on a 19.2 Kbps line. This asynchronous transmission requires 1 start bit and 1 stop bit.

   (a) 192   (b) 240

   (c) 1920   (d) 1966

20. IEEE 1394 is related to

   (a) RS-232   (b) USB

   (c) Firewire   (d) PCI

21. What will be the cipher text produced by the following cipher function for the plain text ISRO with key k = 7. [Consider 'A' = 0, 'B' = 1,... 'Z' = 25] $C_k(M) = (kM + 13) \bmod 26$

   (a) RJCH   (b) QIBG

   (c) GQPM   (d) XPIN

22. Any set of Boolean operators that is sufficient to represent all Boolean expressions is said to be complete. Which of the following is not complete?

   (a) (NOT, OR)   (b) {NOR}

   (c) {AND, OR}   (d) {AND, NOT}

23. Which of the following is the highest isolation level in transaction management?

   (a) Serializable   (b) Repeated Read

   (c) Committed Read   (d) Uncommitted Read

24. Consider the following relational schema:

- Suppliers (<u>sid.integer.</u> sname: string, saddress: string)
- Parts (pid: integer, pname: string, pcolor : string)
- Catalog (<u>sid.integer.pid:integer,</u> pcost: real)

What is the result of the following query?

(SELECT Catalog, pid from Suppliers, Catalog WHERE Suppliers.sid = Catalog.pid)

               MINUS

SELECT Catalog.pid from Suppliers, Catalog WHERE Suppliers.sname<> 'sachin' and Suppliers.sid = Catalog.sid)

   (a) Pid of parts supplied by all except Sachin

   (b) Pid of parts supplied only by Sachin

   (c) Pid of parts available in catalog supplied by Sachin

   (d) Pid of parts available in catalog supplied by all except Sachin

25. Consider the following dependencies and the BOOK table in a relational database design. Determine the normal form of the given relation.

     ISBN → Title

     ISBN → Publisher

     Publisher → Address

   (a) First Normal Form

   (b) Second Normal Form

   (c) Third normal Form

   (d) BCNF

26. Calculate the order of leaf (p_{leaf}) and non leaf (p) nodes of a B^+ tree based on the information given below

Search key field = 12 bytes

Record pointer = 10 bytes

Block pointer = 8 bytes

Block size = 1 KB

   (a) p_{leaf} = 51 and p = 46   (b) p_{leaf} = 47 and p = 52

   (c) p_{leaf} = 46 and p = 51   (d) p_{leaf} = 52 and p = 47

27. The physical location of a record determined by a formula that transforms a file key into a record location is

(a) Hashed file   (b) B-Tree file

(c) Indexed file   (d) Sequential file

28. The most simplified form of the Boolean function $X(A, B, C, D) = \Sigma\,(7, 8, 9, 10, 11, 12, 13, 14, 15)$ (expressed in sum of minterms) is ?

(a) $A + A'BCD$ (b) $AB + CD$

(c) $A + BCD$ (d) $ABC + D$

29. How many programmable fuses are required in a PLA which takes 16 inputs and gives 8 outputs? It has to use 8 OR gates and 32 AND gates,

(a) 1032   (b) 776

(c) 1284   (d) 1536

30. In a three stage counter, using RS flip flops what will be the value of the counter after giving 9 pulses to its input? Assume that the value of counter before giving any pulses is 1.

(a) 1   (b) 2

(c) 9   (d) 10

31. In which of the following shading models of polygons, the interpolation of intensity values is done along the scan line?

(a) Gourard shading

(b) Phong shading

(c) Constant shading

(d) Flat shading

32. Which of the following number of nodes can form a full binary tree?

(a) 8   (b) 15

(c) 14   (d) 13

33. What is the matrix transformation which takes the independent vectors $\begin{pmatrix} 1 \\ 2 \end{pmatrix}$ and $\begin{pmatrix} 2 \\ 5 \end{pmatrix}$ and transforms them to $\begin{pmatrix} 1 \\ 1 \end{pmatrix}$ and $\begin{pmatrix} 3 \\ 2 \end{pmatrix}$ respectively?

(a) $\begin{pmatrix} 1 & -1 \\ 1 & 0 \end{pmatrix}$ (b) $\begin{pmatrix} 0 & 0 \\ 0.5 & 0.5 \end{pmatrix}$

(c) $\begin{pmatrix} -1 & 0 \\ 1 & 1 \end{pmatrix}$ (d) $\begin{pmatrix} -1 & 1 \\ 1 & 0 \end{pmatrix}$

34. In 8086, the jump condition for the instruction JNBE is?

(a) CF=0 or ZF=0   (b) ZF = 0 and SF= 1

(c) CF=0 and ZF=0   (d) CF= 0

35. How many number of times the instruction sequence below will loop before coming out of the loop?

MOV AL, 00H

A1 : INC AL JNZ A1

(a) 1

(b) 255

(c) 256

(d) will not come out the loop

36. In 8085 microprocessor, the ISR for handling trap interrupt is at which location?

(a) 3 CH   (b) 34 H

(c) 74 H   (d) 24 H

37. The voltage ranges for a logic high and a logic low in RS-232 C standard is

(a) Low is 0.0 V to 1.8 V High is 2.0 V to 5.0V

(b) Low is -15.0V to -3.0V High is 3.0 V to 15.0V

(c) Low is 3.0 V to 15.0 V High is -3.0 V to -15.0V

(d) Low is 2.0 V to 5.0 V High is 0.0 V to 1.8V

38. In the Ethernet, which field is actually added at the physical layer and is not part of the frame.

(a) Preamble   (b) CRC

(c) Address   (d) Location

39. Ethernet layer-2 switch is a network element type which gives.

(a) Different collision domain and same broadcast domain.

(b) Different collision domain and different broadcast domain.

(c) Same collision domain and same broadcast domain.

(d) Same collision domain and different broadcast domain.

40. If the frame to be transmitted is 1101011011 and the CRC polynomial to be used for generating checksum is $x^4 + x + 1$, than what is the transmitted frame?

(a) 11010110111011

(b) 11010110111101

(c) 11010110111110

(d) 11010110111001

41. What will be the efficiency of a Stop and Wait protocol, if the transmission time for a frame is 20ns and the propagation time is 30 ns?

(a) 20%   (b) 25%

(c) 40%   (d) 66%

42. IPv6 does not support which of the following addressing modes?

(*a*) Unicast addressing

(*b*) Multicast addressing

(*c*) Broadcast addressing

(*d*) Anycast addressing

43. What is IP class and number of sub-networks if the subnet mask is 255.224.0.0?

(*a*) Class A, 3   (*b*) Class A, 8

(*c*) Class B, 3   (*d*) Class B, 32

44. Which algorithm is used to shape the bursty traffic into a fixed rate traffic by averaging the data rate?

(*a*) Solid bucket algorithm

(*b*) Spanning tree algorithm

(*c*) Hocken helm algorithm

(*d*) Leaky bucket algorithm

45. A packet filtering firewall can

(*a*) Deny certain users from accessing a service

(*b*) Block worms and viruses from entering the network

(*c*) Disallow some files from being accessed through FTP

(*d*) Block some hosts from accessing the network

46. Which of the following encryption algorithms is based on the Fiestal structure?

(*a*) Advanced Encryption Standard

(*b*) RSA public key cryptographic algorithm

(*c*) Data Encryption standard

(*d*) RC4

47. The protocol data unit for the transport layer in the internet stack is

(*a*) Segment   (*b*) Message

(*c*) Datagram   (*d*) Frame

48. The Guass-Seidal iterative method can be used to solve which of the following sets?

(*a*) Linear algebraic equations

(*b*) Linear and non-linear algebraic equations

(*c*) Linear differential equations

(*d*) Linear and non-linear differential equations

49. What is the least value of the function $f(x) = 2x^2 - 8x - 3$ in the interval $[0, 5]$?

(*a*) −15   (*b*) 7

(*c*) −11   (*d*) −3

50. Consider the following set of processes, with arrival times and the required CPU-burst times given in milliseconds.

Process	Arrival Time	Burst Time
P1	0	4
P2	2	2
P3	3	1

What is the sequence in which the processes are completed? Assume round robin scheduling with a time quantum of 2 milliseconds.

(*a*) P1, P2, P3   (*b*) P2, P1, P3

(*c*) P3, P2, P1   (*d*) P2, P3, P1

51. In case of a DVD, the speed of data transfer is mentioned in multiples of?

(*a*) 150KB/s   (*b*) 1.38MB/s

(*c*) 300 KB/s   (*d*) 2.40 MB/s

52. Suppose we have variable logical records of lengths of 5 bytes, 10 bytes and 25 bytes while the physical block size in disk is 15 bytes. What is the maximum and minimum fragmentation seen in bytes?

(*a*) 25 and 5   (*b*) 15 and 5

(*c*) 15 and 0   (*d*) 10 and 5

53. A CPU scheduling algorithm determines an order for the execution of its scheduled processes. Give '*n*' processes to be scheduled on one processor, how many possible different schedules are there?

(*a*) n (*b*) n^2

(*c*) $n!$ (*d*) 2^n

54. Which of the following are the likely causes of thrashing?

(*a*) Page size was very small.

(*b*) There are too many users connected to the system.

(*c*) Least recently used policy is used for page replacement.

(*d*) First in First out policy is used for page replacement.

55. Consider a logical address space of 8 pages of 1024 words each, mapped onto a physical memory of 32 frames. How many bits are there in the physical address and logical address respectively?

(*a*) 5, 3   (*b*) 10, 10

(*c*) 15, 13   (*d*) 15, 15

56. In a 64-bit machine, with 2 GB RAM, and 8 KB page size, how many entries will be there in the page table if its is inverted ?

(*a*) 2^{18} (*b*) 2^{20}

(*c*) 2^{33} (*d*) 2^{51}

57. Which of the following is not a necessary condition for deadlock?

(a) Mutual exclusion

(b) Reentrancy

(c) Hold and wait

(d) No pre-emption

58. Consider the following process and resource requirement of each process.

Process	Type 1		Type 2	
	Used	Max	Used	Max
P_1	1	2	1	3
P_2	1	3	1	2
P_3	2	4	1	4

Predict the state of this system, assuming that there are a total of 5 instances of resource type 1 and 4 instances of resource type 2.

(a) Can go to safe or unsafe state based on sequence

(b) Safe state

(c) Unsafe state

(d) Deadlock state

59. A starvation free job scheduling policy guarantees that no job indefinitely waits for a service. Which of the following job scheduling policies is starvation free?

(a) Priority queing

(b) Shortest job first

(c) Youngest job first

(d) Round robin

60. The state of a process after it encounters an I/O instruction is?

(a) Ready   (b) Blocked

(c) Idle   (d) Running

61. Embedded pointer provides

(a) A secondary access path

(b) A physical record key

(c) An inverted index

(d) A prime key

62. A particular parallel program computation requires 100 seconds when executed on a single CPU. If 20% of this computation is strictly sequential, then theoretically the best possible elapsed times for this program running on 2 CPUs and 4 CPUs respectively are

(a) 55 and 45 seconds

(b) 80 and 20 seconds

(c) 75 and 25 seconds

(d) 60 and 40 seconds

63. Consider the following C code.

```c
#include<stdio.h>
#include<math.h>
void mainQ
{
    double pi = 3.1415926535;
    int a = 1;
    int i;
    for (i = 0; i < 3; i++)
        if(a = cos(pi * i/2))
        printf("%d", 1);
        else printf("%d", 0);
}
```

What would the program print?

(a) 000   (b) 010

(c) 101   (d) 111

64. What is the output of the following Java program?

```java
Class test
{   public static void main (string [ ] args)
    {
    int x = 0;
    int y = 0;
    for (int z = 0; z < 5; z++)
    {
        if ((++x > 2) || (++ y > 2)
        {
            x ++;
        }
    }
    System.out.printIn (x + " " + y);
    }
}
```

(a) 82   (b) 85

(c) 83   (d) 53

65. Consider the list of page references in the time line as below :

9 6 2 3 4 4 4 4 3 4 4 2 5 8 6 8 5 5 3 2 3 3 9 6 2 7

What is the working set at the penultimate page reference if Δ is 5?

(a) {8, 5, 3, 2, 9, 6}   (b) {4, 3, 6, 2, 5}

(c) (3, 9, 6, 2, 7)   (d) {3, 9, 6, 2}

66. What is the cyclomatic complexity of a module which has seventeen edges and thirteen nodes?

(a) 4   (b) 5

(c) 6   (d) 7

67. Which of the following types of coupling has the weakest coupling?

(a) Pathological coupling

(b) Control coupling

(c) Data coupling

(d) Message coupling

68. Which of the following testing methods uses fault simulation technique?

(a) Unit testing

(b) Beta testing

(c) Stress testing

(d) Mutation testing

69. If a program P calls two subprograms $P1$ and $P2$ and $P1$ can fail 50% of the time and $P2$ can fail 40% of the time, what is the failure rate of program P?

(a) 50%   (b) 60%

(c) 70%   (d) 10%

70. Which of the following strategy is employed for overcoming the priority inversion problem?

(a) Temporarily raise the priority of lower priority level process

(b) Have a fixed priority level scheme.

(c) Implement Kernel pre-emption scheme.

(d) Allow lower priority process to complete its job.

71. Let $P(E)$ denote the probability of the occurrence of event E. If $P(A) = 0.5$ and $P(B) = 1$ then the values of $P(A/B)$ and $P(B/A)$ respectively are

(a) 0.5, 0.25   (b) 0.25, 0.5

(c) 0.5, 1   (d) 1, 0.5

72. How many diagonals can be drawn by joining the angular points of an octagon?

(a) 14   (b) 20

(c) 21   (d) 28

73. What are the final states of the DFA generated from the following NFA?

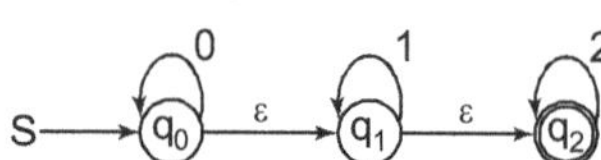

(a) q_0, q_1, q_2

(b) $[q_0, q_1] [q_0, q_2], [\,]$

(c) $q_0, [q_1, q_2]$

(d) $[q_0, q_1], q_2$

74. The number of elements in the power set of the set $\{\{A, B\}, C\}$ is

(a) 7   (b) 8

(c) 3   (d) 4

75. What is the right way to declare a copy constructor of a class if the name of the class is My Class?

(a) My Class (constant My Class*arg)

(b) My Class (constant My Class & arg)

(c) My Class (My Class arg)

(d) My Class (My Class*arg)

76. The number of edges in a 'n' vertex complete graph is?

(a) $\dfrac{n * (n - 1)}{2}$

(b) n^2

(c) $\dfrac{n * (n + 1)}{2}$

(d) $n * (n + 1)$

77. The binary equivalent of the decimal number 42.75 is

(a) 101010.110

(b) 100110.101

(c) 101010.101

(d) 100110.110

78. Which of the following is not provided as a service in cloud computing?

(a) Infrastructure as a service

(b) Architecture as a service

(c) Software as a service

(d) Platform as a service

79. The built-in base class in Java, which is used to handle all exceptions is

(a) Raise

(b) Exception

(c) Error

(d) Throwable

80. In graphics, the number of vanishing points depends on

(a) The number of axes cut by the projection plane

(b) The center of projection

(c) The number of axes which are parallel to the projection plane

(d) The perspective projections of any set of parallel lines that are not parallel to the projection plane

ANSWERS

1. (*b*)	**2.** (*d*)	**3.** (*b*)	**4.** (*c*)	**5.** (*a*)	**6.** (*b*)	**7.** (*c*)	**8.** (*d*)	**9.** (*a*)	**10.** (*c*)
11. (*a*)	**12.** (*a*)	**13.** (*b*)	**14.** (*d*)	**15.** (*d*)	**16.** (*c*)	**17.** (*d*)	**18.** (*a*)	**19.** (*c*)	**20.** (*c*)
21. (*a*)	**22.** (*c*)	**23.** (*a*)	**24.** (*b*)	**25.** (*b*)	**26.** (*c*)	**27.** (*a*)	**28.** (*c*)	**29.** (*c*)	**30.** (*b*)
31. (*a*)	**32.** (*b*)	**33.** (*d*)	**34.** (*c*)	**35.** (*c*)	**36.** (*d*)	**37.** (*c*)	**38.** (*a*)	**39.** (*a*)	**40.** (*c*)
41. (*b*)	**42.** (*c*)	**43.** (*b*)	**44.** (*d*)	**45.** (*d*)	**46.** (*c*)	**47.** (*a*)	**48.** (*a*)	**49.** (*c*)	**50.** (*b*)
51. (*b*)	**52.** (*c*)	**53.** (*c*)	**54.** (*a*)	**55.** (*c*)	**56.** (*a*)	**57.** (*b*)	**58.** (*c*)	**59.** (*d*)	**60.** (*b*)
61. (*a*)	**62.** (*d*)	**63.** (*c*)	**64.** (*a*)	**65.** (*d*)	**66.** (*c*)	**67.** (*d*)	**68.** (*d*)	**69.** (*c*)	**70.** (*a*)
71. (*c*)	**72.** (*b*)	**73.** (*a*)	**74.** (*d*)	**75.** (*b*)	**76.** (*a*)	**77.** (*a*)	**78.** (*b*)	**79.** (*d*)	**80.** (*d*)

Note: * None of the given option is correct Question may contain insufficient data.

EXPLANATIONS

1. Given element (1:8, – 5:5, – 10:5)

   Total put all the values of elements = (UL$_3$ LL$_3$ | 1)

   (UL$_2$ + LL$_2$ + 1) (UL$_1$ + LL$_1$ + 1)

   = (8 – 1 + 1)(5 – (–5) + 1)(5 – (–10) + 1)

   = 8 × 11 × 16

   = 1408

2. Sequence of element is

   9, 6, 5, 7, 8

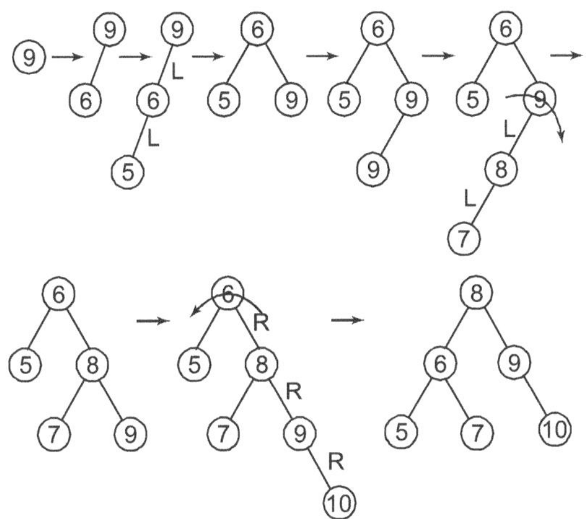

   So, Number of rotations = 3

3. Opportunistic reasoning is addressed by black board knowledge representation.

4. Given step in linked list

   p = get node () // Allocation of space for a new node

   info (p) = 10 // Setting info value of new node to 10

   Next (p) = list // The pointer to the next node is set to list

   list = p // Updation of list field.

   Hence, a new node is inserted to the existing linked list. Get is insecting a node opreation.

5. Shift reduce parsing belongs to the class of bottom-up parsing.

6. Given data,

   $$S \rightarrow Aa \mid b$$
   $$A \rightarrow Ac \mid Sd \mid \varepsilon$$

   After converting into left recursion elimination, the resultant grammar is,

   $$S \rightarrow Aa \mid b$$
   $$A \rightarrow bdA' \mid A'$$
   $$A \rightarrow cA' \mid adA' \mid \varepsilon$$

7. On the code execution, procedure first ( ) is called. Under procedure 'y', the second is called and add is passed as on argument. Due to deep binding, the scope of variables in 'add' gets assigned here. So, usage of 'y' in 'add' will corresponds to 'y' declared in 'first' and not the global 'y'. Similarly due to deep binding 'x' is already binded to the global 'x'.

   So, in function add, global 'x' will be updated as 1 + 3 = 4.

8. XOR logic gate is used to detect overflow in 2's complement arithmetic.

10. Frame buffer = 8 bit/pixel

    Number of entries in the lookup table

    $$= 2^8 = 256$$

    Entry size = 3 × 8 = 24 bits

Total size of the table

$$= \frac{256 \times 24}{8} = 768 \text{ bytes}$$

11. Two BCD numbers: 0×14, 0×08

   Binary representation

   $0 \times 14 + 0 \times 08 \Rightarrow 00100010$

   So, the resultant answer is 0×22

12. Complexity of insertion sort $[O(n)]$ is lower than complexity of quick sort $[O(n \log n)]$. In the best case.

   Complexity of insertion sort $[O(n^2)]$ is higher than complexity of quick sort $[O(n \log n)]$. In average case.

13. Given number

   $(1102)_3 = (123)_x$

   $$1 \times 3^3 + 1 \times 3^2 + 0 \times 3^1 + 2 \times 3^\circ$$
   $$= 1 \times x^2 + 2 \times x + 3$$

   $\Rightarrow \quad 27 + 9 + 0 + 2 = x^2 + 2x + 3$

   $\Rightarrow \quad x^2 + 2x + 3 = 38$

   Solve these equation,

   $\Rightarrow \quad x^2 + 2x - 35 = 0$

   $\Rightarrow \quad x^2 + 7x - 5x - 35 = 0$

   $x = 5, -7$

14. Fetching rate = IMIPS

   Consider data width of the system bus to "be in byte, DMA will run every cycle for every byte.

   $$1 \text{ sec} \rightarrow 10^6 \text{bits}$$
   $$1 \text{ bit} \rightarrow 10^{-6} \text{ sec}$$
   $$9600 \text{ bit} \rightarrow 9600 \times 10^{-6} \text{ sec}$$
   $$9600 \text{ B} \rightarrow 9600 \times 8 \times 10^{-6} \text{ sec} = 1.2 \text{ ms}$$

15. Given, speed up factor = 6

   Efficiency of K-stage pipeline

   efficiency = 70%

   $$= \frac{\text{Speed-up factor}}{\text{Number of stages}}$$

   $\Rightarrow \quad 0.7 = \dfrac{6}{K}$

   $\Rightarrow \quad K = \dfrac{6}{0.7} = 8.57 \approx 9$

16. Speed gain

   $$= \frac{\text{Memory access time without cache}}{\text{Memory access time with cache}}$$

   $$= \frac{T_{\text{memory}}}{T_{\text{cache}} + 0.20 \, T_{\text{memory}}} = \frac{1}{\dfrac{T_{\text{cache}}}{T_{\text{memory}}} + 0.20}$$

Assuming that cache is faster than memory by at least 10 times.

$$\text{Speed gain} = \frac{1}{0.20 + x}$$

Hence, speed gained by using the cache is 4.16.

17. Given, $b_1 = 11000011$, $b_2 = 01001100$

   On adding 11000011 and 01001100, the output is 00001111 with carry 1. Since result in not zero, hence zero flag is 0. We have a carry, hence carry flag will be 1, overflow will be 0 by XOR C_{in} and C_{out} which are both 1, 1.

18. To calculate the number of redundant bits (r) required to correct data bits (d)

   $$2^r = d + r + 1$$

   d is given as 16

   $$2^r = 16 + r + 1$$

   Here r satisfies the value 5 as per the equation.

19. Given bandwidth = 19.2 Kbps

   Number of bits transmitted in 1 sec

   $$= 8 + 1 + 1 = 10 \text{ bits}$$

   Number of character that can be send = 19200/100 = 1920 characters.

20. IEEE 1394 is related to firewall. It is an interface standard for high speed communications and isochronous real time data transfer.

21. Given ciper function,

   Message $\rightarrow$ ISRO

   Considering 'A' = 0, 'B' = 1 and so on, 'I' will be 8. So, the first character is 'I'.

   $C(I) = (KM + 13) \bmod 26$

   $\quad = (7 \times 8 + 13) \bmod 26 = 17,$

   which is the value of R.

   Continuing the same process for the remaining characters, 'S', 'R' and 'D' will result in 'J', 'C' and 'H' respectively. So, the cipher text produced will be 'RJCH'.

22. From the given universal gates i.e., the gates that can be implement any other function are NAND and NOR. So, considering each option.

   Option (a), NOT and OR combines for NOR GATE, option (b)is itself NOR GATE, option (d) actually corresponds to NAND GATE.

23. In transaction management, serializable is considered as the highest isolation level.

24. The first query will result in all those pid which are being supplied. The second query will result in pid for all parts, which are being supplied by any supplier other than supplier whose name is

sachin. By performing a difference operation on the two queries, the result will be the pid of parts supplied only by sachin.

25. From the designed relation table

Finding candidate key:

$(ISBN)^+ \rightarrow$ ISBN, Title, Publisher, Address Hence, ISBN is the candidate key. Considering the third functional dependency, the attribute on both LHS and RHS are non-prime attributes which results in transitive dependency. Hence, the higher normal form is second normal form.

26. To find the order of leaf and non-leaf nodes

For a leaf node, $n(K + R_p) + p_{next} \leq$ Block size

$\Rightarrow n(12 + 10) + 8 \leq 1024$ B

$\Rightarrow n \leq 46.18 \approx 46$

For a non-leaf node, $n(p) + n - 1(k) \leq$ Block size

$\Rightarrow n(8) + n - 1 (12) \leq 1024$ B

$\Rightarrow 8n + 12n - 12 \leq 1024$

$\Rightarrow n \leq 51.8 = 51$

27. A hash file transforms a file key into a record location. By knowing the key and the hash function used, the record location can be known.

28. Booleen function $\times$ (A, B, C, D) $= \Sigma(7, 8, 9, 10, 11, 12, 13, 14, 15)$

Constructing the K-map

AB\CD	00	01	11	10
00	0	1	3	2
01	4	5	1 ⁷	6
11	1 ¹²	1 ¹³	1 ¹⁵	1 ¹⁴
10	1 ⁸	1 ⁹	1 ¹¹	1 ¹⁰

F = A + BCD

29. Input = 16, output = 8

Total programmable fuse = Fuse required by AND GATE + Fuse required by OR GATE Fuse required by AND GATE = 2 × Number of inputs × Number of AND GATE = 2 × 16 × 32 = 1024 fuses

Fuse required by OR GATE = Number of outputs × Number of AND GATE = 8 × 32 = 256

Total fuses = 1024 + 256 = 1280

30. 3 stage counter with RS flip-flop is 3 bit counter, so after every 8 clock pulse, the flip-flip will return to the starting state. As per the question,

initial state is 1, after 8 clock pulse, it will again be 1. Now at 9th, the value will be 2.

32. The full binary tree can be formed

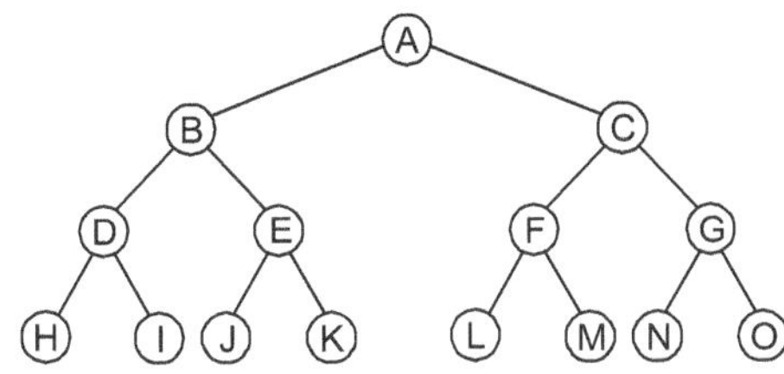

Since, the binary tree must be full hence at every level must be 2^i nodes considering $i = 0$ for the root node.

33. Matrix transformation by

Considering each option,

(a) $\begin{pmatrix} 1 & -1 \\ 1 & 0 \end{pmatrix}\begin{pmatrix} 1 \\ 2 \end{pmatrix} = \begin{pmatrix} -1 \\ 2 \end{pmatrix} = 1\begin{pmatrix} -1 \\ 1 \end{pmatrix} = \lambda \ X \neq \begin{pmatrix} 1 \\ 1 \end{pmatrix}$ or $\begin{pmatrix} 3 \\ 2 \end{pmatrix}$

(b) $\begin{pmatrix} 0 & 0 \\ 0.5 & 0.5 \end{pmatrix}\begin{pmatrix} 1 \\ 2 \end{pmatrix} = \begin{pmatrix} 0 \\ 1.5 \end{pmatrix} \neq \begin{pmatrix} 1 \\ 1 \end{pmatrix}$ or $\begin{pmatrix} 3 \\ 2 \end{pmatrix}$

(c) $\begin{pmatrix} -1 & 1 \\ 1 & 0 \end{pmatrix}\begin{pmatrix} 1 \\ 2 \end{pmatrix} = \begin{pmatrix} -1 \\ 3 \end{pmatrix} \neq \begin{pmatrix} 1 \\ 1 \end{pmatrix}$ or $\begin{pmatrix} 3 \\ 2 \end{pmatrix}$

(d) $\begin{pmatrix} -1 & 1 \\ 1 & 0 \end{pmatrix}\begin{pmatrix} 1 \\ 2 \end{pmatrix} = \begin{pmatrix} 1 \\ 1 \end{pmatrix}$

$\begin{pmatrix} -1 & 1 \\ 1 & 0 \end{pmatrix}\begin{pmatrix} 2 \\ 5 \end{pmatrix} = \begin{pmatrix} 3 \\ 2 \end{pmatrix}$

34. In 8084 the instruction JNBE, carry flag = 0 and zero flag = 0 will be correct.

35. In the given instruction

AL will contain 0000 0000, on incrementing it will be 0000 0001.

36. In 8085 microprocessor, interrupt RST 7.5 will have vector address $(003C)_H$, RST 6.5 will have vector address $(0034)_H$, RST 5.5 will have vector address $(002C)_H$ and TRAP will have vector address $(0024)_H$.

38. In the ethrnet Preamble contains 7 bytes of alternating 1's and O's that informs the receiver about the enable frames and enables it to synchronize its input timing. Preamble is the field that is actually added at the physical layer and is not a part of the frame.

39. A collision domain is a section of network connected by a shared medium or through repeaters where data packets can collide with one another when being sent, particularly when using early versions of Ethernet.

Ethernet layer-2 switch is a network element type which gives different collision domain and same broadcast domain.

40. Generating check sun is, $x^4 + x + 0$

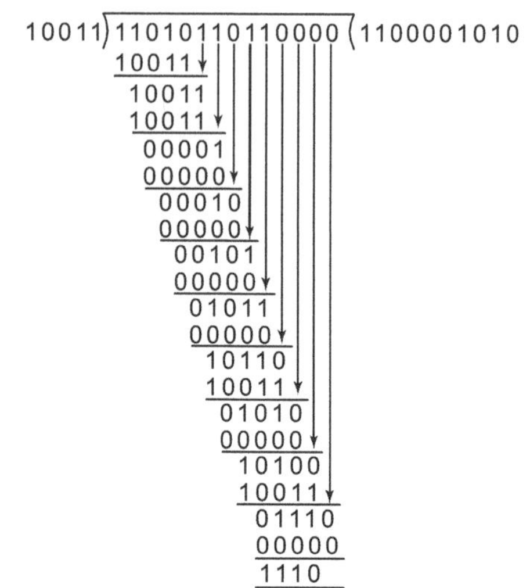

Transmitted frame: 11010110111110.

41. Efficiency of (n) = ?

Transmission time (T_t) = 20 ns

Propagation time (T_p) = 30 ns

$$A = \frac{T_p}{T_t} = \frac{30}{20} = 1.5$$

$$\text{Utilization} = \frac{T_1}{T_1 + 2 \times T_p} = \frac{20}{20 + 60}$$

$$(\eta) = \frac{20}{80} = \frac{1}{4} = 25\%$$

42. IPv6 support unicast, multicast and anycast addressing modes, but not broadcast addressing.

43. Subnet mask = 255.224.0.0

It can be written as, 255.11100000.0.0

Observing the first and second octet, it can be concluded that IP class is A. Since there are three 1's in the second octet which says that, there are 8 subnetworks.

44. A leaky bucket algorithm that may be used to determine whether some sequence of discrete events conforms to defined limits on their average and peak rate of frequency.

45. A packet filtering is a firewall technique used to control network access by monitoring outgoing and incoming packets and allowing them to pass or halt based on source and destination IP addresses, protocols and ports. It blocks worms and viruses from entering the network.

46. Fiestal structure is a symmetric cipher which is used in the construction of block cipher. DES is symmetric, which is based on Fiestal cipher. Although RC4 is symmetric but it is not based on Fiestal cipher.

47. Frame is the PDU for data link layer. Packet is the PDU for network layer and segment is the PDU for transport layer.

48. Gauss Siedal is an iterative method that is used to solve linear algebric equations.

49. Given function,

$$f(x) = 2x^2 - 8x - 3$$

$$f'(x) = 4x - 8$$

$$f''(x) = 4$$

The minimal values is at point $x = 2$, which evaluate to -11.

50. Given set of processes,

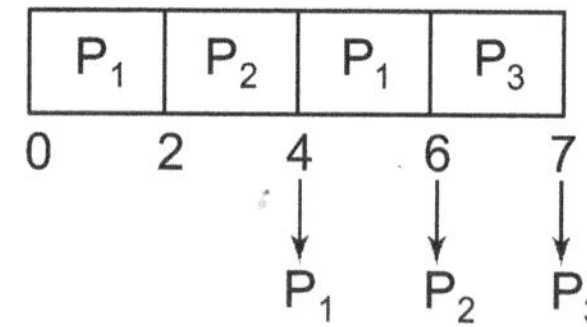

Hence, P_2, P_1, P_3 is the sequence in which processes are completing using round robin with time quantum of 2 milliseconds.

51. In DVD, the speed of data transfer is mentioned in multiples of 1.38MBps.

52. Given block size is 15 B. So, when the logical records are of length 5 B. So, on transferring 5B, remaining will be 10 B, of block, when transferring 10 B, fragmentation will be of 5 B and while transferring records of length 25 B the fragmentation will be of 5 B.

Hence, the maximum fragmentation is of size 10 B and the minimum fragmentation is of size 5 B.

53. In a CPU scheduling algorithm

There are 'n' processes to be scheduled, hence there are $n!$ ways to arrange them in some order. So, total $n!$ schedules are possible.

54. Thrashing condition occur when maximum time is consumed in swapping of the pages compared to the execution of the program.

55. Consider the given addresses

Logical address:

← 3 bits →	← 10 bits →
Pages	Offset

Total bits required for logical address will be 13.

Physical address:

← 5 bits →	← 10 bits →
Frame	Offset

Total bits required for physical address will be 15.

56. In a 64-bit machin,

$$\text{No. of pages} = \frac{\text{Size of memory}}{\text{Page size}}$$

$$= \frac{2 \times 2^{30}}{2^3 \times 2^{10}} = 2^{18}$$

Hence, total number of entries will be 2^{18}.

57. There are four conditions which must simultaneously hold for deadlock are mutual exclusion, hold-and-wait, circular Wait and No preemption.

58. Considering the given process and Calculating the need matrix for the three processes,

Process	Type-1	Type-2
P_1	1	2
P_2	2	1
P_3	2	3

Remaining number of resources

$$= (P_1, P_2, P_3 \rightarrow (1, 1)$$

The number of remaining resources can't satisfy the remaining need of any of the process, so system is in unsafe state.

59. In round robin scheduling algorithm, every process will execute for a fixed time quantum at a time and then the control will be transferred to another process and so on.

Hence, round robin guarantees a starvation free job.

60. The process state diagram is :

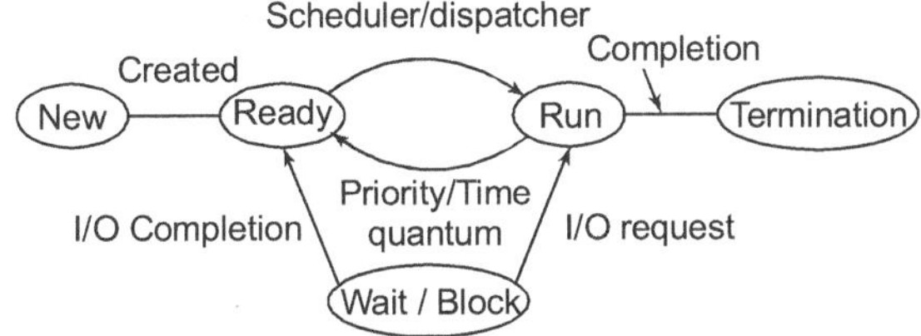

61. Embedded pointers provides a secondary access path.

63. Considering the given C code,

$i = 0 \Rightarrow$ if $(a = \cos 0) \Rightarrow$ Condition satisfied

$\Rightarrow$ Print '1'

$i = 1 \Rightarrow$ if $(a = \cos (\pi/2)) \Rightarrow$ Condition false

$\Rightarrow$ Print '0'

$i = 0 \Rightarrow$ if $(a = \cos (\pi)) \Rightarrow$ Condition satisfy

$\Rightarrow$ Print '1'.

64. Output of the Java program, consider,

Initially, at $z = 0$, the if condition will be false. The for $z = 1$, again the if condition will be false, for $z = 2, 3$ and 4 the condition will be true since

the value will be 4, 6 and 8 respectively and the value of y will be '2' because (++y) will not be executes due to short circuit evaluation.

65. Consider the list of page referece

The working-set reference will be

$9 \rightarrow \{9\}$, $6 \rightarrow (9, 6\}$, $2 \rightarrow \{9, 6, 2\}$, $3 \rightarrow \{9, 6, 2, 3\}$, $4 \rightarrow \{9, 6, 2, 3, 4\}$, $4 \rightarrow \{6, 2, 3, 4)$, $4 \rightarrow \{2, 3, 4\}$, $4 \rightarrow \{3, 4\}$, $3 \rightarrow \{3, 4\}$, $4 \rightarrow \{3, 4\}$, $2 \rightarrow \{2, 3, 4\}$, $5 \rightarrow \{3, 4, 2, 5\}$, $8 \rightarrow \{2, 4, 5, 8\}$, $6 \rightarrow \{2, 4, 5, 6, 8\}$, $8 \rightarrow \{2, 5, 6, 8\}$, $5 \rightarrow \{5, 6, 8\}$, $5 \rightarrow \{5, 6, 8\}$, $3 \rightarrow (3, 5, 6, 8\}$, $2 \rightarrow (2, 3, 5, 8\}$, $3 \rightarrow \{2, 3, 5\}$, $3 \rightarrow \{2, 3, 5\}$, $9 \rightarrow (2, 3, 9\}$, $6 \rightarrow \{2, 3, 9, 6\}$, $2 \rightarrow \{2, 3, 6, 9\}$, $7 \rightarrow \{3, 9, 6, 2, 7\}$

66. Cyclomatic complexity = Number of edges – Number of vertices + 2

$$= 17 - 13 + 2$$

$$= 4 + 2$$

$$= 6$$

67. Out of all the coupling methods asked in options, message coupling is the weakest coupling.

68. In the fault simulation testing, the faults are simulated in the form of mutants. Test cases are prepared to kill the mutants. The objective of mutation testing is to generate efficient and optimized set of test data in order to kill maximum number of mutants to achieve a high mutation score.

69. Program 'p' fails when either P_1 fails or P_2 fails. Failure rate of P = (Failure of P_1 + (Failure of P_2) – (Failure of P_1 ∩ Failure of P_2)

$$= \frac{50}{100} + \frac{40}{100} - \frac{50}{100} \times \frac{40}{100}$$

$$= \frac{90}{100} - \frac{20}{100} = \frac{70}{100}$$

70. In preemptive models like SRTF, priority scheduling, the process with low priority [can be in term of high burst time too] are always preempted by the processes with high priority. There might be some scenario, where a process with low priority will never get a chance which will led to its starvation. To, solve this problem, temporarily raise the priority of low priority level process so that it can complete its job.

71. Given, P(A) = 0.5, P(B) = 1 then

$$P(A/B) = \frac{P(A \cap B)}{P(B)} = \frac{0.5 \times 1}{1} = 0.5$$

$$P(B/A) = \frac{P(A \cap B)}{P(A)} = \frac{0.5}{0.5} = 1$$

72. Octagon $(n) = 8$(side)

Number of diagonals $= \dfrac{n \times (n-3)}{2}$

Value of $n = 8$

Number of diagonal $= \dfrac{8 \times 5}{2} = 20$

73. From the given NFA by observation of state q_0, it can be concluded that string with only any number of 0's can be satisfied by the grammar hence q_0 will also be the final state. Similarly q_1 by giving null-transition, we are reaching a final state, hence q_1 can also be a final state.

So, the set of final state will be (q_0, q_1, q_2).

74. Number of element in the power set

Set $\to \{\{A, B\}\, C\}$.

Number of element in the set $= 2$

Number of elements in power set $= 2^n = 2^2 = 4$

The element will be:

$\{\phi\ \{\{A, B\}\}, \{C\}, \{\{A, B\}C\}\}$

75. My class (constant My class & arg) is the right way to declare a copy constructor of a class, if the name of the class is My class.

76. In a complete graph, every vertex will have an edge to every other vertex. Hence as per the Handshaking theorem, the total number of edges will be $\dfrac{n(n-1)}{2}$, since every edge will correspond to 2 degree.

77. Find Binary equivalent of decimal number = 42.75

2	42	0
2	21	1
2	10	0
2	5	1
2	2	0
	1	

Similarly,

$0.75 \times 2 = 1.5$

$0.5 \times 2 = 1.0$

$0.0 \times 2 = 0.0$

Hence, the binary equivalent is 101010.110.

78. Cloud computing provides three services that are infrastructure as a service, software as a service and platform - as a service.

79. To handle all the exceptions in Java throwable is the built in class. Exception and error are the sub classes of throwable.

80. In graphics, the number of vanishing points depends on the perspective projections of any set of parallel lines that are not parallel to projection plane.

SOLVED PAPER 2014
Computer Science

1. Consider a 33 MHz CPU based system. What is the number of wait states required if it is interfaced with a 60ns memory? Assume a maximum of 10ns delay for additional circuitry like buffering and decoding.
   - (a) 0
   - (b) 1
   - (c) 2
   - (d) 3

2. The number of states required by a Finite State Machine, to simulate the behavior of a computer with a memory capable of storing 'm' words, with each word being 'n' bits long is
   - (a) $m \times 2^n$
   - (b) 2^{m+n}
   - (c) 2^{mn}
   - (d) $m + n$

3. What is the output of the following C program?

```
# include <stdio.h>
# define SQR(x)(x*x)
int main ()
{
    int a;
    int b = 4;

    a = SQR(b + 2);
    printf ("%d\n", a);
    return 0;
}
```

   - (a) 14
   - (b) 36
   - (c) 18
   - (d) 20

4. Consider the following pseudo-code

```
while (m < n)
if (x > y) and (a < b) then
    a = a + 1
    y = y - 1
end if
    m = m + 1
end while
```

   What is cyclomatic complexity of the above pseudo-code?
   - (a) 2
   - (b) 3
   - (c) 4
   - (d) 5

5. What is the number of steps required to derive the string ((() ()) ()) for the following grammar?
   - $S \rightarrow SS$
   - $S \rightarrow (S)$
   - $S \rightarrow \varepsilon$

   - (a) 10
   - (b) 15
   - (c) 12
   - (d) 16

6. The process of modifying IP address information in IP packet headers while in transit across a traffic routing device is called
   - (a) Port address translation (PAT)
   - (b) Network address translation (NAT)
   - (c) Address mapping
   - (d) Port mapping

7. What does a pixel mask mean?
   - (a) string containing only 1's
   - (b) string containing only 0's
   - (c) string containing two 0's
   - (d) string containing 1's and 's

8. In the standard IEEE 754 single precision floating point representation, there is 1 bit for sign, 23 bits for fraction and 8 bits for exponent. What is the precision in terms of the number of decimal digits?
   - (a) 5
   - (b) 6
   - (c) 7
   - (d) 8

9. LET R be the radius of a circle. What is the angle substended by an arc of length R at the centre of the circle?
   - (a) 1 degree
   - (b) 1 radian
   - (c) 90 degrees
   - (d) π radians

10. The number of logical CPUs in a computer having two physical quad-core chips with hyper threading enabled is ________.
    - (a) 1
    - (b) 2
    - (c) 8
    - (d) 16

11. An aggregation association is drawn using which symbol?
    - (a) A line which loops back on to the same table
    - (b) A small open diamond at the end of a line connecting two tables
    - (c) A small closed diamond at the end of a line connecting two tables
    - (d) A small closed triangle at the end of a line connecting two tables

12. How many states are there in a minimum state deterministic finite automaton accepting the language $L = \{w \mid w \; \varepsilon \; \{0, 1\}^*$, number of 0's is divisible by 2 and number of 1's is divisible by 5, respectively\}?
    - (a) 7
    - (b) 9
    - (c) 10
    - (d) 11

13. Which of the following is true with respect to a reference?

(a) A reference can never be NULL

(b) A reference needs an explicit dereferencing mechanism

(c) A reference can be reassigned after it is established

(d) A reference and pointer are synonymous

14. There are 200 tracks on a disk platter and the pending requests have come in the order-36, 69, 167, 76, 42, 51, 126, 12 and 199. Assume the arm is located at the 100th track and moving towards track 200. If sequence of disc access is 126,167, 199, 12, 36, 42, 51, 69 and 76 then which disc access scheduling policy is used?

(a) Elevator

(b) Shortest Seek-time first

(c) C-SCAN

(d) First Come First Served

15. Consider the logic circuit given below:

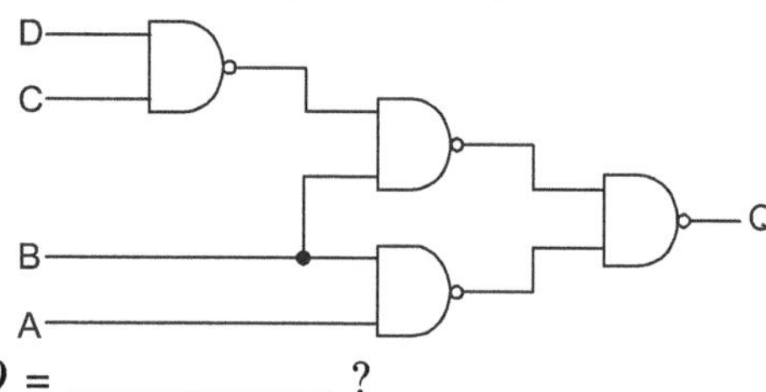

$Q =$ __________ ?

(a) $\bar{A}C + B\bar{C} + CD$ (b) $ABC + \bar{C}D$

(c) $AB + B\bar{C} + B\bar{D}$ (d) $A\bar{B} + A\bar{C} + \bar{C}D$

16. What is routing algorithm used by OSPF routing protocol?

(a) Distance vector   (b) Flooding

(c) Path vector   (d) Link state

17. If each address space represents one byte of storage space, how many address lines are needed to access RAM chips arranged in a 4 × 6 array, where each chip is 8 K × 4 bits?

(a) 13   (b) 15

(c) 16   (d) 17

18. Consider the following segment table in segmentation scheme:

Segment Id	Base	Limit
0	200	200
1	5000	1210
2	1527	498
3	2500	50

What happens if the logical address requested is- Segment ID 2 and Offset 1000?

(a) Fetches the entry at the physical address 2527 for Segment Id 2

(b) A trap is generated

(c) Deadlock

(d) Fetches the entry at offset 27 in Segment Id 3

19. The number of bit strings of length 8 that will either start with 1 or end with 00 is ______.

(a) 32   (b) 128

(c) 160   (d) 192

20. Which of the following is not a maturity level as per Capability Maturity Model?

(a) Initial   (b) Measurable

(c) Repeatable   (d) Optimized

21. Consider the following sequential circuit.

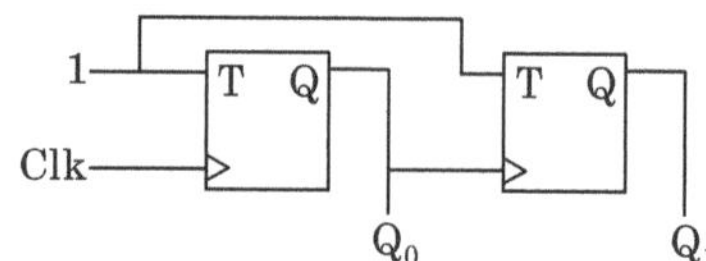

What are values of Q_0 and Q_1 after 4 clock cycles, if initial values are 00?

(a) 11   (b) 01

(c) 10   (d) 00

22. Consider the schema $R(A, B, C, D)$ and the functional dependencies $A \to B$ and $C \to D$. If the decomposition is made as $R_1(A, B)$ and $R_2(C, D)$, then which of the following is TRUE?

(a) Preserves dependency but cannot perform lossless join

(b) Preserves dependency and performs lossless join

(c) Does not preserve dependency and cannot performs lossless join

(d) Does not preserve dependency but performs lossless join

23. The test suite (set of test input) used to perform unit testing on a module could cover 70% of the code. What is the reliability of the module if the probability of success is 0.95 during above testing?

(a) 0.665 to 0.95

(b) At the most 0.665

(c) At the most 0.95

(d) At least 0.665

24. In a system an RSA algorithm with $p = 5$ and $q = 11$, is implemented for data security. What is the value of the decryption key if the value of the encryption key is 27?

(a) 3   (b) 7

(c) 27   (d) 40

25. Suppose you want to build a memory with 4 byte words and a capacity of 2^{21} bits. What is type of decoder required if the memory is built using $2 \text{ K} \times 8$ RAM chips?

(a) 5 to 32   (b) 6 to 64

(c) 4 to 16   (d) 7 to 128

26. The output of a tristate buffer when the enable input in 0 is

(a) Always 0

(b) Always 1

(c) Retains the last value when enable input was high

(d) Disconnected state

27. How many different BCD numbers can be stored in 12 switches? (Assume two position or on-off switches).

(a) 2^{12} (b) $2^{12} - 1$

(c) 10^{12} (d) 10^3

28. Suppose there are 11 items in sorted order in an array. How many searches are required on the average, if binary search is employed and all searches are successful in finding the item?

(a) 3.00   (b) 3.46

(c) 2.81   (d) 3.33

29. Consider the following Java code fragment. Which of the following statement is true?

Line No.	Code Statement
1.	Public class While
2.	{
3.	Public void loop()
4.	{
5.	int x = 0;
6.	while(1)
7.	{
8.	system.out.println ("x plus one is" + (x + 1));
9.	}
10.	}
11.	}

(a) There is syntax error in line no. 1

(b) There are syntax errors in line nos. 1 and 6

(c) There is syntax error in line no. 8

(d) There is syntax error in line no 6

30. Every time the attribute A appears, it is matched with the same value of attribute B but not the same value of attribute C. Which of the following is true?

(a) $A \rightarrow (B, C)$

(b) $A \rightarrow B, A \rightarrow\!\!> C$

(c) $A \rightarrow B, C \rightarrow\!\!> A$

(d) $A \rightarrow\!\!> B, B \rightarrow C$

31. A IP packet has arrived in which the fragmentation offset value is 100, the value of HLEN is 5 and the value of total length field is 200. What is the number of the last byte?

(a) 194   (b) 394

(c) 979   (d) 1179

32. What is the output of the following C program?

```
# include <stdio.h>
void main (void)
{
    int shifty;
    shifty = 0570;
    shifty = shifty >> 4;
    shifty = shifty << 6;
    printf ("The value of shifty is %0\n", shifty);
}
```

(a) The value of shifty is 1500

(b) The value of shifty is 4300

(c) The value of shifty is 5700

(d) The value of shifty is 2700

33. The following Finite Automaton recognizes which of the given languages?

(a) {1, 0} * {0 1}

(b) {1, 0} * {1}

(c) {1}{1, 0} * {1}

(d) 1*0*{0, 1}

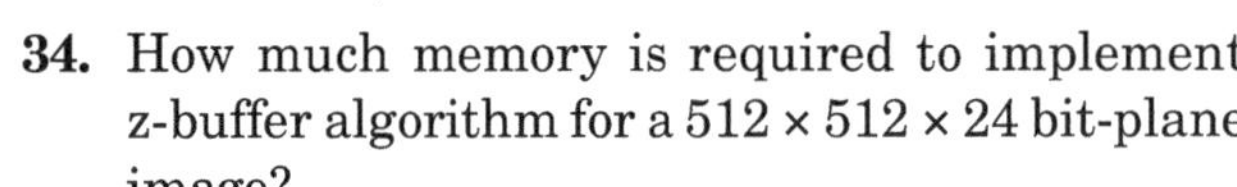

34. How much memory is required to implement z-buffer algorithm for a $512 \times 512 \times 24$ bit-plane image?

(a) 768 KB   (b) 1 MB

(c) 1.5 MB   (d) 2 MB

35. Using the page table shown below, translate the physical address 25 to virtual address. The address length is 16 bits and page size is 2048 words while the size of the physical memory is four frames.

Page	Present (1-In, 0-out)	Frame
0	1	3
1	1	2
2	1	0
3	0	–

(a) 25   (b) 6169

(c) 2073   (d) 4121

36. Consider a standard Circular queue 'q' implementation (which has same condition for queue full and queue empty) whose size is 11 and the elements of the queue are $q[0], q[1],..., q[10]$.

The front and rear pointers are initialized to point at q [2]. In which position will the ninth element be added?

(a) $q[0]$ (b) $q[1]$

(c) $q[9]$ (d) $q[10]$

37. The probability that two friends are born in the same month is _______?

(a) 1/6   (b) 1/12

(c) 1/144   (d) 1/24

38. How many lines of output does the following C code produce?

```
# include <stdio.h>

float i = 2.0;
float j = 1.0;
float sum = 0.0;

main()
{    while (i /j> 0.001)
     {
         j + = j;
         sum = sum + (i / j);
         printf ("%f\n", sum);
     }
}
```

(a) 8   (b) 9

(c) 10   (d) 11

39. If only one memory location is to be reserved for a class variable, no matter how many objects are instantiated, then the variable should be declared as _______.

(a) extern   (b) static

(c) volatile   (d) const

40. Assume that a 16-bit CPU is trying to access a double word starting at an odd address. How many memory operations are required to access the data?

(a) 1   (b) 2

(c) 3   (d) 4

41. Consider the following binary search tree T given below : Which node contains the fourth smallest element in T?

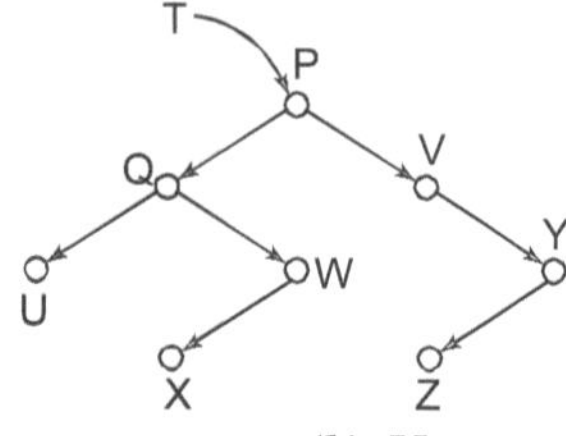

(a) Q (b) V

(c) W (d) X

42. Let x, y, z, a, b, c be the attributes of an entity set E. If $\{x\}, \{x, y\}, \{a, b\}, \{a, b, c\}, \sim \{x, y, z\}$ are superkeys then which of the following are the candidate keys?

(a) $\{x, y\}$ and $\{a, b\}$

(b) $\{x\}$ and $\{a, b\}$

(c) $\{x, y, z\}$ and $\{a, b, c\}$

(d) $\{z\}$ and $\{c\}$

43. The five items : A, B, C, D and E are pushed in a stack, one after other starting from A. The stack is popped four times and each element is inserted in a queue. Then two elements are deleted from the queue and pushed back on the stack. Now, one item is popped from the stack. The popped item is _______.

(a) A (b) B

(c) C (d) D

44. A computer has 16 pages of virtual address space but the size of main memory is only four frames. Initially the memory is empty. A program references with the virtual pages in the order of 0, 2, 4, 5, 2, 4, 3, 11, 2, 10. How many page faults occur if LRU page replacement algorithm is used?

(a) 3   (b) 5

(c) 7   (d) 8

45. Consider a 50 kbps satellite channel with a 500 milliseconds round trip propagation delay. If the sender wants to transmit 1000 bit frames, how much time will it take for the receiver to receive the frame?

(a) 250 milliseconds (b) 20 milliseconds

(c) 520 milliseconds (d) 270 milliseconds

46. If the maximum output voltage of a DAC is V volts and if the resolution is R bits then the weight of the most significant bit is_____.

(a) $\dfrac{V}{(2^R - 1)}$ (b) $(2^{R-1}).\dfrac{V}{(2^R - 1)}$

(c) $(2^{R-1}).V$ (d) $\dfrac{V}{(2^R - 1)}$

47. The following three 'C' language statements is equivalent to which single statement?

```
y = y + 1;
z = x + y;
x = x + 1;
```

(a) $z = x + y + 2;$

(b) $z = (x{+}{+}) + ({+}{+}y);$

(c) $z = ({+}{+}x) + (y{+}{+});$

(d) $z = (x{+}{+}) + ({+}{+}y) + 1;$

48. A frame buffer array is addressed in row-major order for a monitor with pixel locations starting from (0, 0) and ending with (100, 100). What is address of the pixel (6, 10)? Assume one bit storage per pixel and starting pixel location is at 0.

(a) 1016 (b) 1006

(c) 610 (d) 616

49. Consider a single linked list where F and L are pointers to the first and last elements respectively of the linked list. The time for performing which of the given operations depends on the length of the linked list?

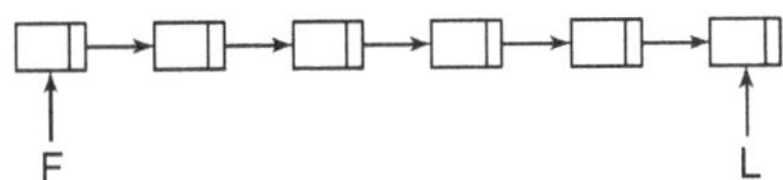

(a) Delete the first element of the list

(b) Interchange the first two elements of the list

(c) Delete the last element of the list

(d) Add an element at the end of the list

50. Let A be a finite set having x elements and let B be a finite set having y elements. What is the number of distinct functions mapping B into A.

(a) x^y (b) $2^{(x+y)}$

(c) y^x (d) $\dfrac{y!}{(y-x)!}$

51. Which of the following is NOT represented in a subroutine's activation record frame for a stack-based programming language?

(a) Values of local variables

(b) Return address

(c) Heap area

(d) Information needed to access non local variables

52. Consider the following grammar.

- $S \rightarrow AB$
- $A \rightarrow a$
- $A \rightarrow BaB$
- $B \rightarrow bbA$

Which of the following statements is FALSE?

(a) The length of every string produced by this grammar is even

(b) No string produced by this grammar has three consecutive a's

(c) The length of substring produced by B is always odd

(d) No string produced by this grammar has four consecutive b's

53. Consider the logic circuit given below.

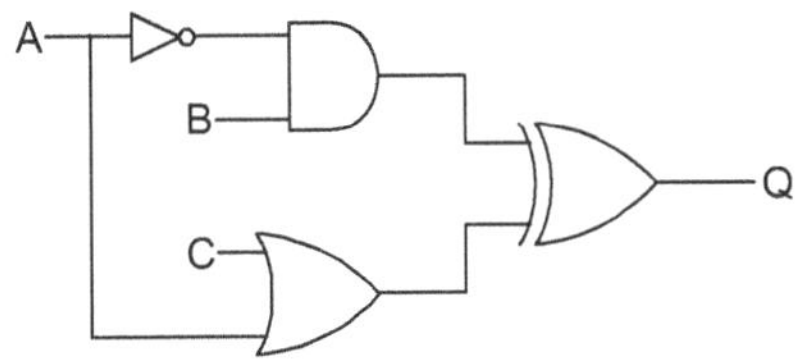

The inverter, AND and OR gates have delays of 6, 10 and 11 nanoseconds respectively. Assuming that wire delays are negligible, what is the duration of glitch for Q before it becomes stable?

(a) 5 (b) 11

(c) 16 (d) 27

54. The conic section that is obtained when a right circular cone is cut through a plane that is parallel to the side of the cone is called ______.

(a) parabola (b) hyperbola

(c) circle (d) ellipse

55. An IP packet has arrived with the first 8 bits as 0100 0010. Which of the following is correct?

(a) The number of hops this packet can travel is 2.

(b) The total number of bytes header is 16 bytes

(c) The upper layer protocol is ICMP

(d) The receiver rejects the packet

56. Which of the following is not a valid Boolean algebra rule?

(a) $X.X = X$ (b) $(X+Y).X = X$

(c) $\bar{X} + XY = Y$ (d) $(X+Y).(X+Z) = X + YZ$

57. A supernet has a first address of 205.16.32.0 and a supernet mask of 255.255.248.0. A router receives 4 packets with the following destination addresses. Which packet belongs to this supernet?

(a) 205.16.42.56 (b) 205.17.32.76

(c) 205.16.31.10 (d) 205.16.39.44

58. Assume the following information.

- Original timestamp value = 46
- Receive timestamp value = 59
- Transmit timestamp value = 60
- Timestamp at arrival of packet = 69

Which of the following statements is correct?

(a) Receive clock should go back by 3 milliseconds

(b) Transmit and Receive clocks are synchronized

(c) Transmit clock should go back by 3 milliseconds

(d) Receive clock should go ahead by 1 millisecond

59. Which of the following is FALSE with respect to possible outcomes of executing a Turning Machine over a given input?

(a) It may halt and accept the input

(b) It may halt by changing the input

(c) It may halt and reject the input

(d) It may never halt

60. Suppose you are browsing the world wide web using a web browser and trying to access the web servers. What is the underlying protocol and port number that are being used?

(a) UDP, 80

(b) TCP, 80

(c) TCP, 25

(d) UDP, 25

61. A mechanism or technology used in Ethernet by which two connected devices choose common transmission parameters such as speed, duplex mode and flow control is called

(a) Autosense

(b) Synchronization

(c) Pinging

(d) Auto negotiation

62. Consider the following sorting algorithms.

1. Quicksort

2. Heapsort

3. Mergesort

Which of them perform in least time in the worst case?

(a) 1 and 2 only

(b) 2 and 3 only

(c) 3 only

(d) 1, 2 and 3

63. Consider the following table

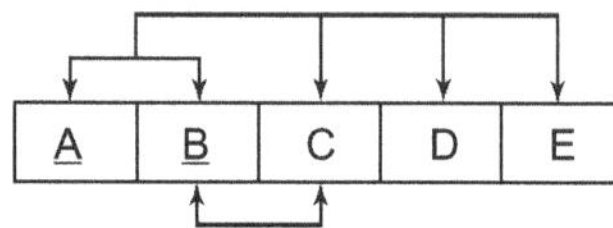

The table is in which normal form?

(a) First Normal Form

(b) Second Normal Form

(c) Third Normal Form but not BCNF

(d) Third Normal Form and BCNF

64. Consider a 13 element hash table for which $f(\text{key}) = \text{key mod } 13$ is used with/integer keys. Assuming linear probing is used for collision resolution, at which location would the key 103 be inserted, if the keys 661, 182, 24 and 103 are inserted in that order?

(a) 0

(b) 1

(c) 11

(d) 12

65. A cube of side 1 unit is placed in such a way that the origin coincides with one of its top vertices and the three axes run along three of its edges. What are the co-ordinates of the vertex which is diagonally opposite to the vertex whose co-ordinates are $(1, 0, 1)$?

(a) $(0, 0, 0)$

(b) $(0, -1, 0)$

(c) $(0, 1, 0)$

(d) $(1, 1, 1)$

66. Consider a system where each file is associated with a 16 bit number. For each file, each user should have the read and write capability. How much memory is needed to store each user's access data?

(a) 16 KB

(b) 32 KB

(c) 64 KB

(d) 128 KB

67. What is the time complexity for the following C module? Assume that $n > 0$.

```
int module (int n)
{
    if (n == 1)
        return 1;
    else
        return (n + module (n – 1 ));
}
```

(a) $O(n)$

(b) $O(n^2)$

(c) $O(\log n)$

(d) $O(n!)$

68. What is the minimum number of resources required to ensure that deadlock will never occur, if there are currently three process P_1, P_2 and P_3 running in a system whose maximum demand for the resources of same type are 3, 4 and 5 respectively.

(a) 3

(b) 7

(c) 9

(d) 10

69. For a software project, the spiral model was employed. When will the spiral stop?

(a) When the software product is retired

(b) When the software product is released after Beta testing

(c) When the risk analysis is completed

(d) After completing five loops

70. Dirty bit is used to indicate which of the following?

(a) A page fault has occurred

(b) A page has corrupted data

(c) A page has been modified after being loaded into cache

(d) An illegal access of page

71. Which of the following is not a valid multicast MAC address?

(a) 01 : 00 : 5E ; 00 : 00 : 00

(b) 01 : 00 : 5E : 00 : 00 : FF

(c) 01 : 00 : 5E : 00 : FF : FF

(d) 01 : 00 : 5E : FF : FF : FF

72. The rank of the matrix $A = \begin{pmatrix} 1 & 2 & 1 & -1 \\ 9 & 5 & 2 & 2 \\ 7 & 1 & 0 & 4 \end{pmatrix}$

is __________

(a) 0   (b) 1

(c) 2   (d) 3

73. How many different trees are there with four nodes A, B, C and D?

(a) 30   (b) 60

(c) 90   (d) 120

74. What is the median of data if its mode is 15 and the mean is 30?

(a) 20   (b) 25

(c) 22.5   (d) 27.5

75. An organization is granted the block 130.34.12. 64/26. It needs to have 4 subnets. Which of the following is not an address of this organization?

(a) 130.34.12.124   (b) 130.34.12.89

(c) 130.34.12.70   (d) 130.34.12.132

76. Consider the following scenario.

A web client sends a request to a web server. The web server transmits a program to that client and is executed at client. It creates a web document. What are such web documents called?

(a) Active

(b) Static

(c) Dynamic

(d) Passive

77. What is the size of the physical address space in a paging system which has a page table containing 64 entries of 11 bit each (including valid/invalid bit) and a page size of 512 bytes?

(a) 2^{11} (b) 2^{15}

(c) 2^{19} (d) 2^{20}

78. Which of the following is not an optimization criterion in the design of a CPU scheduling algorithm?

(a) Minimum CPU utilization

(b) Maximum throughput

(c) Minimum turnaround time

(d) Minimum waiting time

79. Consider the following Deterministic Finite Automaton M.

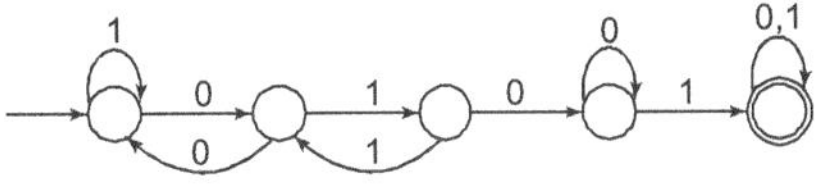

Let S denote the set of eight bit strings whose second, third, sixth and seventh bits are 1. The number of strings in S that are accepted by M is

(a) 0   (b) 1

(c) 2   (d) 3

80. A computing architecture, which allows the user to use computers from multiple administrative domains to reach a common goal is called as

(a) Grid Computing

(b) Neural Networks

(c) Parallel Processing

(d) Cluster Computing

ANSWERS

1. (d)	2. (c)	3. (a)	4. (c)	5. (a)	6. (b)	7. (d)	8. (c)	9. (b)	10. (d)
11. (b)	12. (c)	13. (a)	14. (c)	15. (c)	16. (d)	17. (d)	18. (b)	19. (c)	20. (b)
21. (d)	22. (a)	23. (b)	24. (a)	25. (a)	26. (d)	27. (d)	28. (a)	29. (d)	30. (b)
31. (c)	32. (d)	33. (a)	34. (c)	35. (d)	36. (d)	37. (b)	38. (d)	39. (b)	40. (c)
41. (c)	42. (b)	43. (d)	44. (c)	45. (d)	46. (b)	47. (b)	48. (a)	49. (c)	50. (a)
51. (c)	52. (d)	53. (a)	54. (a)	55. (d)	56. (c)	57. (d)	58. (a)	59. (b)	60. (b)
61. (d)	62. (b)	63. (c)	64. (b)	65. (b)	66. (a)	67. (a)	68. (d)	69. (a)	70. (c)
71. (d)	72. (c)	73. (*)	74. (b)	75. (d)	76. (a)	77. (c)	78. (a)	79. (c)	80. (a)

Note: * None of the given option is correct. Question may contain insufficient data.

EXPLANATIONS

1. Given frequency of CPU = 33 MHz

   Total memory access delay = Memory time + additional delay = (16 + 10) = 70 ns

   CPU time = 1 / Frequency

   $$= 1/33 \text{ MHz}$$

   $$= 30.30 \text{ ns}$$

   So, number of cycles (i.e., wait state)

   $$= \left\lceil \frac{70}{30.30} \right\rceil = 3 \text{ wait state}$$

2. Each m words length = m bits

   So, total number of bits = $m \times n$

   Since for n bits there are 2^n bits are possible.

   So, for nm bits = 2^{mn}.

3. Output of the given program

   int a = SQR (b + 2);

   int a = (b + 2 × b + 2);

   int a = (4 + 2 × 4 + 2);

   int a = 14;

   print f ("%d / n", a); = 14

4. Considering the given pseudo code

   Cyclomatic complexity of program = Predicate statement + 1 = 3 + 1 = 4

5. Given string: (((()())())

   $S \rightarrow (S) \rightarrow (SS) \rightarrow (S(S)) \rightarrow (S()) \rightarrow ((S)()) \rightarrow ((SS)())$
   $\rightarrow (((S)S)()) \rightarrow ((()S)()) \rightarrow ((()(S))()) \rightarrow ((()())())$

6. In the process of modifying information, the network address translator is used to convert private IP into public IP and for vice-versa.

7. Pixel mask means, it is formed by using string of 0's and 1's.

8. In IEEE-754 format data is stored into normalized format i.e., 1.M so total number of bit for mantissa is 24.

   With 24 bit we can represent 2^{24} numbers.

   In decimal representation,

   $$2^{24} = 10^x$$
   $$\log_2 2^{24} = \log_2 10^x$$
   $$24 = x \log_2 10$$
   $$24 = x(3.321)$$
   $$x = 7.226$$
   $$x = 7$$

9. Given, Radius = R

   One radian is the angle of an arc created by wrapping the radius of a circle around it circumference.

   So, it should be 1 radian = 57.28 degree.

10. Every physical CPU corresponding to 2 logical CPU.

    It is given there are 2 quad core chips.

    So, total number of physical CPU = 2 × 4 = 8.

    Number of logical CPU = 2 × 8 = 16.

11. An aggregation is a directional association between objects. Aggregation is also called 'Has-a' relationship.

    Represents bus have many passengers.

12. 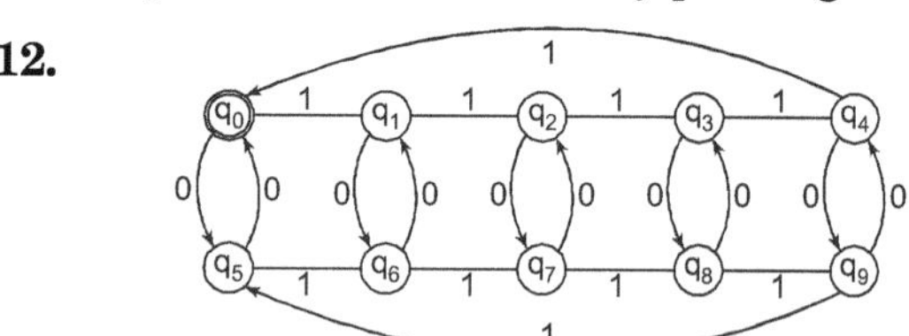

    Minimum 10 states are required for DFA.

13. From the given option.

    A reference can never be NULL, every reference have some objects to refer.

14. Tracks on a desk = 200

    In access sequence head goes in one direction till end i.e., 199 the come back to small request '12' and goes to serve all other remaining request in increasing order. So it is nothing but C-SCAN.

    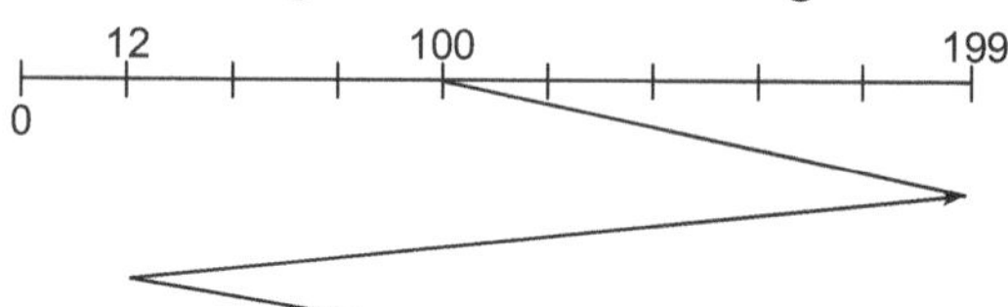

15. Considering the logical circuit

    D NAND $C = (DC)'$

    B NAND $A = (BA)'$

    $(DC)'$ NAND $B = (B(DC)')'$

    Then finally, $((B(DC)')'$ NAND $(BA)')'$

    $$= ((B(DC)')'(BA)')' = ((B(DC)' + BA)$$

    $$= AB + B(D' + C') = AB + B\bar{D} + B\bar{C}$$

16. Open source shortest path first routing protocol using by link state routing.

17. Total number of location = 4 × 6 = 24

    # bits used to represent = $\log_2 24 = 5$

    Here, each address space represented by one byte. So, number of addresses

    $$= \frac{8K \times 4 \text{ bit}}{8 \text{ bit}} = \frac{2^{13+2}}{2^3}$$

    $$= 2^{12} = 12 \text{ bits}$$

    Total bits needed = 12 + 5 = 17 bits,

18. Since 1000 > 498 so trap is generated to OS.

19. Given data, string of length = 8, starting with 1 i.e., place 1 and rest 7 position can be filled = 2^7 = 128.

String of length 8, Ending with 00 i.e. place 00 and rest 6 position can be filled = 2^6 = 64.

String of length 8, starting with 1 and Ending with 00 i.e. place 1 at start and place 00 in end then rest 5 position can be filled = 2^5 = 32.

$$n(A \cup B) = n(A) + n(B) - n(A \cap B)$$
$$\text{Total} = 128 + 64 - 32 = 160$$

20. Measurable is not a maturity level as per Capability Maturity Model.

21. In the given sequential circuit,

We know that T flip flop toggles the state if input T is 1, and does not change state if input T is 0.

Initial: 00 States Q_0 and Q_1 are zero

After Clock-1: State Q_0 changed to 1 because input T is 1 and previous state was 0 and State Q_1 changed to 1 because input T is 1 and previous state was 0. So output at end of clock 4 is 11.

After Clock-2: State Q_0 changed to 0 because input T is 1 and previous state was 1 and State Q_1 remains same because clock value is 0.

So output at end of clock 4 is 01.

After Clock-3: State Q_0 changed to 1 because input T is 1 and previous state was 0 and State Q_1 changed to 0 because input T is 1 and previous state was 1. So output at end of clock 4 is 10.

After Clock-4: State Q_0 changed to 0 because input T is 1 and previous state was 1 and State Q_1 remains same because clock value is 0.

So output at end of clock 4 is 00.

22. Sciena(A, B, C, D)

$R(A, B, C, D)$ with functional dependency

$$A \to B \text{ and } C \to D.$$

Decomposition into $R_1(A, B)$ with functional dependency $A \to B$ and $R_2(C, D)$ functional dependency $C \to D$. Since dependency is preserved but decomposition relation are not lossless since R_1 intersection R_2 = Phi.

23. As given in question

Unit testing of the module is covering = 70% of the code

Probability of success = 0.95

Reliability $\leq 0.7 * 0.95 = 0.665$.

24. RSA algorithm

$$p = 5, q = 11, e = 27$$

We know that

$$n = p \times q = 5 \times 11 = 55$$

We also know that

$$e \times d \bmod \phi(n) = 1$$
$$27 \times d \bmod 40 = 1$$
$$d = 3.$$

25. Want to Built a memory with 4 byte words,

Capacity = 2^{21}

RAM = 2K × 8 = $2^{11} \times 8$

Capacity = $2^{21} / 2^3 = 2^{18}$ byte

Decoder size = $2^{18}/4 \times 2^{11} = 2^5$

So decoder size = 5 to 2^5 = 5 to 32.

26. When the enable input (E) is not active, i.e. there is no electrical current flows through. Hence it is in disconnected state.

27. Total switches = 12

By using 4 bit number of BCD number represent = 10.

So, 12 bit number contain number of 4 bit pair

$$= 3(111111111111)$$

Total = 10 × 10 × 10 = 1000 BCD no.

28. If binary search tree is constructed by using some random numbers then,

For root element number of comparison = 1 (since at level 1 only 1 element is present) For second levels each element need number of comparison = 2 (since at level 2 only 2 element is present)

For third levels number of comparison = 3 (since at level 3 only 4)

For fourth levels number of comparison = 4 (since at level 4 only 4 element is present)

So, average number of comparisons

$$= \frac{(1 \times 1 + 2 \times 2 + 4 \times 3 + 4 \times 4)}{11} = \frac{33}{11} = 3$$

as for level we need comparisons to reach there.

29. Considering the given Java code fragment,

In Java language, while (1) will give compiler time error as it treats as type mismatch to convert from integer to Boolean value.

30. Every time the attribute A appears, it is matched with the same value of attribute B means functional dependency $A \to B$ where b is candidate key.

Every time the attribute A appears, is not matched the same value of attribute C i.e. A is repeating for many value of C and C also repeating so $A \to C$.

31. Offset value = 100, Length(L) = 200

Header length is 5 so number of byte used for header = 4 × 5 = 20

Data length = Total length – Header length

$$= 200 - 20 = 180(0 \text{ to } 179)$$

Starting number of first byte of fragment = 100 × 8 = 800 (since each offset is multiple of 8)

Number of last byte = 800 + 1 79 = 979

32. Output of the C program,

Assuming there is no error in program:

Given values in octal (0570) = 000 101 111 000

Shifty $\geq$ 4 (left shift the bits 4 times) = 100 000 010 111

Shifty $\leq$ 6 (right shift the bits 6 times) = 010 111 000 000 = (2700).

Octal representation of (010 111 000 000) = (2700).

33. All option accepts language contain minimum string 1 which is not accepted by DFA so we can eliminate (b), (c) and (d) option.

35. Automaton recognize by the given languages,

Virtual Address is given = 16 bit = 2^{16} byte

Physical Address = 4 (physical frame) × 2048

$$= 13 \text{ bit}$$

Number of pages = $2^{16} / 2048 = 2^5$

Physical Address 25 = 00 (frame number) 00000011001 (binary in 13 bit)

In table frame 00 is mapped = page number 2

Page number 2 is represented = 00010

Physical address = 00010 00000011001

Decimal representation = 00010 00000011001 (16 bit) = 4121.

36. In a standard circular queue when (Front = Rear) then queue is empty.

We check if ((rear+1) mod $n ==$ front) then queue is full.

So 1st element inserted at q [2], 2nd inserted at q [2+1], 3rd element inserted at q [3+1]... and so on so 9th element inserted at q/[9+1] = q[10].

37. Assume the 1st friend born in any of the 12 months.

For the 2nd friend there is only one possibility i.e., same as 1st friend.

So, probability = (12 / 12) × (1 /12) = 1/12

38. Output of the following C code is,

Initial condition $j = 1$ and $i = 2$

While ($i / j > 0.001$) (here j should be > 2000), j increases in power of 2.

So $2n > 2000$ i.e 2048. So value of $n = 11$ for $n = 12$ while ($i / j < 0.001$) so condition false so we exit from loop.

39. Static members of a class share same memory by all the object which is assign at compile time itself.

41. In the Binary search tree T,

In order traversal of Binary search tree gives elements in increasing order.

Inordor traversal = $U\,Q\,X\,W\,P\,V\,Z\,Y$

So 4th smallest element is W

42. Given attributes at an entity set E = {x, y, z, a, b, c}

Superkey are form by adding any number of attribute in candidate key. So, minimal superkey is called candidate key. So, {x} and {a, b} are candidate keys.

43. Four items are pushed into stack A, B, C, D where Top is pointing E. Now 4 elements are deleted and enqueue into queue. So queue contain E, D, C, B where Rear is pointing B and Front pointing E.

Now two elements are deleted from the queue i.e. E and D respectively and pushed back on the stack i.e., e, d where stack Top pointing D now delete one element from stack gives D.

44. Four frames are given with reference string: 0, 2, 4, 5, 2, 4, 3, 11, 2, 10.

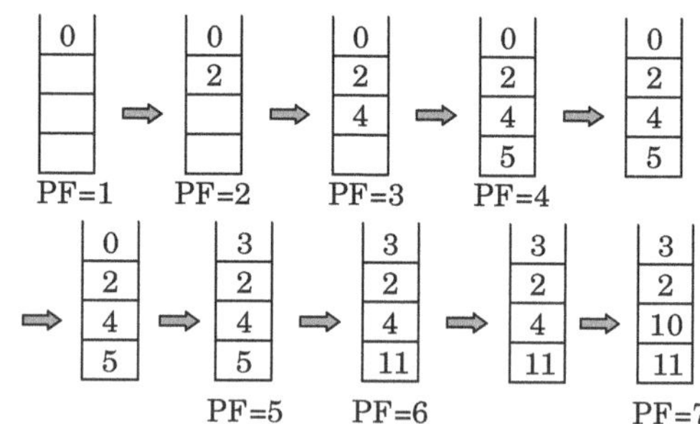

Hence 7 page fault are present.

45. Round trip propagation delay = 500 ms

Total time = Transmission time of Message + Propagation time

Round trip time = 2 × Propagation time.

So, Propagation time = 500 / 2 = 250 ms

Transmission time = Frame size/bandwidth

$$= 1000 \text{ bits} / 50 \text{ kbps} = 20 \text{ ms}$$

Total time to receive the frame by the receiver

$$= 250 + 20 = 270 \text{ ms}$$

47. Given three 'C' language statement

$$Y = y + 1;$$
$$Z = x + y;$$
$$X - x + 1;$$

Here y is incremented then z is updated by new value of y and old value of x, then x is updated by incremented its old value by 1. Which is represented by $z = (x++) + (++y)$, here ++y is pre-incremented and x++ is post-incremented.

48. Starting location $(0, 0)$, ending location $= (100, 100)$

Address of pixel $(6, 10)$ in row major order is

$$= 0 + 1 ((6 - 0) + 101(10 - 0)) = 1016$$

49. Single linked list where F and L , painters

To delete the last element of the list we need to get the address of the node just before the last node, because we after deleting last element we cannot point to new last element since we can go only in one direction.

So we have to do linear search on the linked list to get the second last element then delete last element and make second last node (of initial linked list) as last node and so it depends on length of linked list.

50. A have x elements and B set have y elements then number of distinct functions mapping from B to $A = x^y$.

51. Heap area is not represented in a subroutine's activation record frame for a stack-based programming language because if we create memory dynamically it would be created in the heap area.

52. Given grammar

$$S \rightarrow AB$$
$$S \rightarrow aB$$
$$S \rightarrow abbA$$
$$S \rightarrow abbBaB$$
$$S \rightarrow abbbbAabbA$$
$$S \rightarrow abbbbaabba$$

Given Grammar can produce a string which has 4 consecutive b's.

So given grammar can produce string which contain 4 consecutive b's.

53. Given logic circuit is the Inverter and the AND gate will take total of $6 + 10 = 16$ ns.

OR gate will take 11 ns. The output of OR gate will comes at XOR.

$16 - 11 = 5$ ns because $11 < 1 6$ so 5 ns more will be required to get the actual output.

So the duration of glitch is 5 ns.

54. The conic section that is obtained when a right circular cone is cut through a plane that is parallel to the side of the cone is called parabola.

55. As the HLEN is of 4 bit but (0000 to 0100) is treated as don't care condition. Receiver accepts when HLEN (0101 to 1111).

56. We get $\bar{X} + XY = (\bar{X} + X)(\bar{X} + Y) = \bar{X} + Y$

which is not equal to y so this is invalid.

57. Given the details

Destination address $= 205.16.39.44$

Supernet mask $= 255.255.248.0$

First address $= 205.16.32.0$

58. **Original Time stamp:** Time at which sender sent packet according to its own clock.

Receiving Time stamp: Time at which receiver receives that packet according to its own clock.

Transmit Time stamp: Time at which receiver sent a reply of that packet according to its own clock.

Returned Time stamp: Time at which sender of receives the reply according to its own clock.

Sending Time = Receiving Time – Original Time

Receiving Time = Return Time – Transmit Time

Round Trip Time = Sending Time + Receiving Time

One way time should be RTT2 = 10 ms

Sender sent the packet at 46 and receiver should have received it at 56 , but instead he receiving it at 59. So $59 - 56 = 3$ ms ahead.

So it should set its clock 3 ms behind to synchronize with sender.

59. There are 3 possible outcome of turing machine when an input is given to it :

1. It may halt and accept the input.

2. It may halt and reject the input.

3. It may never halt.

So, option (b) is incorrect since it cannot modify the content by halting.

60. The underlying protocol for browsing web server is TCP. HTTP uses TCP is its underlying transport layer protocol and is used to access the web server.

The HTTP runs at 8080 i.e. 80 port address.

61. Auto-negotiation is an Ethernet procedure by which two connected devices choose common transmission parameters, such as speed, duplex mode, and flow control.

62. Worst case time complexity of Quick sort $= O(n^2)$ when input is already sorted.

Worst case time complexity of Heap sort $= O(n \log n)$.

Worst case time complexity of Merge sort $= O(n \log n)$.

63. 3rd normal form but not BCNF since the dependencies $AB \rightarrow CDE$, $C \rightarrow B$ where C is not a Super key.

64.

0	1	2	3	4	5	6	7	8	9	10	11	12
182	103										661	24

So, 103 mod 13 = 12 since 12 already filled, so by using linear hashing it goes to (12 + 1) mod 13 = 0 which is already filled, so (12 + 2) mod 13 = 1 which s empty so filled with 103.

65.

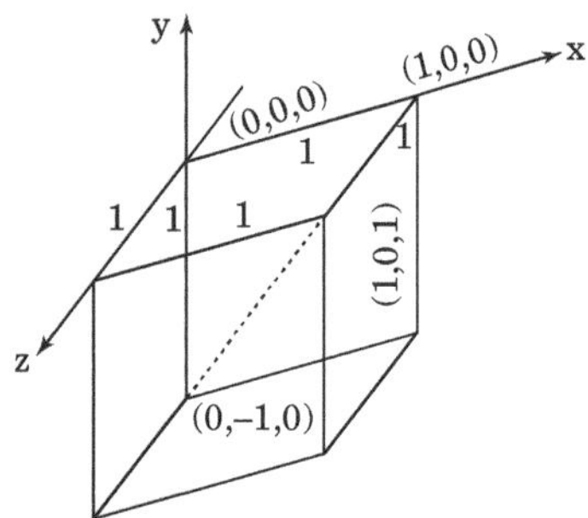

So vertex point of diagonally opposite vertex of c is $(0, -1, 0)$.

66. For 2^{16} files, there are 4 different combinations of read (R) and write (W) i.e., read, write, no read, no write.

So bits required for 1 file to store access info = 2 (since four combinations are needed)

Bits required for 2^{16} files = $(2^{16}) \times 2$ bits

$$= 128 \text{ KB}$$

Converting this bits into bytes

$$= 128 \text{ KB}/(8 \text{ bits/Byte}) = 16 \text{ KB}$$

67. Recurrence relation for above program:

$$T(n) = T(n - 1) + 1$$
$$= T(n - 2) + 1 + 1$$
$$= T(n - 3) + 1 + 1 + 1$$

By doing in this way we get

$$= T(n - k) + k \times c \text{ where } n - k = 1$$

so, $k = n - 1$

$$= T[n - n + 1) + (n - 1) \times c$$
$$= T(1) + (n - 1) \times c$$
$$= O(n)$$

68. In worst case all processes holding just one resource less than their completion (max need).

So, $P_1 = 2, P_2 = 3, P_3 = 4$

Total resource = 2 + 3 + 4 = 9.

Now 1 more resource will needed so that any one of these process will execute and release all its resources.

Hence 9 + 1 = 10 resources will ensure there will not be deadlock.

69. For a software project, the spiral model was employed. When the software product is retired the spiral is stop.

70. Dirty bit is used to indicate a page has been modified after being loaded into cache so before modified that block check the dirty bit if bit is 1 then update it in main memory otherwise direct update that block.

71. Multicast MAC Address range of 01-00-5E-00-00-00 to 01-00-5E-7F-FF-FF i.e. all lower bit should be 1.

72. Here rank of matrix is number of rows which are having atleast one non-zero digit. By solving it we get 2 non-zero rows.

73. Using Cayley's formula: It states that for every positive integer n, the number of trees on n labeled vertices is n^{n-2}.

So here $n = 4$, $4^{(4-2)}$ i.e. 16.

74. We know that 3 median = mode + 2 mean

$$3x = 15 + 60$$
$$3x = 75$$
$$x = 75 / 3 = 25$$

76. An active web document consists of a computer program that the server sends to the browser and that the browser must run locally.

When it runs, the active document program can interact with the user and change the display continuously.

77. Page table entry = Frame bits + Others

$$= 10 \text{ frame bits} + 1 \text{ (valid, invalid bit)}$$
$$= 10 + 1 = 11 \text{ bits}$$

So, number of frame bit = 10 bit

Page size = 512 B; so page offset bit = 9 bit.

So physical address = Frame bit + Offset bit.

$$= 10 + 9 = 19 \text{ bit}$$

So, physical address space size = 2^{19} byte.

78. Minimum CPU utilization not an optimization criterion in the design of a CPU scheduling algorithm.

79. The number of eight bit strings in S that are accepted by M.

a. 01110111

b. 01110110

Since we have to reach final state so only 8th bit will be change.

80. Grid computing is the collection of computer resources from multiple locations to reach a common goal.

1. Which of the given number has its IEEE-754 32-bit floating point representation as (0 10000000 110 0000 0000 0000 0000 0000)

   (a) 2.5   (b) 3.0

   (c) 3.5   (d) 4.5

2. The range of integers that can be represented by an n bit 2's complement number system is :

   (a) -2^{n-1} to $(2^{n-1} - 1)$ (b) $-2(-2^{n-1} - 1)$ to $(2^{n-1} - 1)$

   (c) -2^{n-1} to 2^{n-1} (d) $-2(2^{n-1} + 1)$ to $(2^{n-1} - 1)$

3. How many 32 K × 1 RAM chips are needed to provide a memory capacity of 256 K-bytes?

   (a) 8   (b) 32

   (c) 64   (d) 128

4. A modulus-12 ring counter requires a minimum of

   (a) 10 flip-flops   (b) 12 flip-flops

   (c) 8 flip-flops   (d) 6 flip-flops

5. The complement of the Boolean expression

   $$AB(\bar{B}C + AC)$$

   (a) $(\bar{A} + \bar{B}) + (B + \bar{C}).(\bar{A} + \bar{C})$

   (b) $(\bar{A}.\bar{B}) + (B\bar{C} + \bar{A}\bar{C})$

   (c) $(\bar{A} + \bar{B}).(B + \bar{C}) + (A + \bar{C})$

   (d) $(A + B).(\bar{B} + C) + (A + C)$

6. The code which uses 7 bits to represent a character is:

   (a) ASCII   (b) BCD

   (c) EBCDIC   (d) Gray

7. If half adders and full adders are implements using gates, then for the addition of two 17 bit numbers (using minimum gates) the number of half adders and full adders required will be

   (a) 0, 17   (b) 16, 1

   (c) 1, 16   (d) 8, 8

8. Minimum number of 2 × 1 multiplexers required to realize the following function, $f = \bar{A}\bar{B}C + \bar{A}\bar{B}\bar{C}$. Assume that inputs are available only in true form and Boolean a constant 1 and 0 are available,

   (a) 1   (b) 2

   (c) 3   (d) 7

9. The number of 1s in the binary representation of 3 × 4096 + 15 × 256 + 5 × 16 + 3) are:

   (a) 8   (b) 9

   (c) 10   (d) 12

10. The boolean expression $AB + AB' + A'C + AC$ is independent of the boolean variable

    (a) A   (b) B

    (c) C   (d) None of these

11. If the sequence of operations-push(1), push(2), pop, push(1), push(2), pop, pop, pop, push(2), pop are performed on a stack, the sequence of popped out values

    (a) 2, 2, 1, 1, 2   (b) 2, 2, 1, 2, 2

    (c) 2, 1, 2, 2, 1   (d) 2, 1, 2, 2, 2

12. A machine needs a minimum of 100 sec to sort 1000 names by quick sort. The minimum time needed to sort 100 names will be approximately

    (a) 50.2 sec   (b) 6.7 sec

    (c) 72.7 sec   (d) 11.2 sec

13. Six files F1, F2, F3, F4, F5 and F6 have 100, 200, 50, 80, 120, 150 records respectively. In what order should they be stored so as to optimize act. Assume each file is accessed with the same frequency

    (a) F3, F4, F1, F5, F6, F2

    (b) F2, F6, F5, F1, F4, F3

    (c) F1, F2, F3, F4, F5, FQ

    (d) Ordering is immaterial as all files are accessed with the same frequency.

14. A hash table with ten buckets with one slot per bucket is depicted in fig. The symbols S1 and S7 initially entered using a hashing function with linear probing. The maximum number of comparisons needed in searching an item that is not present is

0	S7
1	S1
2	
3	S4
4	S2
5	
6	S5
7	
8	S6
9	S3

    (a) 4   (b) 5

    (c) 6   (d) 3

15. The queue data structure is to be realized by using stack. The number of stacks needed would be

(a) It cannot be implemented

(b) 2 stacks

(c) 4 stacks

(d) 1 stack

16. Consider the following Entity Relationship Diagram (ERD)

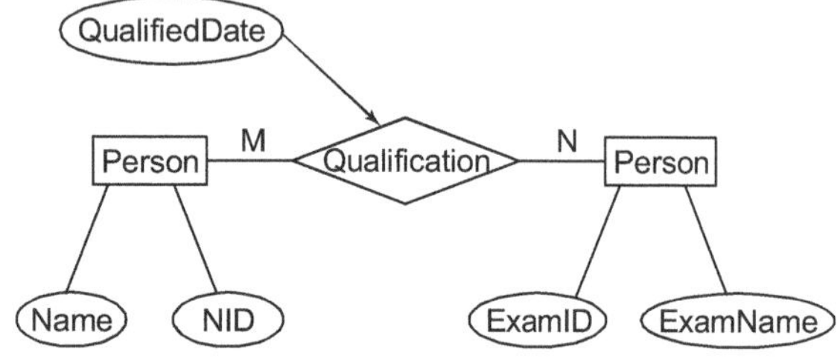

Which of the following possible relations will not hold if the above ERD is mapped into a relation model?

(a) Person (NID, Name)

(b) Qualification (NID. ExamlD. Qualified Date)

(c) Exam (ExamlD. NID. Exam Name)

(d) Exam (ExamlD. Exam Name)

17. Consider the following log sequence of two transactions on a bank account, with initial balance 12000, that transfer 2000 to a mortgage payment and then apply a 5% interest.

1. T1 start

2. T1 B old = 1200 new = 10000

3. T1 M old = 0 new = 2000

4. T1 commit

5. T2 start

6. T2 B old = 10000 new = 10500

7. T2 commit

Suppose the database system crashed just before log record 7 is written. When the system is restarted, which one statement is true of the recovery procedure?

(a) We must redo log record 6 set B to 10500

(b) We must undo log record 6 to set B to 10000 and then redo log record 2 and 3

(c) We need not redo log record 2 and 3 because transaction T1 has committed.

(d) We can apply redo and undo operations in arbitrary order because they are idempotent.

18. Given a block can hold either 3 records or 10 key pointers. A database contains n records, then how many blocks do we need to hold the data file and the dense index

(a) 13 $n/30$

(b) $n/3$

(c) $n/10$

(d) $n/30$

19. The maximum length of an attribute of type text is

(a) 127

(b) 255

(c) 256

(d) It is variable

20. Let $R = (A, B, C, D, E, F)$ be a relation scheme with the following dependencies $C \rightarrow F, E \rightarrow A, EC \rightarrow D, A \rightarrow B$. Which of the following is a key of R?

(a) CD

(b) EC

(c) AE

(d) AC

21. If $D_1, D_2, \dots D_n$ are domains in a relational model, then the relation is a table, which is a subset of

(a) $D_1 \oplus D_2 \oplus \dots \oplus D_n$

(b) $D_1 \times D_2 \times \dots \times D_n$

(c) $D_1 \cup D_2 \cup \dots \cup D_n$

(d) $D_1 \cap D_2 \cap \dots \cap D_n$

22. Consider the following relational query on the above database:

SELECT S.sname

FROM Suppliers S

Where S.sid NOT IN (SELECT C.sid

    FROM Catalog C

    WHERE C.pid NOT IN (SELECT P.pid

    FROM Parts P

    WHERE P.color < > "blue"))

Assume that relations corresponding to the above schema are not empty. Which of the following is the correct interpretation of the above query?

(a) Find the names of all suppliers who have supplied non-blue part.

(b) Find the names of all suppliers who have not supplied a non-blue part.

(c) Find the names of all suppliers who have supplied only non-blue parts

(d) Find the names of all suppliers who have not supplied only non-blue parts.

23. Consider the following schema:

Emp (Empcode, Name, Sex, Salary, Deptt)

A simple SQL query is executed as follows :

    SELECT dept FROM Emp

    WHERE sex = 'M'

    GROUP by Dept

Having avg (Salary) > {select avg (Salary) from Emp}

The output will be

(a) Average salary of male employee is the average salary of the organization

(b) Average salary of male employee is less than the average salary of the organization

(c) Average salary of male employee is equal to the average salary of the organization

(d) Average salary of male employee is more than the average salary of the organization

24. Given the following expression grammar:

$$E \rightarrow E * F | F + E | F$$
$$F \rightarrow F - F | id$$

Which of the following is true?

(a) * has higher precedence than +

(b) − has higher precedence than *

(c) + and − have same precedence

(d) + has higher precedence than *

25. The number of token the following C statements is

printf("i = %d, & i = %x", i & i);

(a) 13   (b) 6

(c) 10   (d) 11

26. Which grammar rules violate the requirement of the operator grammar? $A, B,$ C are variables and a, b, c are terminals

(i) $A \rightarrow BC$ (ii) $A \rightarrow CcBb$

(iii) $A \rightarrow BaC$ (iv) $A \rightarrow \varepsilon$

(a) (i) only   (b) (i) and (ii)

(c) (i) and (iii)   (d) (i) and (iv)

27. Which one of the following is a top-down parser?

(a) Recursive descent parser

(b) Shift left associative parser

(c) SLR (k) parser

(d) LR(k) parser

28. Yacc stands for

(a) yet accept compiler constructs

(b) yet accept compiler compiler

(c) yet another compiler constructs

(d) yet another compiler compiler

29. Which statements is true?

(a) LALR parser is more powerful and costly as compare to other parsers

(b) All CFG's are LP and not all grammars are uniquely defined

(c) Every SLR grammar is unambiguous but not every unambiguous grammar is SLR

(d) LR(K) is the most general back tracking shift reduce parsing method

30. Semaphores are used to solve the problem of

1. Race Condition

2. Process Synchronization

3. Mutual Exclusion

4. None of the above

(a) 1 and 2   (b) 2 and 3

(c) All of these   (d) None of these

31. If there are 32 segments, each size 1 k bytes, then the logical address should have

(a) 13 bits   (b) 14 bits

(c) 15 bits   (d) 16 bits

32. In a lottery scheduler with 40 tickets, how we will distribute the tickets among 4 processes P_1, P_2, P_3 and P_4 such that each process gets 10%, 5%, 60% and 25% respectively?

	P_1	P_2	P_3	P_4
(a)	12	4	70	30
(b)	7	5	20	10
(c)	4	2	24	10
(d)	8	5	30	40

33. Suppose a system contains n processes and system uses the round-robin algorithm for CPU scheduling then which data structure is best suited ready queue of the processes

(a) stack   (b) queue

(c) circular queue   (d) tree

34. A hard disk system has the following parameters

• Number of track = 500

• Number of sectors/track = 100

• Number of bytes/sector = 500

• Time taken by the head to move from one track to adjacent track = 1 ms

• Rotation speed = 600 rpm.

What is the average time taken for transferring 250 bytes from the disk?

(a) 300.5 ms   (b) 255.5 ms

(c) 255 ms   (d) 300 ms

35. At a particular time of computation the value of a counting semaphore is 7. Then 20 P operations and 15 V operations were completed on this semaphore. The resulting values of the semaphore is

(a) 42   (b) 2

(c) 7   (d) 12

36. Increasing the RAM of a computer typically improves performance because

(a) Virtual Memory increases

(b) Larger RAMs are faster

(c) Fewer page faults occur

(d) Fewer segmentation faults occur

37. Consider the following program.

```
main ()
{
    fork();
    fork();
    fork();
}
```

How many new processes will be created?

(a) 9   (b) 6

(c) 7   (d) 5

38. Suppose two jobs, each of which needs 10 minutes of CPU time, start simultaneously, Assume 50% I/O wait time. How long will it take for both to complete, if they run sequentially?

(a) 10   (b) 20

(c) 30   (d) 40

39. If a node has K children in B tree, then the node contains exactly _____ keys,

(a) K^2 (b) $K - 1$

(c) $K + 1$ (d) $\sqrt{K}$

40. The time complexity of the following C function is (assume $n > 0$)

```
int recursive (int n){
if (n==1)
return (1);
else
return (recursive (n – 1 )+recursive (n – 1 ));
}
```

(a) $O(n)$ (b) $O(n \log n)$

(c) $O(n^2)$ (d) $O(2^n)$

41. The number of spanning trees for a complete graph with seven vertices is

(a) 2^5 (b) 7^5

(c) 3^5 (d) $2^{2 \times 5}$

42. If one uses straight two-way merge sort algorithm to sort the following elements in ascending order:

20, 47, 25, 8, 9, 4, 40, 30, 12, 17

then the order of these elements after second pass of the algorithms is

(a) 8, 9, 15, 20, 47, 4, 12, 7, 30, 30

(b) 8, 15, 20, 47, 4, 9, 30, 40, 12, 17

(c) 15, 20, 47, 4, 8, 9, 12, 30, 40, 17

(d) 4, 8, 9, 15, 20, 47, 12, 17, 30, 40

43. Let $R1$ and $R2$ be regular sets defined over the alphabet, then

(a) $R_1 \cap R_2$ is not regular

(b) $R_1 \cup R_2$ is not regular

(c) $\Sigma^* - R_1$ is regular

(d) R^*_1 is not regular

44. The DNS maps the IP addresses to

(a) A binary address as strings

(b) An alphanumeric address

(c) A hierarchy of domain names

(d) A hexadecimal address

45. To add a background color for all <h1> elements, which of the following HTML syntax is used

(a) $h1$ {background-color: #FFFFFF}

(b) (background-color: #FFFFFF}.$h1$

(c) $h1$ {background-color : #FFFFFF}.$h1$ (all)

(d) $h1$ all {bgcolor = #FFFFFF}

46. The correct syntax to write "Hi there" in Javascript is

(a) jscript.write ("Hi There")

(b) response.write("Hi There")

(c) print ("Hi There")

(d) print.jscript ("Hi There")

47. To declare the version of XML, the correct syntax is

(a) <?xml version = '1.0'/>

(b) <*xml version = '1.0'/>

(c) <?xml version = "1.0"/>

(d) <xml version = '1.0'/>

48. A T-switch is used to

(a) Control how messages are passed between computers

(b) Echo every character that is received

(c) Transmit characters one at a time

(d) Rearrange the connections between computing equipments

49. What frequency range is used for microwave communications, satellite and radar?

(a) Low frequency : 30 kHz to 300 kHz

(b) Medium frequency : 300 kHz to 3 MHz

(c) Super high frequency : 3000 MHz to 30000 MHz

(d) Extremely high frequency : 30000 kHz

50. How many bits internet address is assigned to each host on a TCP/IP internet which is used in all communication with the host?

(a) 16 bits   (b) 32 bits

(c) 48 bits   (d) 64 bits

51. How many characters per sec (7 bits + 1 parity) can be transmitted over a 2400 bps line if the transfer is synchronous (1 start and 1 stop bit)?

(a) 300   (b) 240

(c) 250   (d) 275

52. In CRC if the data unit is 100111001 and the divisor is 1011 then what is dividend at the receiver?

(a) 100111001101 (b) 100111001011

(c) 100111001 (d) 100111001110

53. An ACK number of 1000 in TCP always means that

(a) 999 bytes have been successfully received

(b) 1000 bytes have been successfully received

(c) 1001 bytes have been successfully received

(d) None of the above

54. In a class B subnet, we know the IP address of one host and the mask as given below:

IP address: 125.134.112.66

Mask: 255.255.224.0

What is the first address (Network address)?

(a) 125.134.96.0 (b) 125.134.112.0

(c) 125.134.112.66 (d) 125.134.0.0

55. A certain population of ALOHA users manages to generate 70 request/sec. If the time is slotted in units of 50 msec, then channel load would be

(a) 4.25 (b) 3.5

(c) 450 (d) 350

56. Which statements is false?

(a) PING is a TCP/IP application that sends datagrams once every second in the hope of an echo response from the machine being PINGED

(b) If the machine is connected and running a TCP/IP protocol stack, it should respond to the PING datagram with a datagram of its own.

(c) If PING encounters an error condition, an ICMP message is not returned

(d) PING display the time of the return response in milliseconds or one of several error message

57. A router uses the following routing table :

Destination	Mask	Interface
144.16.0.0	255.255.0.0	eth0
144.16.64.0	255.255.224.0	ethl
144.16.68.0	255.255.255.0	eth2
144.16.68.64	255.255.255.224	eth3

A packet bearing a estimation address 144.16.68.117 arrives at the router. On which interface will it be forwarded?

(a) eth0 (b) ethl

(c) eth2 (d) eth3

58. Which layers of the OSI reference model are host-to-host layers?

(a) Transport, session, presentation, application

(b) Session, presentation, application

(c) Datalink, transport, presentation, application

(d) Physical, datalink, network, transport

59. Alpha and Beta testing are forms of

(a) Acceptance testing

(b) Integration testing

(c) System testing

(d) Unit testing

60. If in a software project the number of user input, user output, enquiries, files and external interfaces are (15, 50, 24, 12, 8), respectively, with complexity average weighing factor. The productivity if effort = 70 person-month is

(a) 110.54 (b) 408.74

(c) 304.78 (d) 220.14

61. The contents of the flag register after execution of the following program by 8085 microprocessor will be Program

$SUB\,A$

$MVI\,B, (01)_H$

$DCR\,B$

HLT

(a) $(54)_H$ (b) $(00)_H$

(c) $(01)_H$ (d) $(45)_H$

62. The minimum time delay between the initiation of two independent memory operations is called

(a) Access time (b) Cycle time

(c) Rotational time (d) Latency time

63. Which of the following compression algorithms is used to generate a.png file?

(a) LZ78 (b) Deflate

(c) LZW (d) Huffman

64. Dirty bit for a page in a page table

(a) helps avoid unnecessary writes on a paging device

(b) helps maintain LRU information

(c) allows only read on a page V'D'

(d) None of these

65. Which of the following is not an image type used in MPEG?

(a) A frame

(b) B frame

(c) D frame

(d) P frame

66. Consider an uncompressed stereo audio signal of CD quality which is sampled at 44.1 kHz and quantized using 16 bits. What is required storage space if a compression ratio of 0.5 is achieved for 10 seconds of this audio?

   (a) 172 KB   (b) 430 KB

   (c) 860 KB   (d) 1720 KB

67. What is compression ratio in a typical mp3 audio files?

   (a) 4 : 1   (b) 6 : 1

   (c) 8 : 1   (d) 10 : 1

68. Consider the following program fragment

```
if (a > b)
if (b > c)
      s1;
else s2;
```

s2 will be executed if

   (a) $a <= b$

   (b) $b > c$

   (c) $b >= c$ and $a <= b$

   (d) $a > b$ and $b <= c$

69. If n has the value 3, then the statement $a[++n] = n++;$

   (a) assigns 3 to $a[5]$

   (b) assigns 4 to $a[5]$

   (c) assigns 4 to $a[4]$

   (d) what is assigned is compiler dependent

70. The following program

```
main()
{
    inc() ; inc() ; inc() ;
}
inc()
{
    static int x;
    print f("%d", ++x);
}
```

   (a) prints 012

   (b) prints 123

   (c) prints 3 consecutive, but unpredictable numbers

   (d) prints 111

71. Consider the following program fragment

```
i = 6720; j = 4;
while (i % j) == 0
    {
        i = i / j;
        j = j + 1;
    }
```

On termination j will have the value

   (a) 4   (b) 8

   (c) 9   (d) 6720

72. Consider the following declaration :

   int a, $*b$ = & a, $**c$ = &b;

The following program fragment

   $a = 4; **C = 5;$

   (a) does not change the value of a

   (b) assigns address of c to a

   (c) assigns the value of b to a

   (d) assigns 5 to a

73. The output of the following program is

```
main()
{
    static int x[ ] = {1, 2, 3, 4, 5, 6, 7, 8};
    int i;
    for (i = 2; i < 6; ++i)
        x[x[i]] = x[i];
    for (i = 0; i < 8; ++ i)
        print f("%d", x[i]);
}
```

   (a) 1 2 3 3 5 5 7 8   (b) 1 2 3 4 5 6 7 8

   (c) 8 7 6 5 4 3 2 1   (d) 1 2 3 5 4 6 7 8

74. Which of the following has the compilation error in C ?

   (a) int $n = 17;$

   (b) char $c = 99;$

   (c) float $f = $ (float) 99.32;

   (d) #include <stdio.*h*>

75. The for loop

```
for (i = 0; i < 10; ++ i)
    print fl("%d", i &1);
```

prints

   (a) 0101010101

   (b) 0111111111

   (c) 0000000000

   (d) 1111111111

76. Consider the following statements

   # define hypotenuse (a, b) sqrt $(a * a + b * b);$

   The macro call hypotenuse $(a + 2, b + 3)$

   (a) Finds the hypotenuse of a triangle with sides $a + 2$ and $b + 3$

   (b) Finds the square root of $(a + 2)^2 + (b + 3)^2$

   (c) Is invalid

   (d) Find the square root of $3 * 2 + 4 * b + 5$

77. In $X = \dfrac{(M + N \times O)}{(P \times Q)}$, how many one-address instructions are required to evaluate it?

(a) 4

(b) 6

(c) 8

(d) 10

78. The decimal number has 64 digits. The number of bits needed for its equivalent binary representation is?

(a) 200

(b) 213

(c) 246

(d) 277

79. Consider the following C declaration

```
struct {
    short S[5];
    union {
        float y,
        long z;
    } u;
}t;
```

Assume that the objects of the type short, float and long occupy 2 bytes, 4 bytes and 8 bytes, respectively. The memory requirement for variable t, ignoring alignment consideration, is

(a) 22 bytes   (b) 14 bytes

(c) 18 bytes   (d) 10 bytes

80. Consider the following code segment.

```
void foo(int x, int y)
{
    x + = y ;
    y + = x ;
}
main ()
{
    int x = 5.5 ;
    foo(x, x) ;
}
```

What is the final value of x in both call by value and call by reference, respectively?

(a) 5 and 16   (b) 5 and 12

(c) 5 and 20   (d) 12 and 20

ANSWERS

1. (c)	**2.** (a)	**3.** (c)	**4.** (b)	**5.** (a)	**6.** (a)	**7.** (c)	**8.** (b)	**9.** (c)	**10.** (b)
11. (a)	**12.** (b)	**13.** (a)	**14.** (b)	**15.** (b)	**16.** (c)	**17.** (b)	**18.** (a)	**19.** (*)	**20.** (b)
21. (b)	**22.** (a,c)	**23.** (d)	**24.** (b)	**25.** (c)	**26.** (d)	**27.** (a)	**28.** (d)	**29.** (c)	**30.** (c)
31. (c)	**32.** (c)	**33.** (c)	**34.** (d)	**35.** (b)	**36.** (c)	**37.** (c)	**38.** (d)	**39.** (b)	**40.** (d)
41. (b)	**42.** (b)	**43.** (c)	**44.** (c)	**45.** (a)	**46.** (b)	**47.** (c)	**48.** (d)	**49.** (d)	**50.** (b)
51. (a)	**52.** (b)	**53.** (d)	**54.** (a)	**55.** (b)	**56.** (c)	**57.** (c)	**58.** (a)	**59.** (a)	**60.** (b)
61. (a)	**62.** (b)	**63.** (b)	**64.** (a)	**65.** (a)	**66.** (c)	**67.** (d)	**68.** (d)	**69.** (d)	**70.** (b)
71. (c)	**72.** (d)	**73.** (a)	**74.** (*)	**75.** (a)	**76.** (d)	**77.** (c)	**78.** (b)	**79.** (c)	**80.** (c)

*Note: * None of the given option is correct. Question may contain insufficient data.*

EXPLANATIONS

1. IEE-754 32-bit floating point representation
$(-1)^5 (1.M) 2^{(E-127)}$

$\Rightarrow$ $(1.110...)\, 2^{(128-127)}$

$\Rightarrow$ $(1 + 0.5 + 0.25)\, 2$

$\Rightarrow$ $(1.75) \times 2$

$\Rightarrow$ 3.5

2. The range of integers that can be represented by n-bit 2's complement number system is -2^{n-1} to $(2^{n-1} - 1)$.

3. Given chip size = $32\,K \times 1$

Required structure = $256\,K \times 8$

To increase memory capacity

So, Number of RAM $= \dfrac{256\,K \times 8}{32\,K \times 1} = \dfrac{2^{18} \times 2^3}{2^{15} \times 2^0} = 64$

It require 8 parallel line and in each parallel line 8 serial RAM chips are required.

4. In a modulus ring counter, to generate 'n' states, n-flip flops are required.

Hence 12 flip-flops are required for modulus 12 counter.

5. Given expression $AB(\bar{B}C + AC)$ so, complement

$\overline{AB(\bar{B}C + AC)}$

$\Rightarrow$ $\overline{(AB)} + \overline{(\bar{B}C + AC)}$

$\Rightarrow$ $(\bar{A} + \bar{B}) + \overline{(\bar{B}C)} + \overline{(AC)}$

$\Rightarrow$ $(\bar{A} + \bar{B}) + ((B + \bar{C})(\bar{A} + \bar{C}))$

6. To repsent 7 bit character ASCII encodes 128 specified characters into 7-bit integers.

7. Since, we need to add two 17-bit numbers. Hence the LSB (s) of both the numbers can be added using a half adder and for rest of the 16-bits, full adders are needed.

8. Given function

$f = \bar{A}\bar{B}C + \bar{A}\bar{B}\bar{C}$

$\quad = \bar{A}\bar{B}(C + \bar{C}) \quad [C + \bar{C} = 1]$

$\quad = \bar{A}\bar{B} = \overline{A + B}$

Hence, two 2×1 multiplication are required to realize the function.

9. Binary representation

$3 \times 4096 + 15 \times 256 + 5 \times 16 + 3$

$\quad = (3F53)_{16}$ (Hera representation)

$\quad = (0011111101010011)_2$

Hence, total ten 1's are required in the binary representation.

10. Boolean expression
$AB + AB' + A'C + AC$

$\quad = A(B + \bar{B}) + C(A + \bar{A})\ [B + \bar{B} = 1, A + \bar{A} = 1]$

$\quad = A + C$

Hence, the boolean expression is independent of the boolean variable 'B'.

11. 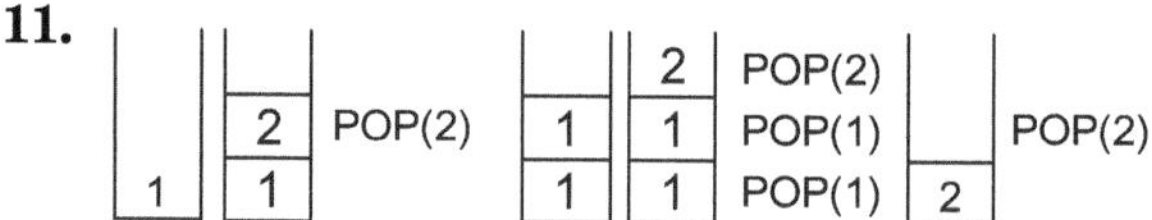

Sequence of popped out values: 2, 2, 1, 1, 2.

12. Given minimum of 100 sec to sort 1000 names.

Running time of quick sort = $n \log_2 n$

$\qquad n = 1000$

$\quad 100 \text{ sec} = c \times 1000 \times \log 1000$

$\qquad c = 0.01$

For 100 names,

$\qquad$ Time $= 0.01 \times 100 \times \log 100 = 6.7$ sec

13. 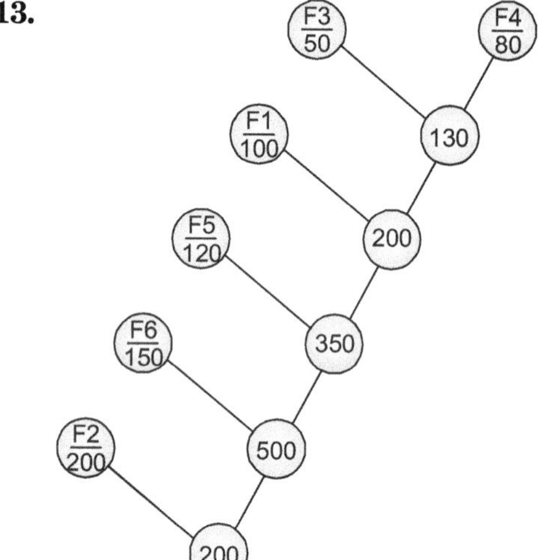

So, the order is $F3$, $F4$, $F1$, $F5$, $F6$ and $F2$.

14. From the hash table, it can be observed that, four elements are in succession in the hash table. Hence, maximum 5 comparisons are needed to search an item that is not present.

15. A queue data structure can be implemented with the help of 2 stacks.

16. As given in the E-R diagram it can be observed that for entity type exam, only the attributes Exam ID and Exam Name are enough. There is no need to insert NID.

17. After considering the following sequence in data base transaction system if transaction perform commit then it becomes permanent there is no effect of any failure so we need not redo log records 2 and 3 because transaction T_1 has committed.

18. Block can hold either 3 records or 10 key point.

Blocks required by data file = $n/3$

No. of records needed by pointer = $n/10$

Total blocks needed = $\dfrac{n}{3} + \dfrac{n}{10} = \dfrac{13n}{30}$.

20. Given dependencies

$$C \to F, E \to A, EC \to D, A \to B.$$

$$(EC)^+ = ABCDEF$$

So, 'EC' is the key for R.

21. If $D_1, D_2, \dots D_n$ are domain in a relational model, then the relation is a table, which is a subset of $D_1 \times D_2 \times \dots \times D_n$.

23. Select deptName

from employee

where sex = 'M'

grouply dept Name

$$\underbrace{\text{having avg (salary)}}_{\substack{\text{[Avg salary of male employees}\\\text{in each department]}}} > \underbrace{\text{(select avg (salary)}\\\text{from employees)}}_{\substack{\text{[Avg salary of male employees}\\\text{in each department]}}}$$

It returns the names of departments in which the average salary of male employees is more than the average salary of the organization.

24. Given expression

$$E \to E * F | F + E | F, F \to E - F | io$$

Since, '$*$' and '$+$' are at same level and '$-$' is at lower level. Hence '$-$' has higher precedence in comparison to '$*$' and '$+$'.

25. The number of token in the statements is,

$$\text{print } f \dfrac{(\text{``}i = \%d, \& i = \%x\text{''}, i, \& i);}{1\,2\,3\,4\,5\,6\,7\,8\,9\,10}$$

26. According to operator grammar which does not contain: (a) Nullable variable (b) 2 adjacent non-terminals on RHS of the production. So, production (i) and (iv) violate the rules.

27. A recursive descent parser is an example of top-down parser.

28. Yacc stands for yet another compiler compiler.

29. From given option consider

- LR(0) < SLR(1) < LALR(1) < CLR(1) is the order of parser for most powerful and costly compiler.
- The grammar generated by LP are CFG, but that does not all CFG's are LP.
- LR(k) is the most general non-backtracking shift reduce parsing method.

30. Semaphores are used to solve the problem of all three, race condition, process synchronization and mutual exclusion.

31. Given data,

Number of segments = 32

Number of bits needed for segment = 5

Size of each segment = 1 K

Hence, logical address will have 15 bits.

32. Given,

$$P_1 = 10\%, P_2 = 5\%, P_3 = 60\%, P_4 = 25\%$$

So, P_1 : $10\% = 40 \times \dfrac{10}{100} = 4$

For P_2 : $5\% = 40 \times \dfrac{5}{100} = 2$

For P_3 : $60\% = 0 \times \dfrac{60}{100} = 24$

For P_4 : $25\% = 40 \times \dfrac{25}{100} = 10$

33. If the time quantum for a particular process expires, then the process is swapped out of the CPU to the rear end of the ready queue. When, all the process have their turn, then the first process gets another turn. Hence, circular queue data structure is best suited in round robin algorithm.

34. Considering the given parameters

Average time to transfer

= Average seek time + Average rotational delay + Data transfer time

Time taken by the head to move from 1 track to adjacent track = 1 ms.

Average seek time

$$= \dfrac{0 + 1 + 2 + 3 + \dots + 499}{500}$$

$$= \dfrac{499(499 + 1)}{2 \times 500}$$

$$= 249.5 \text{ ms}$$

Average rotational delay

$$= \dfrac{0.1 \text{ sec}}{2} = 50 \text{ ms}$$

Data transfer time = 0.1 sec $\to$ 50,000 B

250 B = 0.5 ms

Average time = 249.5 + 0.5 + 50 = 300 ms.

35. Given initial value of semaphore is 7. After performing 20 P operations, $7 - 20 = -13$, value of semaphore is now '-13'. After then 15 V operation, $-13 + 15 = 2$. Resulting value of semaphore is 2.

36. Increasing the RAM means so more number of pages can be there is RAM which will result is less number of page faults.

37. After considering the program,

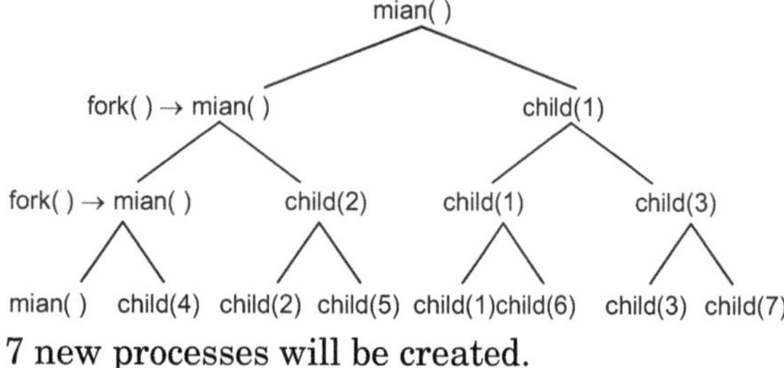

7 new processes will be created.

38. Two jobs, each of which needs 10 minutes.

Since, 20 mins of CPU time is needed by both the processes. Hence, 20 mins of CPU time is required.

As per the question, 50% I/O wait time means out of total time taken, 50% was spend in input output.

Hence, total 40 mins are required.

39. If, a node has K children in B-tree, then the node contains exactly $K - 1$ keys.

40. The time complexity of the following function is
$$T(n) = T(n - 1) + T(n - 1) + 1$$
$$[\text{recursive } (n - 1) = T(n - 1)]$$
$$= 2T(n - 1) + 1$$
$$= O(2^n) \quad [\text{using substitution method}]$$

41. Number of spanning tree possible with n-node
$$= n^{n-2}.$$

where, $n = 7$

Total number of spanning trees $= 7^5$

42. Given array:

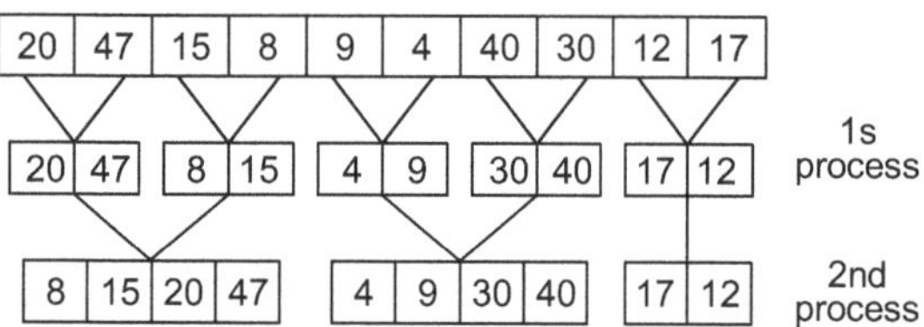

So, the order of elements after second pass of the algorithm is 8, 15, 20, 47, 4, 9, 30, 40, 12, 17.

43. $\Sigma^* - R_1$

Regular set is closed under intersection, union, complement and Kleen star.

44. The domain name system (DNS) maps the IP addresses to a hierarchy of domain names.

45. To add a background color for all

    $h1$ {background-color: #FFFFFF}

This HTML syntax is used to add a background color for all <h1 > elements.

46. Response, write ("Hi There"). This is the syntax to write "Hi There" in JavaScript.

47. To declare the version of XML,

    <?xml version = "1.0"/>

This syntax is used to declare the version of xml.

48. A T-switch is used to rearrange the connections between computing equipments.

49. Microwaves frequency wavelength ranges from 1 meter to 1 millimeter with frequencies between 300 MHz (100 cm) and 300 GHz (0.1 cm). This broad radiation Includes both ultra high frequency and extremely high frequency.

50. IPv4 standard specifies that each host is assigned a unique 32-bit number also called as internet address.

51. A character consist of (7 bits + 1 parity) bit.

Hence, total 8 bits are transmitted per character. Since on the line, 2400 bits are transmitted per second.

Hence number of character transmitted per
$$\text{second} = \frac{2400}{8} = 300.$$

52. Given data unit = 100111001

    Divisor is = 1011

Applying CRC:

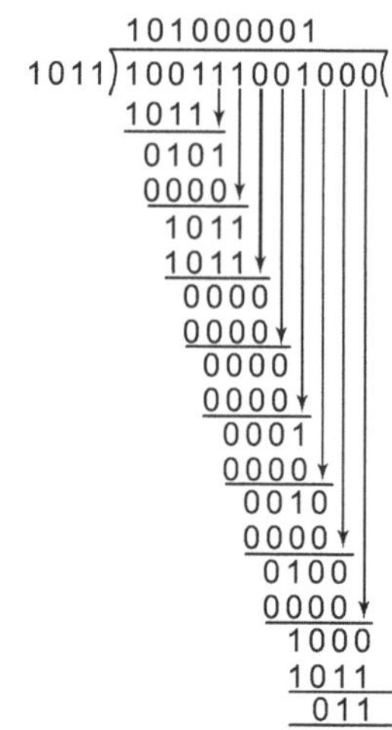

Divided at the receiver: 100111001011.

53. Acknowledgement number specifies the next expected byte. Now, since Ack number is 1000, it says that byte '999' has been received but the initial sequence number is not specified.

54. Mask : 255.2SS.224.0

    255.255.<u>11</u>100000.00000000

IP address:

    125.134.112.66

    125.134.011110000.66

Hence first address is,

    125.134.01100000.0 = 125.134.96.0

55. Population of ALOHA user manages to generate

Number of request in 1 sec = 70

Time slot per second = 20

$$\text{Channel load} = \frac{\text{Number of request}}{\text{Time slot}}$$

$$= \frac{70}{20} = 3.5$$

56. If PING encounters an error condition, an ICMP message is returned.

The PING command is a command prompt command used to test the ability of the source computer to reach a specified destination computer.

57. Considering eth2, the mask given is 255.255.255.0, hence 144.16.68.117 can be forwarded to this interface.

Considering eth3, the mask given is 255.255.255.224 = 255.255.255.11100000, IP of the destination is 144.16.68.64 = 144.16.68.01000000.

Hence, 144.16.68.117 can't be forwarded to this interface.

58. Application layer, presentation layer, session layer and transport layer are the host layers of the OSI reference model.

59. I. The difference is alpha testing is done at develope site and beta testing is done at client site.

II. Alpha and Beta testing are forms of acceptance testing.

61. SUB A:

S	P	X	Z	X	AC	X	CY	
0	1	0	1	0	1	0	1	Flag registers

A = 01 H

DCR B:

S	P	X	Z	X	AC	X	CY	
0	1	0	1	0	1	0	1	= (5 4) H

62. The minimum time delay between the initiation of two independent memory operations is called cycle time.

63. To genrate a.png file, PNG uses a non-patented lossless data compre-ssion method known as DEFLATE.

64. A modified bit or dirty bit is a bit that is associated with a block of computer memory and indicates whether or not the corresponding block has been modified.

65. From the given option.

A frame is not an image type used in MPEG.

66. Given data of CD quality

Sample frequency = 44.1 kHz = 44100 bps.

Since it's sterio audio signal.

Hence 2 channel are needed bit rate

$$= 2 \times 16 \times 44100 = 1411200 \text{ bps}$$

Compression ratio = 0.5

Compressed bit rate = 705600 bps

In 10 sec → 7056000 bits = 882000 B = 861.33KB

67. The compression ratio in typical mp3 audio file is 10 : 1.

68. The program fragment can be written as:

```
if (a > b)
{
    if (b > c)
    {
        s1:
    }
    else
    {
        s2;
    }
}
```

Hence $s2$ will be executed when first if condition is true and second is false.

Hence, if $(a > b)$ and $(b <= c)$, s2 will execute.

69. $a[++n] = n++$ Here, n is updated twice before the sequence point is reached. It is compiler dependent. Different result can be obtained at different compilers.

70. Given programme where

Variable 'x' is static and hence will be initialized to 0.

inc ()→ print '1'

inc ( )→ print '2'

inc ( )→ print '3'

inc ( )→ print '123'

Hence, it print '123'

71. Consider the program fragment than

$i = 6720, j = 4$

$(i \% j) = 0 ;$	$i = 1680$	$j = 5$
$(i \% j) = 0;$	$i = 336$	$j = 6$
$(i \% j) = 0;$	$i = 56$	$j = 7$
$(i \% j) = 0;$	$i = 8$	$j = 8$
$(i \% j) = 0;$	$i = 1$	$j = 9$
$(i \% j) \neq 0$		

On termination the value of 7 is 9.

72. Given declaration

The value of integer 'a' is 4. 'b' is a pointer pointing to b.

$$** c = 5$$
$$a = 5$$

The program fragment will assign 5 to a.

73. The output of the given program

$x[\ ] =$ | 1 | 2 | 3 | 4 | 5 | 6 | 7 | 8 |

      0 1 2 3 4 5 6 7

$i = 2, x[x[2]] = x\,[2] \Rightarrow x\,[3] = 3$

$i = 3, x[x[3]] = x\,[3] \Rightarrow x\,[3] = 3$

$i = 4, x[x[4]] = x\,[4] \Rightarrow x\,[5] = 5$

$i = 5, x[x[5]] = x\,[5] \Rightarrow x\,[5] = 5$

$x[\ ] =$ | 1 | 2 | 3 | 3 | 5 | 5 | 7 | 8 |

74. All the options given in the questions are correct. None of them have any kind of compilation error.

75. The for loop in the given program.

The operation is 'Bitwise AND operations'

0000 & 0001 = 0

0001 & 0001 = 1

0010 & 0001 = 0

0011 & 0001 = 1

0100 & 0001 = 0

0101 & 0001 = 1

0110 & 0001 = 0

0111 & 0001 = 1

1000 & 0001 = 0

1001 & 0001 = 1

Hence, the output is 01010101.

76. Given statement,

define hypotenuse $(a,\ b)$ sqrt $(a*a + b*b)$; hypotenuse $(a + 2, b + 3)$.

$\Rightarrow$ sqrt $(a + 2 * a + 2 + b + 3 * b + 3)$

$\Rightarrow$ $a + 2a + 2 + b + 3b + 3$

$\Rightarrow$ sqrt $(3a + 4b + 5)$

Hence, it find the square root of $3 * a + 4 + b + 5$.

77. Given

$$X = \frac{(M + N \times O)}{(P \times Q)}$$

One-address instruction required

1. Load P;

2. MUL Q;

3. STORE A;

4. Load N;

5. MUL O;

6. ADD M;

7. DIV A;

8. STORE X

Hence, total 8 1-address instructions are required to evaluate it.

78. Consider the decimal number and assume that 'n' bit binary number requires 'd' digit in decimal representation.

$$d > n \log_{10} 2$$

Given $d = 64$

$\Rightarrow$ $64 > n * 0.3010$

$\Rightarrow$ $n = 64 \% 0.3010$

        $n = 213$

79. Consider the declaration and given structure creates the minimum of array and union, but union only creates the minimum for only 'long z' which is max. So total minimum required = 18.

80. After consider the code segment

Since, it's an integer variable, but the value provided is of floating type. Hence '5' will get stored.

Call by value: The value returned will not effect actual 'x' so the final value will remain 5.

Call by reference: In this, the reference to original memory location is passed.

$$x = x + y = 5 + 5 = 10$$
$$y = y + x = 10 + 10 = 20$$

The final value of 'x' will be 20.

SOLVED PAPER 2016
Computer Science

1. Which of the following is true?
   (a) $\sqrt{3} + \sqrt{7} = \sqrt{10}$
   (b) $\sqrt{3} + \sqrt{7} \leq \sqrt{10}$
   (c) $\sqrt{3} + \sqrt{7} < \sqrt{10}$
   (d) $\sqrt{3} + \sqrt{7} > \sqrt{10}$

2. What is the sum to infinity of the series,
   $3 + 6x^2 + 9x^4 + 12x^6 + \dots$ given $|x| < 1$?
   (a) $\dfrac{3}{(1 + x^2)}$
   (b) $\dfrac{3}{(1 + x^2)^2}$
   (c) $\dfrac{3}{(1 - x^2)^2}$
   (d) $\dfrac{3}{(1 - x^2)}$

3. $\lim\limits_{x \to \infty} \dfrac{\sqrt{1 + x} - \sqrt{1 - x}}{x}$ is given by
   (a) 0
   (b) –1
   (c) 1
   (d) $\dfrac{1}{2}$

4. If $(G,.)$ is a group such that $(ab)^{-1} = a^{-1} b^{-1}, a, b,$ $\in G$, then G is a/an
   (a) Commutative semi group
   (b) Abelian group
   (c) Non-abelian group
   (d) None of these

5. A given connected graph G is a Euler Graph if and only if all vertices of G are of
   (a) Same degree
   (b) Even degree
   (c) Odd degree
   (d) Different degree

6. The maximum number of edges in a n-nodes undirected graph without self loops is
   (a) n^2
   (b) $\dfrac{n(n-1)}{2}$
   (c) $n - 1$
   (d) $\dfrac{n(n+1)}{2}$

7. The minimum number of NAND gates required to implement the boolean function $A + A\bar{B} + A\bar{B}C$ is equal to
   (a) 0 (zero)
   (b) 1
   (c) 4
   (d) 7

8. The minimum Boolean expression for the following circuit is

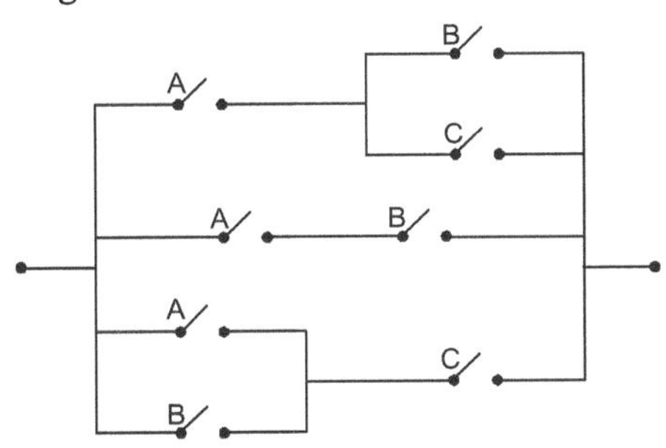

   (a) $AB + AC + BC$
   (b) $A + BC$
   (c) $A + B$
   (d) $A + B + C$

9. For a binary half-subtractor having two inputs A and B, the correct set of logical expression for the outputs $D (= A$ minus $B)$ and $X(=$borrow$)$ are
   (a) $D = AB + \bar{A}B, X = \bar{A}B$
   (b) $D = \bar{A}B + A\bar{B}, X = A\bar{B}$
   (c) $D = \bar{A}B + A\bar{B}, X = \bar{A}B$
   (d) $D = AB + \bar{A}B, X = A\bar{B}$

10. Consider the following gate network

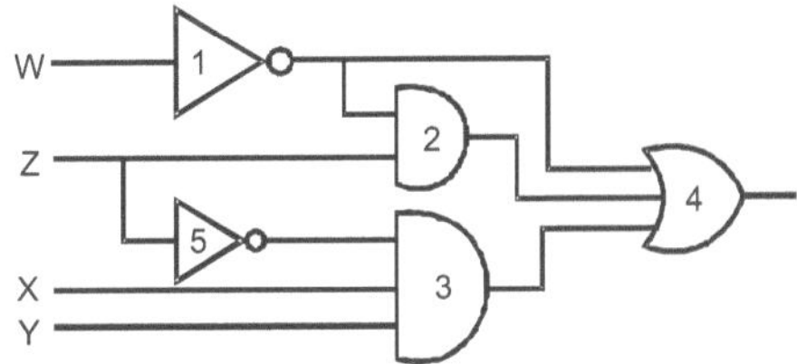

   Which one of the following gates is redundant?
   (a) Gate No. 1
   (b) Gate No. 2
   (c) Gate No. 3
   (d) Gate No. 4

11. The dynamic hazard problem occurs in
   (a) Combinational circuit alone
   (b) Sequential circuit only
   (c) Both (a) and (b)
   (d) None of the above

12. The logic circuit given below converts a binary code y_1, y_2, y_3 into

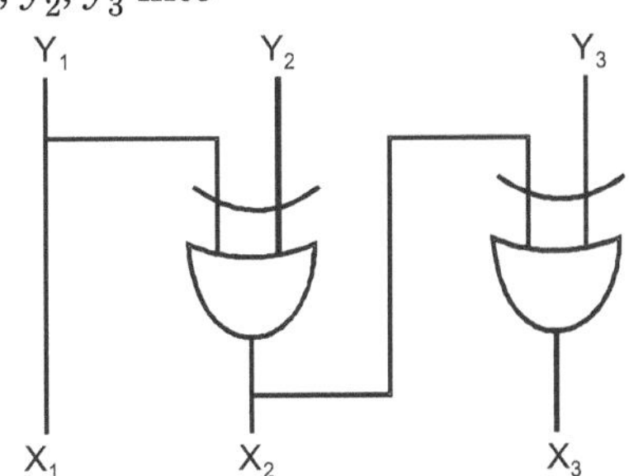

   (a) Excess-3 code
   (b) Gray code
   (c) BCD code
   (d) Hamming code

13. The circuit shown in the figure below is

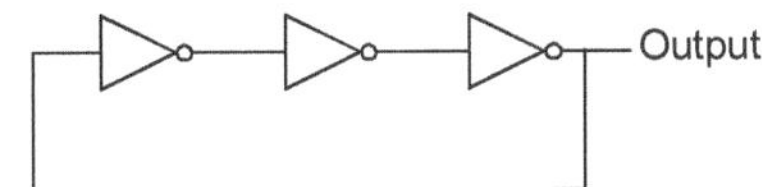

    (a) An oscillating circuit and its output is square wave

    (b) The one whose output remains stable in '1' state

    (c) The one having output remains stable in '0' state

    (d) Has a single pulse of three times propagation delay

14. If $12\,A7\,C_{16} = X_8$ then the value of X is

    (a) 224174   (b) 425174

    (c) 6173   (d) 225174

15. The Excess-3 code is also called

    (a) Cyclic Redundancy Code

    (b) Weighted Code

    (c) Self-Complementing Code

    (d) Algebraic Code

16. The simplified Sum of Product of the following Boolean expression $(P + \bar{Q} + \bar{R})(P + Q + R)$ $(P + Q + \bar{R})$ is

    (a) $(\bar{P}Q + R)$ (b) $(P + Q\bar{R})$

    (c) $(P\bar{Q} + R)$ (d) $(PQ + R)$

17. Which of the following binary number is the same as its 2's complement?

    (a) 1010   (b) 0101

    (c) 1000   (d) 1001

18. The functional difference between SR flip-flop and JK flip-flop is that

    (a) JK flip-flop is faster than SR flip-flop

    (b) JK flip-flop has a feedback path

    (c) JK flip-flop accepts both inputs 1

    (d) None of above

19. Consider a non-pipelined processor with a clock rate of 2.5 GHz and average cycles per instruction of four. The same processor is upgraded to a pipelined processor with five stages; but due to the internal pipeline delay, the clock speed is reduced to 2 GHz. Assume that there are no stalls in the pipeline. The speed up achieved in this pipelined processor is

    (a) 3.2   (b) 3.0

    (c) 2.2   (d) 2.0

20. What is the output of the C code?

```
#include<stdio.h>
void main()
{
    int k=5;
    int *p = & k;
    int **m = &p;
    printf("%d %d% d \n", k, *p,**m);
}
```

    (a) 5 5 5   (c) 5 5 junk

    (b) 5 junk junk   (d) compile time error

21. Consider a disk pack with 16 surfaces, 128 tracks per surface and 256 sectors per track. 512 bytes of data are stored in a bit serial fashion in a sector. The capacity of the disk pack and the number of bits required to specify a particular eector in the disk respectively;

    (a) 256 MB; 19 bits (b) 256 MB, 28 bits

    (c) 512 MB, 20 bits (d) 64 GB, 28 bits

22. Let the page fault service time be 10 ms in a computer with average memory access time being 20 ns. If one page fault is generated for every 10^6 memory accesses, what is the effective access time for the memory?

    (a) 21.4 ns   (b) 29.9 ns

    (c) 23.5 ns   (d) 35.1 ns

23. Register renaming is done is pipelined processors

    (a) As an alternative to register allocation at compile time

    (b) For efficient access to function parameters and local variables

    (c) To eliminate certain kinds of hazards

    (d) As part of address translations

24. In which class of Flynn's taxanomy, Von Neumann architecture belongs to?

    (a) SISD   (b) SIMD

    (c) MIMD   (d) MISD

25. What will be output of the following program? Assume that you are running this program in little-endian processor.

```
#include<stdio.h>
int main ( ){
short a = 320;
char*ptr;
    ptr = (char*)&a;
    printf("%d",*ptr);
return 0;
}
```

    (a) 1   (b) 320

    (c) 64   (d) compilation error

26. Consider the following segment of C code:

```
int j, n;
j = 1;
while (j <= n)
    j = j * 2
```

The number of comparisons made in the execution of the loop for any $n > 0$ is

    (a) $\lfloor \log_2 n \rfloor * n$ (b) n

    (c) $\lfloor \log_2 n \rfloor$ (d) $\lfloor \log_2 n \rfloor + 1$

27. The following postfix expression with single digit operands is evaluated using a stack:

$$8\ 2\ 3\ \wedge\ /\ 2\ 3\ *\ +\ 5\ 1\ *\ \_$$

(Note that $\wedge$ is the exponentiation operator)

The top two elements of the stack after the first * operator is evaluated are
(a) 6, 1 (b) 5, 7
(c) 3, 2 (d) 1, 5

28. Average number of comparison required for a successful search for sequential search on n items is
(a) $\dfrac{n}{2}$ (b) $\dfrac{n-1}{2}$
(c) $\dfrac{n+1}{2}$ (d) None of the above

29. A Hash Function f is defined as $f(\text{key}) = \text{key mod } 7$. With linear probing, while inserting the keys 37, 38, 72, 48, 98, 11, 56 into a table indexed from 0, in which location the key 11 will be stored (Count table index 0 as 0th location)?
(a) 3 (b) 4
(c) 5 (d) 6

30. A complete binary tree with n non-leaf nodes contains
(a) $\log_2 n$ nodes (b) $n + 1$ nodes
(c) $2\,n$ nodes (d) $2n + 1$ nodes

31. Algorithm design technique used in quick sort algorithm is?
(a) Dynamic programming
(b) Backtracking
(c) Divide and conquer
(d) Greedy method

32. An FSM (finite state machine) can be considered to be a turing machine of finite tape length
(a) Without rewinding capability and unidirectional tape movement
(b) Rewinding capability and unidirectional tape movement
(c) Without rewinding capability and bidirectional tape movement
(d) Rewinding capability and bidirectional tape movement

33. Let $L = \{w \in (0 + 1)^* \mid w$ has even number of 1s$\}$, i.e. L is the set of all bit strings with even number of 1s. Which one of the regular expression below represents L?
(a) $(0^*10^*1)^*$ (b) $(0^*10^*10)^*$
(c) $0^*(10^*1^*)^*0^*$ (d) $0^*1(10^*1)^*10^*$

34. Consider the following recurrence:
$$T(n) = 2T(\sqrt{n}) + 1,\ T(1) = 1$$
Which one of the following is true?
(a) $T(n) = O(\log \log n)$
(b) $T(n) = O(\log n)$
(c) $T(n) = O(\sqrt{n})$
(d) $T(n) = O(n)$

35. Consider the following statements about the context free grammar
$$G = \{S \to SS, S \to ab, S \to ba, S \to \wedge]$$
1. G is ambiguous
2. G produces all strings with equal number of a's and b's
3. G can be accepted by a deterministic PDA.
Which combinations below expresses all the true statements about G?
(a) 1 only (b) 1 and 3 only
(c) 2 and 3 only (d) 1, 2 and 3

36. If L and $\overline{L}$ are recursively enumerable then L is
(a) Regular (b) Context-free
(c) Context-sensitive (d) Recursisve

37. $S \to aSa \mid bSb \mid a \mid b$
The language generated by the above grammar over the alphabets {a, b} is the set of
(a) All palindromes
(b) All odd length palindromes
(c) Strings that begin and end with the same symbol
(d) All even length palindromes

38. What is the highest type number that can be assigned to this following grammar?
$$S \to Aa,\ A \to Ba,\ B \to abc$$
(a) Type 0 (b) Type 1
(c) Type 2 (d) Type 3

39. Access time of the symbolic table will be logarithmic, if it is implemented by
(a) Linear list (b) Search tree
(c) Hash table (d) Self-organization list

40. Recursive descent parsing is an example of
(a) Top-down parsers (b) Bottom-up parsers
(c) Predictive parsers (d) None of the above

41. A top-down parser generates
(a) Rightmost derivation
(b) Rightmost derivation in reverse
(c) Leftmost derivation
(d) Leftmost derivation in reverse

42. Relative mode of addressing is most relevant to writing
(a) Co-routines
(b) Position-independent code
(c) Sharable code
(d) Interrupt Handlers

43. A simple two-pass assembler does which of the following in the first pass :
(a) Checks to see if the instructions are legal in the current assembly mode
(b) It allocates space for the literals.
(c) It builds the symbol table for the symbols and their values.
(d) All of these

44. Peephole optimization is a form of
(a) Loop optimization
(b) Local optimization
(c) Constant folding
(d) Data flow analysis

45. At a particular time of computation the value of a counting semaphore is 7. Then 20 P operations and x V operations were completed on this semaphore. If the final value of semaphore is 5, x will be
(a) 18   (b) 22
(c) 15   (d) 13

46. With single resource, deadlock occurs
(a) If there are more than two processes competing for that resource
(b) If there are only two processes competing for that resource
(c) If there is a single process competing for that resource
(d) None of these

47. A system has 3 processes sharing 4 resources. If each process needs a maximum of 2 units, then
(a) Deadlock can never occur
(b) Deadlock may occur
(c) Deadlock has to occur
(d) None of these

48. Determine the number of page faults when references to pages occur in the following order:
1, 2, 4, 5, 2, 1, 2, 4
Assume that the main memory can accommodate 3 pages and the main memory already has the pages 1 and 2, with page one having brought earlier than page 2. (LRU page replacement algorithm is used)
(a) 3   (b) 5
(c) 4   (d) None of these

49. Working Set (t, k) at an instant of time t is
(a) The set of k future references that the Operating System OS will make
(b) The set of future references that the OS will make in next t unit of time
(c) The set of k references with high frequency
(d) The k set of pages that have been referenced in the last t time units

50. A CPU generates 32-bit virtual addresses. The page size is 4 KB. The processor has a translation look-aside buffer (TLB) which can hold a total of 128 page table entries and is 4-way set associative. The minimum size of the TLB tag is
(a) 11 bits   (b) 13 bits
(c) 15 bits   (d) 20 bits

51. The real-time operating system, which of the following is the most suitable scheduling scheme?
(a) Round robin   (b) First come first server
(c) Pre-emptive   (d) Random scheduling

52. In which one of the following page replacement policies, Balady's anomaly may occur?
(a) FIFO   (b) Optimal
(c) LRU   (d) MRU

53. Consider join of a relation R with a relation S. If R has m tuples and S has n tuples then the maximum and minimum sizes of the join respectively are
(a) $m + n$ and 0
(b) mn and 0
(c) $m + n$ and $|m - n|$
(d) mn and $m + n$

54. Let $R(a, b, c)$ and $S(d, e, f)$ be two relations in which d is the foreign key of S that refers to the primary key of R.
Consider the following four operations R and S
1. Insert into R 2. Insert into S
3. Deletion from R 4. Deletion from S
Which of the following can cause violation of the relational integrity constraint above?
(a) Both 1 and 4   (b) Both 2 and 3
(c) All of these   (d) None of these

55. The relation book (title, price) contains the titles and prices of different books. Assuming that no two books have same price, what does the following SQL query list?
[select title from book as B where (select count(*) from book as T where T.price > B.price) < 5]
(a) Titles of the four most expensive books
(b) Title of the fifth most inexpensive book
(c) Title of the fifth most expensive book
(d) Titles of the five most expensive books

56. Goals for the design of the logical schema include
(a) Avoiding data inconsistency
(b) Being able to construct queries easily
(c) Being able to access data efficiently
(d) All of the above

57. Given the relations:
- employee (name, salary, deptno), and
- department (deptno, deptname, address).

Which of the following queries cannot be expressed using the basic relational algebra operations $(U, -, x, \pi, \sigma, p)$?
(a) Department address of every employee
(b) Employees whose name is the same as their department name
(c) The sum of all employees' salaries
(d) All employees of a given department

58. Trigger is
(a) Statement that enables to start any DBMS
(b) Statement that is executed by the user when debugging an application program
(c) The condition that the system tests for the validity of the database user
(d) Statement that is executed automatically by the system as a side effect a modification of the database

59. The order of a leaf node in a B$^+$ tree is the maximum number of (value, data record pointer) pairs it can hold. Given that the block size is 1 Kbytes, data record pointer is 7 bytes long, the value field is 9 bytes long and a block pointer is 6 bytes long, what is the order of the leaf node?
(a) 63   (b) 64
(c) 67   (d) 68

60. A clustering index is defined on the fields which are of type _________.
(a) Non-key and ordering
(b) Non-key and non-ordering
(c) Key and ordering
(d) Key and non-ordering

61. The extent to which the software can continue to operate correctly despite the introduction of invalid inputs is called as
(a) Reliability   (b) Robustness
(c) Fault tolerance   (d) Portability

62. Which one of the following is a functional requirement?
(a) Maintainability   (b) Portability
(c) Robustness   (d) None of the mentioned

63. Configuration management is not concerned with
(a) Controlling changes to the source code
(b) Choice of hardware configuration for an application
(c) Controlling documentation changes
(d) Maintaining versions of software

64. A company needs to develop a strategy for software product development for which it has a choice of two programming language $L1$ and $L2$. The number of lines of code (LOC) developed using $L2$ is estimated to be twice the LOC developed with $L1$. The product will have to be maintained for five years. Various parameters for the company are given in the table below.

Parameter	Language L1	Language L2
Man years needed for development	LOC/10000	LOC/10000
Development cost per man year	₹ 10,00,000	₹ 7,50,000
Maintenance time	5 years	5 years
Cost of maintenance per year	₹ 1,00,000	₹ 50,000

Total cost of the project includes cost of development and maintenance. What is the LOC for $L1$ for which of the cost of the project using $L1$ is equal to the cost of the project using $L2$?
(a) 10,000   (b) 5,000
(c) 7,500   (d) 75,000

65. A company needs to develop a digital signal processing software for one of its newest inventions. The software is expected to have 20000 lines of code. The company needs to determine the effort in person-months needed to develop this software using the basic COCOMO model. The multiplicative factor for this model is given as 2.2 for the software development on embedded systems, while the exponentiation factor is given as 1.5. What is the estimated effort in person-months?
(a) 196.77   (b) 206.56
(c) 199.56   (d) 210.68

66. In the Spiral model of software development, the primary determinant in selecting activities in each iteration is
(a) Iteration size
(b) Cost
(c) Adopted process such as Rational Unified process or Extreme Programming
(d) Risk

67. Bit stuffing refers to

(a) Inserting a 0 in user stream to differentiate it with a flag

(b) Inserting a 0 in flag stream to avoid ambiguity

(c) Appending a nipple to the flag sequence

(d) Appending a nipple to the user data stream

68. Dynamic routing protocol enable routers to

(a) Dynamically discover and maintain routes

(b) Distribute routing updates to other routers

(c) Reach agreement with other routers about the network topology

(d) All of the above

69. In Ethernet CSMA/CD, the special bit sequence transmitted by media access management to handle collision is called

(a) Preamble   (b) Postamble

(c) Jam   (d) None of these

70. Which network protocol allows hosts to dynamically get a unique IP number on each bootup

(a) DHCP   (b) BOOTP

(c) RARP   (d) ARP

71. In a token ring network the transmission speed is 10^7 bps and the propagation speed is 200 m/μs. Then 1 bit delay in this network is equivalent to:

(a) 500 m of cable   (b) 200 m of cable

(c) 20 m of cable   (d) 50 m of cable

72. The address of a class B host is to be split into subnets with a 6 bit subnet number. What is the maximum number of subnets and the maximum number of hosts in each subnet?

(a) 62 subnets and 262142 hosts

(b) 64 subnets and 262142 hosts

(c) 62 subnets and 1022 hosts

(d) 64 subnets and 1024 hosts

73. The message 11001001 is to be transmitted using the CRC polynomial $x^3 + 1$ to protect it from errors. The message that should be transmitted is:

(a) 11001001000   (b) 11001001011

(c) 11001010   (d) 110010010011

74. What is the maximum size of data that the application layer can pass on to the TCP layer below?

(a) Any size

(b) (2^{16} bytes the size of TCP header)

(c) 2^{16} bytes

(d) 1500 bytes

75. Frames of 1000 bits are sent over a 10^6 bps duplex link between two hosts. The propagation time is 25 ms. Frames are to be transmitted into this link to maximally pack them in transit (within the link). What is the minimum number of bits (i) that will be required to represent the sequence numbers distinctly? Assume that no time gap needs to be given between transmission of two frames.

(a) $i = 2$ (b) $i = 3$

(c) $i = 4$ (d) $i = 5$

76. Which of the following is TRUE only of XML but not for HTML?

(a) It is derived from SGML

(b) It describes content and layout

(c) It allows user defined tags

(d) It is restricted only to be used with web browsers

77. Consider a system with 2 level cache. Access times of Level-1 cache, Level-2 cache and main memory are 1 ns, 10 ns, and 500 ns respectively. The hit rates of Level-1 and Level-2 caches are 0.8 and 0.9, respectively. What is the average access time of the system ignoring the search time within the cache?

(a) 13.0 ns   (b) 12.8 ns

(c) 12.6 ns   (d) 12.4 ns

78. If a class C is derived from class B, which is derived from class A, all through public inheritance, then a class C member function can access

(a) Only protected and public data of C and B

(b) Only protected and public data of C

(c) All data of C and private data of A and B

(d) Public and protected data of A and B and all data of C

79. Which one of the following is correct about the statements given below?

I. All function calls are resolved at compile-time in C language.

II. All function calls are resolved at compile-time in C++.

(a) Only II is correct

(b) Both I and II are correct

(c) Only I is correct

(d) Both I and II are incorrect

80. When a DNS server accepted and uses incorrect information from a host that has no authority giving that information, then it is called

(a) DNS lookup

(b) DNS hijacking

(c) DNS spoofing

(d) None of the mentioned

ANSWERS

1. (d)	**2.** (c)	**3.** (c)	**4.** (b)	**5.** (b)	**6.** (b)	**7.** (a)	**8.** (a)	**9.** (c)	**10.** (b)
11. (c)	**12.** $(*)$	**13.** (a)	**14.** (d)	**15.** (c)	**16.** (b)	**17.** (c)	**18.** (c)	**19.** (a)	**20.** (a)
21. (a)	**22.** (b)	**23.** (c)	**24.** (a)	**25.** (c)	**26.** (d)	**27.** (a)	**28.** (c)	**29.** (c)	**30.** (d)
31. (c)	**32.** (a)	**33.** (b)	**34.** (b)	**35.** (b)	**36.** (d)	**37.** (b)	**38.** (d)	**39.** (b)	**40.** (a)
41. (c)	**42.** (b)	**43.** (d)	**44.** (b)	**45.** (a)	**46.** (d)	**47.** (a)	**48.** (c)	**49.** (d)	**50.** (c)
51. (c)	**52.** (a)	**53.** (b)	**54.** (b)	**55.** (d)	**56.** (d)	**57.** (c)	**58.** (d)	**59.** (a)	**60.** (a)
61. (b)	**62.** (d)	**63.** (b)	**64.** (b)	**65.** (a)	**66.** (d)	**67.** (a)	**68.** (d)	**69.** (c)	**70.** (a)
71. (c)	**72.** (c)	**73.** (b)	**74.** (a)	**75.** (d)	**76.** (c)	**77.** (a, c)	**78.** (d)	**79.** (d)	**80.** (c)

Note: * None of the given option is correct. Question may contain insufficient data.

EXPLANATIONS

1. Considering all the option
$$\sqrt{3} + \sqrt{7}(=, \leq, <, >)\sqrt{10}$$
Solving LHS by taken square at both sides.
$$\text{LHS} = (\sqrt{3} + \sqrt{7})^2$$
$$= (\sqrt{3})^2 + (\sqrt{7})^2 + 2\sqrt{3}\sqrt{7}$$
$$= 3 + 7 + 2\sqrt{3}\sqrt{7}$$
$$= 10 + 2\sqrt{3}\sqrt{7}$$
$$= 10 + 9.165 = 19.165$$
Now, $\text{RHS} = (\sqrt{10})^2 = (\sqrt{10})^2 = 10$
So, LHS is greater than RHS.
$$\sqrt{3} + \sqrt{7} > \sqrt{10}$$

2. Sum of the infinity of the series
$3 + 6x^2 + 9x^4 + 12x^6 + ... \infty$ is AP-GP series.
Assume,
$$F(x) = 3 + 6x^2 + 9x^4 + 12x^6 + ... \infty \qquad ...(1)$$
Multiple equation (1) by $-x^2$
$$-x^2 F(x) = -3x^2 - 6x^4 - 9x^6 - 12x^8 - ... \infty \ ...(2)$$
Multiple equation (2) from eq.(1)
$$F(x) = 3 + 6x^2 + 9x^4 + 12x^6 + ... \qquad ...(1)$$
$$-x^2 F(x) = 0 - 3x^2 - 6x^4 - 9x^6 - ... \qquad ...(2)$$
$$(1 + x^2) F(x) = 3 + 3x^2 + 3x^4 + 3x^6 + ...$$
$$F(x) = \frac{3 + 3x^2 + 3x^4 + 3x^6 + ...}{(1 + x^2)}$$
$$F(x) = \frac{3(1 + x^2 + x^4 + x^6 + ...)}{(1 + x^2)}$$
$$= \frac{3}{(1 + x^2)^2(1 + x^2)} = \frac{3}{(1 + x^2)^3}$$

4. If $(a \cdot b) = (b \cdot a)$ i.e., commutative $(G, .)$ is abelian
Given $(ab)^{-1} = a^{-1} b^{-1}$
We know $(ab)^{-1} = b^{-1} a^{-1}$
By the property of commutative $a^{-1}b^{-1} = b^{-1} a^{-1}$.
So, $(G, .)$ is abelian group.

5. Connected graph is Euler if all vertices of G are of even degree i.e.,

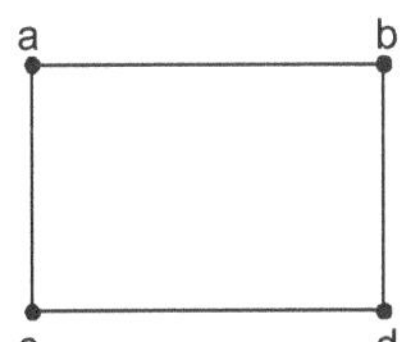

Here a, b, c, d are all of degree 2.

6. n-node each having degree $(n - 1)/2$; such each edge so maximum number of edges $= n(n - 1)/2$.

7. Required NAND gates for,
$$A + A\bar{B} + A\bar{B}C = A[1 + \bar{B} + \bar{B}C] = A$$
So, NAND gate is not required.

8. Given circuit

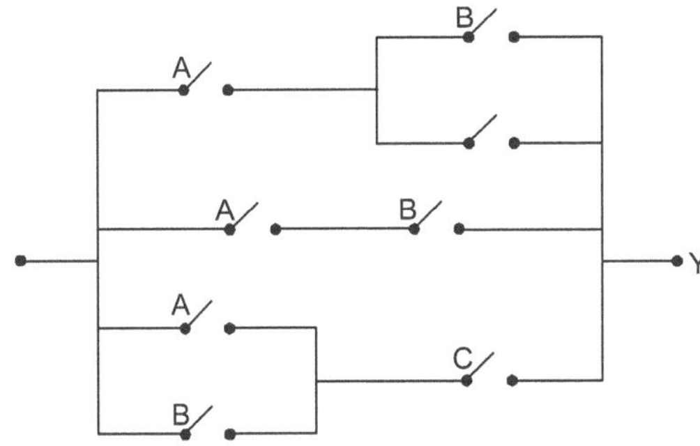

We have to evaluate the value for Y between parallel edges '+' should be used to functioning of the given circuit and in series '.'.
$$= A(B + C) + A.B + (A + B).C$$
$$= AB + AC + AB + AC + BC$$
$$= AB + AC + BC$$

9. For Binary half-subtractor circuit,

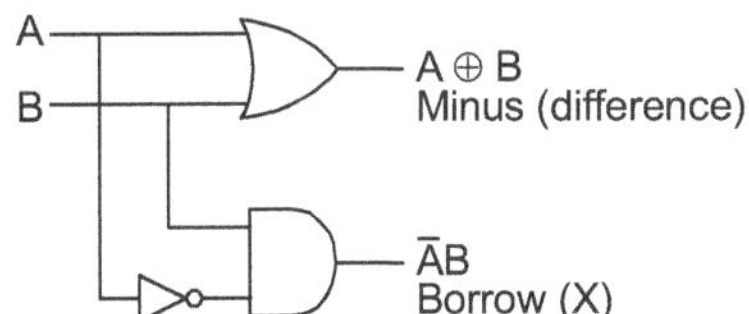

So, $D = A \oplus B = \bar{A}B + A\bar{B}$ (Difference)

$X = \bar{A}B$ (Borrow)

10. From the given gate network

Output of Gate 1 = $\bar{w}$

Output of Gate 2 = $\bar{w}z$

Output of Gate 3 = $\bar{z}xy$

Output of Gate 4 = $\bar{w} + \bar{w}z + \bar{z}xy$

$$= \bar{w}(1 + 2) + \bar{z} + xy$$

$$= \bar{w} + \bar{z}xy$$

Since $\bar{w}$ absorbe $\bar{w}z$ and results in $\bar{w}$ only. So here Gate 2 is redundant.

11. Dynamic Hazard can occur in both combination circuit and sequential circuit i.e., in both circuit output can change more than one time as a result of single input change (delay can be due to gates or flip flops).

13. If input is 0 then it returns 1 and then 1 goes to feedback as input and produce 0 as output, will happen infinite times and hence produce square waves.

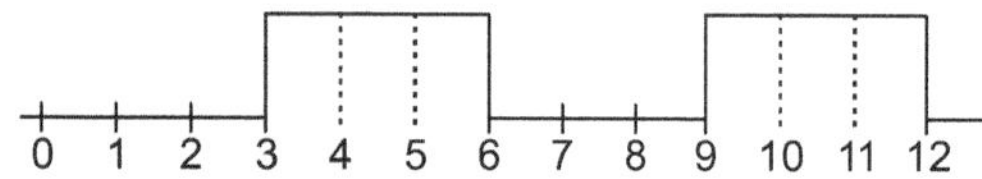

14. Given $(12A7C)_{16} = X_8$

Repsent $(12A7C)_{16}$ in so the hexadecimal.

0001001010100111 1100

for octal 3 bit representation needed (0-7)

000010010101001111100 i.e., $(225174)_8$.

15. Excess-3 code also called **self complementry non-weighted code** because 1's complement of an excess-3 number is the excess-3 code for 9's complement of the corresponding decimal number.

16. Given SOP form of booleen expression

$$(P + \bar{Q} + \bar{R}).(P + Q + R).(P + Q + \bar{R})$$

R\PQ	00	01	11	10
0	X	1	1	1
1	1	0	1	1

Hence, the expression is $(P + Q\bar{R})$.

17. From the given option,

1000 is the number which is same as its 2's complement i.e., 1000's 1 's complement 0111. Adding 1 to 0111 gives 1000 back.

18. The function difference between JK and SR FF's is JK flip flop accepts both input as 1 where as S-R flip flop given different output when both inputs are 1 i.e., undefined behavior when both input are 1.

19. Lets consider a non-pipeline processor

$$\text{Cock rate} = 2.5\text{GHz}$$

$$\text{For } n\text{-instruction} = \frac{n \times 4 \times 1}{2.5 \text{ GHz}} = 1.6 \text{ ns}$$

For pipeline processor:

$$\text{Clock speed} = \text{GHz}$$

$$\text{For } n\text{-instruction} = \frac{n \times 1}{2 \text{ GHz}} = 0.5 \text{ ns}$$

$$\text{Speed up} = \frac{1.6 \, ns}{0.5 \, ns} = 3.2$$

20. Output of C code

$$k\boxed{5}\;\boxed{100}\!*p\boxed{200}\!*\!*m$$

So, $k = 5, *p = *(100) = 5$

$**m = **(200) = *(100) = 5$

5, 5, 5 will be printed.

21. From the given data

Surfaces = 16

Tracks/Surface = 128

Sectors = 256

Capacity of disk

$$= \text{\#surfaces} \times \text{\#tracks} \times \text{\# sectors} \times \text{\# data}$$

$$= 16 \times 128 \times 256 \times 512 \text{ B}$$

$$= 2^4 \times 2^7 \times 2^8 \times 2^9 \text{ B} = 2^{28} \text{ B}$$

$$= 256 \text{ MB} \qquad [\because 2^{20} = 1 \text{ M}]$$

Number of bits to specify particular sector

$$= \text{\# surface} \times \text{\# tracks} \times \text{\# sectors}$$

$$= 16 \times 128 \times 256$$

$$= 24 \times 27 \times 28 = 2^{19} = 19 \text{ bits}$$

22. Given, service time = 10 ms

Effective access time

$$= P \times (\text{Page fault service time})$$

$$+ (1 - P) \text{ Memory access time}$$

$$= \frac{1}{10^6} \times 10 \text{ m sec} + \left(1 - \frac{1}{10^6}\right) \times 20 \text{ n sec}$$

$$= \frac{1}{10^6} \times \frac{10 \times 10}{10^6} \text{ n sec} + \left(1 - \frac{1}{10^6}\right) \times 20 \text{ n sec}$$

$$= 29.99 \text{ nsec}$$

23. Register renaming is done is pipelined processors to handle certain kind of hazards i.e., RAW hazard, WAR hazard and WAW hazard.

24. Single data stream in which single uni-core processor, executes a single instruction stream, to operate on data stored in a single memory, which belongs to von-Neumann architecture.

25. Output of the given program running in little-endian processor, is used so least significant byte is stored at smallest address.

a	320
	1000

Storage of 320 in bits forms:

Higher byte	Lower byte
00000001	01000000
1001	1000

Char*ptr = (char*) & a;

now 'a' is Type casted into character type from short. So now *ptr points to only single byte, print (ptr) will print 64.

26. Considering the segment of C code.

Since $j = j * 2$, from $j = 1$ to $j = n$ run for $\log_2 n$ times and 1 more time condition check when it fails.

So, it will be $[\log_2 n] + 1$. It can be check by taking 2-3 example.

27. Given expression : 8 2 3 ^ / 2 3 * + 5 1 * –.

		3					3	
	2	2	8			2	2	6
8	8	8	8	1		1	1	1
8	2	3	2^3	8/8	2	3	2×3

When '*' is evaluated, so stack contain two element i.e., 6 and 1.

28. Average number of comparision required on n items.

Number of comparison in worst case = n

Number of comparison in best case = 1

So, average number of comparison

$$= \frac{\text{Worst} + \text{Best}}{2} = \left(\frac{n+1}{2}\right)$$

29. Given, f(key) = key mod 7

98	56	72	38	32	11	48
0	1	2	3	4	5	6

1. 32% 7 = 4
2. 38% 7 = 3
3. 72% 7 = 2
4. 48% 7 = 6
5. 98% 7 = 0
6. 11% 7 = 4
7. 56% 7 = 0

11 will be placed at 5th index.

30. In a complete binary tree, there are,

Number of internal nodes = No. of leaf node –1

So total number of nodes

$$= \text{Internal nodes} + \text{Leaf nodes}$$
$$= n + n + 1$$
$$= 2n + 1$$

Internal node = 3

Leaf node = 4

Total nodes = 3 + 4 = 7

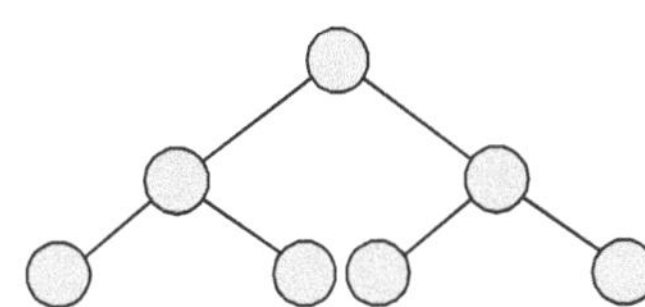

31. Quick sort algorithm is based on divide an conquer approach.

Since we conquer the array by dividing it on the basis of pivot elements till the sorted array is obtained.

32. A FSM can be considered to be a turing machine of finite tape length without rewinding capability and unidirectional tape movement.

33. $L = \{w \in (0 + 1)^* \mid w$ have even number of 1'$\}$ We have to check all option which accepts one 1 's two 1's, four 1's ... $2n$ 1's in any order.

Only option (b) accepts even number of 1's in any order.

34. Given recurrence

$$T(n) = 2T(\sqrt{n}) + 1$$

Substitute $n = 2m$, so $m = \log_2 n$

$$T(2^m) = 2T(2^{m/2}) + 1$$

Substitute $T(2^m) - S(m)$

$$S(m) = 2S(m/2) + 1$$

on applying Master theorem, we get

$$S(m) = \Theta(m)$$

on back substituting $S(m)$ to $T(2^m)$.

$$T(n) = \Theta(\log_2 n)$$

35. Given contert free grammar

$$G = \{S \rightarrow SS, S \rightarrow ab, S \rightarrow ba, S \rightarrow \in\}$$

- For null string, grammar has more than 1 derivation tree, which proves its ambiguity.

- Since grammar does not produce '$aabb$' so it not produce all strings with equal number of a's and b's. So false.

- Given grammar generate $(ab + ba)^*$ i.e., 'ab' and 'ba' in any order which is regular, so DCFL. PDA can be design for every DCFL. So true.

36. When L and $\bar{L}$ are recursively enumerable then L must be recursive language.

Since regular $\subseteq$ CFL $\subseteq$ CSL $\subseteq$ Recursive.

37. Given, $S \to aSa|bSa|a|b$

Language generated by above grammar is "the set of all odd length palindromes strings" i.e., $\{a, b, aba, aaa, ...\}$.

38. $S \to Aa$, $A \to Ba$, $B \to abc$

Given grammar is of "type3" i.e., of form

$$V \to V\,T^*,\ V \to T^*$$

39. Search trees like "B-tree search", "AVL search", will take logarithmic search time.

40. Recursive descent parser is an example of top down parser.

41. A top down parser generate left most derivation.

42. **Relative mode of addressing** is most relevant to writing position independent code i.e., by passing base address only we can reach to any address by the use of displacement.

43. A two-pass compiler does lexical analysis, syntax analysis, semantic analysis and intermediate code generation in 1st pass. Symbol table management and space allotment for literals is also done at first pass.

44. Peephole optimization is form of local optimization.

45. Given

Initial value of counting semaphore = 7

Number of wait operation = $20P$

Number of signal operation = xV

Final value of counting semaphore = 5

i.e., $\quad 5 = 7 - 20 + x$

$$x = 5 - 7 + 20$$
$$x = 25 - 7$$
$$x = 18$$

46. With single resource, other information like resource instances etc. is not given. So we can't say anything about deadlock.

47. System has,

3 processes let's say $P_1\,P_2$ and P_3.

Resources = 4.

Each process needs maximum of 2 unit (resource)

$P_1\ P_2\ P_3$

1   1   1

1

So deadlock never occur since the process which will be assigned last resource will complete its execution and will release those resources after execution.

48. Number of page faults when given

References pages: 1, 2, 4, 5, 2, 1, 2, 4

			4	4	4	1	1	1
2	2	2	2	2	2	2	2	2
1	1	1	1	5	5	5	5	4
Hit	HiL	Miss	Miss	Hit	Miss	Hit	Miss	

Number of page fault are 4.

49. Working set (t, k) is the set of pages used by the K-most recent memory references in the last f-times unit.

50. Virtual addresses = 32-bit

15	5	12

($\longleftarrow$ 32 bit $\longrightarrow$)

Page size = 4 KB = 2^{12} B

128 page table with 4 way associative.

$$= \frac{2^7}{2^2} = 2^5 \Rightarrow 5 \text{ bits for sets.}$$

So total bits for TAG

$$= 32 - (12 + 5)$$
$$= 32 - 17 = 15 \text{ bits}$$

51. For real time operating system pre-emptive scheduling is used.

52. Belady's Anamoly is generally observed in FIFO page replacement policy. With increase in the number of page frames, there is a possibility that the number of page faults also increases.

53. Consider the relation R with relation S

If R has m tuples and S has n tuple.

Maximum size of join = mn

Minimum size of join = 0 (when nothing in common)

54. Given relations, foreign key = d

R(a, b, c)   S($\underline{d}$, e, f)

Since foreign key is present in S. So insertion into R, does not cause any problem and deletion from S does not cause any violation. But insertion into S and deletion from R, can cause violation.

55. Lets assume a database 'Book'

Title	Price
ALGO	100
PDS	200
CD	300
CN	400
CO	500
DL	600
MATH	700

On execution of the query on given database output obtained will be the "title of five most expensive books" i.e., Math, DL, CO, CN and CD whose prices are more than 4 other books.

56. Goal for the design of the logical scheme include avoiding data inconsistency, being able to construct query easily and being able to access data efficiently.

57. Given relations

To calculate sum of all employee's salaries, we have to use aggregate function. So it cannot be expressed using basic relational algebra operation.

58. Trigger is the statement that is executed automatically by the system as a side effect of a modification of the database.

59. Given, block size = 1 k bytes, record painter = 7 byte

Structure of B^+ tree leaf node:

P(Key + Record pointer) + Block pointer $\leq$ Block size

$$P\,(7 + 9) + 6 \leq 1024 \text{ B}$$
$$16\,P \leq 1024 - 6$$
$$16\,P \leq 1018$$
$$P \leq 63.625$$

P will be 63 maximum.

60. Clustering index is defined on the fields which are of non-keys (i.e., values are repeated) and ordering type.

61. The extent to which the software can continue to operate correctly despite the introduction of invalid inputs is called robustness.

62. Functional requirement specify 'what' the system should do. None of the above is a functional requirement.

63. It is not concerned with hardware configuration for an application.

64. From the given table

Let the LOC for $L_1 = x$

The, LOC for $L_2 = 2x$

Given that; cost of project using L_1 = Cost of project using L_2

$\Rightarrow$ Development cost of L_1, + Maintenance cost of L_1 = Development cost of L_2 + Maintenance cost of L_2

$$\Rightarrow \quad \frac{x}{10000} \times 1000000 + 5 \times 100000$$
$$\Rightarrow \quad \frac{2x}{100000} \times 750000 + 5 \times 500000$$
$$\Rightarrow \quad 100x + 500000 = 150x + 250000$$
$$50x = 250000$$

$x = 5000$

$\therefore$ The LOC for project using L_1 = 5000

65. Effort is formulated $E = a(\text{KLOC})^b$

where $\qquad a = 2.2$

and $\qquad b = 1.5$

KLOC is given as 20000 LOC = 20 KLOC

$$E = 2.2\,(20)^{1.5}$$
$$= 196.77 \text{ person month.}$$

66. In spiral model of software development, the primary determinant is in selecting activity in each iteration is risk.

67. Bit stuffing refers to inserting 0 in user stream to differentiate it with a flag,

i.e., $\qquad$ flag = 1111111

user stream = 1111111011110

Output after bit stuffing 1111110011110

68. Dynamic routing protocol enable routers to dynamicaly discover and maintain routes between routers, when their is a change routing updates are distributed through flooding to other routers to share knowledge about current situation of network.

69. The ethernet CSMA/CD, the special bit sequence (JAM signal) is transmitted by media access management to handle collision.

70. From the given options DHCP network protocal allows hosts to dynamically get a unique IP number on each bootup. Since all other results in static assignment.

So DHCP is used.

71. Transmission delay

$$= \frac{\text{Length (frame or token)}}{\text{Bandwidth}}$$
$$= \frac{1}{10^7} = 1 \times 10^{-7} = 0.1\ \mu\text{sec}$$

Propagation speed = 200 meter/μsec

So 1 bit delay = 0.1 × 200 meter/μsec

$$= 20 \text{ mtr.}$$

72. Since 6 bit subnet number = 2^6 = 64

Usable subnets = 64 − 2 (one for network and one for broadcast) = 62 subnet.

Number of host = 2^{10}

$$= 1024 - 2 \text{ (DBA, network address)}$$
$$= 1022 \text{ hosts.}$$

73. Given message = 1100100

CRC polynomial = $x^3 + 1$ = 1001

```
1001)11001001000 (11010011
     1001
     1011
     1001
     0100
     0000
     1000
     1001
     0011
     0000
     0110
     0000
     1100
     1001
     1010
     1001
     011
```

So message should be 11001001011.

74. Since application layer does not have any restriction of size of data (maximum), it can send any size of data to transport layer.

75. Given data,

Propagation time = 25 msec

In 1 second it can send = 10^6 bits

So in 25 msec = $25 \times 10^{-3} \times 10^6$ = 25000 bits

1 frame = 1000 bits

Number of frame is 25000 bits

$$= \frac{25000 \text{ bits}}{1000 \text{ bits}} = 25 \text{ bits}$$

Hence, number of bits for sequence number

$$= [\log_2 25] = 5$$

76. HTML does not support user defined TAGs but XML supports.

77. Assuming hierarchical access:

$$= H_1 T_1 + (1 - H_1) H_1 (T_1 + T_2) + (1 - H_1)$$
$$(1 - H_2)(T_1 + T_2 + T_1)$$
$$= 0.8 \times 1 + (0.2)(0.9)(11) + (0.2 \times 0.1)(511)$$
$$= 13$$

Assuming simultaneous access:

$$= H_1 T_1 + (1 - H_1)H_2 T_2 + (1 - H_1)(1 - H_2)T_3$$
$$= 0.8 \times 1 + (0.2)(0.9) \times 10 + (0.2)(0.1) \times 500$$
$$= 12.6 \text{ nsec}$$

Both are present in options.

78. Table showing the derived class.

Access	Public	Protected	Private
Same class	Yes	Yes	Yes
Derived class	Yes	Yes	No
Outside class	Yes	No	No

79. Branch address is not known at compile time so all function call are not resolved at compile time. Because branch address are known at runtime in both C and C++ (in branch condition).

80. In DNS spoofing the user is cheated of the URL that he tried to access but he is redirected to a fake website with same URL (which look same as original website).

■■

SOLVED PAPER 2017
Computer Science

1. If A is a skew symmetric matrix then A^t is
   (a) Diagonal matrix (b) A
   (c) O (d) $-A$

2. Let A and B be any two arbitrary events, then, which one of the following is true?
   (a) $P(A \cap B) = P(A)\,P(B)$
   (b) $P(A \cup B) = P(A) + P(B)$
   (c) $P(A \mid B) = P(A \cap B)\,P(B)$
   (d) $P(A \cup B) \leq P(A) + P(B)$

3. Using Newton-Raphson method, a root correct to 3 decimal places of $x^3 - 3x - 5 = 0$.
   (a) 2.222 (b) 2.275
   (c) 2.279 (d) None of the above

4. What does a data dictionary will identify?
   (a) Field name (b) Field format
   (c) Field types (d) All of the above

5. Which of the following concurrency control protocol ensures both conflict and free from deadlock?
   (a) Time stamp ordering
   (b) 2 Phase locking
   (c) Both (a) and (b)
   (d) None of the above

6. ACID properties of a transactions are
   (a) Atomicity, consistency, isolation, database
   (b) Atomicity, consistency, isolation, durability
   (c) Atomicity, consistency, integrity, durability
   (d) Atomicity, consistency, integrity, database

7.

Employee	Department	OT_allowance
RAMA	Mechanical	5000
GOPI	Electrical	2000
SINDHU	Computer	4000
MAHESH	Civil	1500

   Which is the output of the following SQL query?

   select count(*) from

   ((select Employee, Department from Overtime_allowance) natural join

   (select department, OT_allowance from Overtime_allowance) as T);
   (a) 16 (b) 4
   (c) 8 (d) None of the above

8. Which symbol denote derived attributes in ER Model?
   (a) Double ellipse
   (b) Dashed ellipse
   (c) Squared ellipse
   (d) Ellipse with attribute name underlined

9. The symmetric difference of sets and $A = \{1, 2, 3, 4, 5, 6, 7, 8\}$ and $B = \{1, 3, 5, 6, 7, 8, 9\}$ is
   (a) $\{1, 3, 5, 6, 7, 8\}$ (b) $\{2, 4, 9\}$
   (c) $\{2, 4\}$ (d) $\{1, 2, 3, 4, 5, 6, 7, 8, 9\}$

10. The problem 3-SAT and 2-SAT are
   (a) both in P
   (b) both NP complete
   (c) NP-complete and in P respectively
   (d) undecidable and NP complete respectively

11. Given the following statements
   - S1: Every context-sensitive language L is recursive
   - S2: There exists a recursive language that is not context-sensitive

   Which statements are true?
   (a) Only S1 is correct
   (b) Only S2 is correct
   (c) Both S1 and S2 are not correct
   (d) Both S1 and S2 are correct

12. Which one of the following is FALSE?
   (a) There is a unique minimal DFA for every regular language
   (b) Every NFA can be converted to an equivalent PDA.
   (c) Complement of every context-free language is recursive.
   (d) Every nondeterministic PDA can be converted to an equivalent deterministic PDA.

13. In some programming language, an identifier is permitted to be a letter followed by any number of letters or digits. If L and D denote the sets of letters and digits respectively, which of the following expressions defines an identifier?
   (a) $(L + D)^+$ (b) $(L \cdot D)^*$
   (c) $L(L + D)^*$ (d) $L(L \cdot D)^*$

14. The recurrence relation that arises in relation with the complexity of binary search is:

(a) $T(n) = 2T\left(\dfrac{n}{2}\right) + k$, k is a constant

(b) $T(n) = T\left(\dfrac{n}{2}\right) + k$, k is a constant

(c) $T(n) = T\left(\dfrac{n}{2}\right) + \log n$

(d) $T(n) = T\left(\dfrac{n}{2}\right) + n$

15. Which one of the following in-place sorting algorithms needs the minimum number of swaps?

(a) Insertion Sort   (b) Quick Sort

(c) Heap Sort   (d) Selection Sort

16. Given two statements

I. Insertion of an element should be done at the last node of the circular list

II. Deletion of an element should be done at the last node of the circular list

(a) Both are true

(b) Both are false

(c) First is flase and second is true

(d) None of the above

17. Which of the following data structure is useful in traversing a given graph by breadth first search?

(a) Stack   (b) Queue

(c) List   (d) None of the above

18. How many 128×8 bit RAMs are required to design 32 K $\times 32$ bit RAM?

(a) 512   (b) 1024

(c) 128   (d) 32

19. The most appropriate matching for the following pairs:

X: Indirect Addressing   1. Loop

Y: Immediate Addressing   2. Pointers

Z: Auto Decrement Addressing   3. Constants

(a) X-3, Y-2, Z-1   (b) X-2, Y-3, Z-1

(c) X-3, Y-1, Z-2   (d) X-2, Y-1, Z-3

20. Which interrupt in 8085 Microprocessor is unmaskable?

(a) RST 5.5   (b) RST 7.5

(c) TRAP   (d) Both (a) and (b)

21. A cache memory needs an access time of 30 ns and main memory 150 ns, what is average access time of CPU (assume hit ratio = 80%)?

(a) 30 ns   (b) 30 ns

(c) 150 ns   (d) 70 ns

22. Which one of the following Boolean expressions is NOT a tautology?

(a) $((a \to b) \wedge (b \to c) \to (a \to c)$

(b) $(a \leftrightarrow c) \to (\sim b \to (a \wedge c))$

(c) $(a \wedge b \wedge c) \to (c \vee a)$

(d) $a \to (b \to a)$

23. What is the minimum number of two-input NAND gates used to perform the function of two-input OR gate?

(a) One   (b) Two

(c) Three   (d) Four

24. When two n-bit binary numbers are added the sum will contain at the most

(a) n bits   (b) $n + 2$ bits

(c) $n + 3$ bits   (d) $n + 1$ bits

25. The 2-input XOR has a high output only when the input values are

(a) low   (b) high

(c) same   (d) different

26. Advantage of synchronous sequential circuits over asynchronous one is:

(a) Lower hardware requirement

(b) Better noise immunity

(c) Faster operation

(d) All of the above

27. Physical topology of FDDI is?

(a) Bus   (b) Ring

(c) Star   (d) None of the above

28. In networking terminology UTP means

(a) Uniquitous teflon port

(b) Uniformly terminating port

(c) Unshielded twisted pair

(d) Unshielded T-connector port

29. The default subnet mask for a class B network can be

(a) 255.255.255.0   (b) 255.0.0.0

(c) 255.255.192.0   (d) 255.255.0.0

30. If there are n devices (nodes) in a network, what is the number of cable links required for a fully connected mesh and a star topology respectively

(a) $n(n-1)/2, n-1$ (b) $n, n-1$

(c) $n-1, n$ (d) $n-1, n(n-1)/2$

31. Which of the following protocol is used for transferring electronic mail messages from one machine to another?

(a) TELNET   (b) FTP

(c) SNMP   (d) SMTP

32. Which media access control protocol is used by IEEE 802.11 wireless LAN?

(a) CDMA   (b) CSMA/CA

(c) ALOHA   (d) None of the above

33. An Ethernet frame that is less than the IEEE 802.3 minimum length of 64 octets is called

(a) Short frame   (b) Small frame

(c) Mini frame   (d) Runt frame

34. Match with the suitable one:

List-I	**List-II**
A. Multicast group membership	1. Distance vector routing
B. Interior gateway protocol	2. IGMP
C. Exterior gateway protocol	3. OSPF
D. RIP	4. BGP

(a) A-2, B-3, C-4, D-1 (b) A-2, B-4, C-3, D-1

(c) A-3, B-4, C-1, D-2 (d) A-3, B-1, C-4, D-2

35. MD5 is a widely used hash function for producing hash value of

(a) 64 bits   (b) 128 bits

(c) 512 bits   (d) 1024 bits

36. Which protocol suite designed by IETF to provide security for a packet at the Internet layer?

(a) IPSec   (b) NetSec

(c) PacketSec   (d) SSL

37. Pretty Good Privacy (PGP) is used in:

(a) Browser security (b) FTP security

(c) Email security   (d) None of the above

38. What is WPA?

(a) wired protected access

(b) wi-fi protected access

(c) wired process access

(d) wi-fi process access

39. Estimation at software development effort for organic software in basic COCOMO is:

(a) $E = 2.0 \, (KLOC)^{1.05} \, PM$

(b) $E = 3.4 \, (KLOC)^{1.06} \, PM$

(c) $E = 2.4 \, (KLOC)^{1.05} \, PM$

(d) $E = 2.4 \, (KLOC)^{1.07} \, PM$

40. XPath is used to navigate through elements and attributes in

(a) XSL document

(b) XML document

(c) XHTML document

(d) XQuery document

41. What is the output of the C++ program?

```cpp
#include <iostream>
using namespace std;
void square(int *X){
    *X = (*X)++ * (*X);
}
void square (int *X, int *y){
    *X = (*X) * - - (*Y);
}
int main()
{
    int number = 30;
    square (& number, & number);
    cout << number;
    return 0;
}
```

(a) 910   (b) 920

(c) 870   (d) 900

42. Which of the following operator(s) cannot be overloaded?

(a) .(member Access or Dot operator)

(b) ?: (ternary or Conditional Operator)

(c) :: (Scope Resolution Operator)

(d) All of the above

43. Which of the following UML 2.0 diagrams capture behavioral aspects of a system?

(a) Use case diagram, Object diagram, Activity diagram and state machine diagram

(b) Use case diagram, Activity diagram and state machine diagram

(c) Object diagram, Communication Diagram, Timing diagram and Interaction diagram

(d) Object diagram, Composite structure diagram, package diagram and Deployment diagram

44. Which of the following is associated with objects?

(a) State   (b) Behavior

(c) Identity   (d) All of the above

45. Which of these is characteristic of RAID 5?

(a) Dedicated parity

(b) Double parity

(c) Hamming code parity

(d) Distributed parity

46. SATA is the abbreviation of

(a) Serial Advanced Technology Attachment

(b) Serial Advanced Technology Architecture

(c) Serial Advanced Technology Adapter

(d) Serial Advanced Technology Array

47. Capability Maturity Model (CMM) is the methodology to

(a) develop and refine an organization's software development process

(b) develop the software

(c) test the software

(d) All of the above

48. What problem is solved by Dijikstra banker' algorithm?

(a) Mutual exclusion

(b) Deadlock recovery

(c) Deadlock avoidance

(d) Cache coherence

49. The number of swappings needed to sort the numbers 8 , 22, 7, 9, 31, 5, 13 in ascending order using bubble sort is

(a) 11   (b) 12

(c) 13   (d) 10

50.

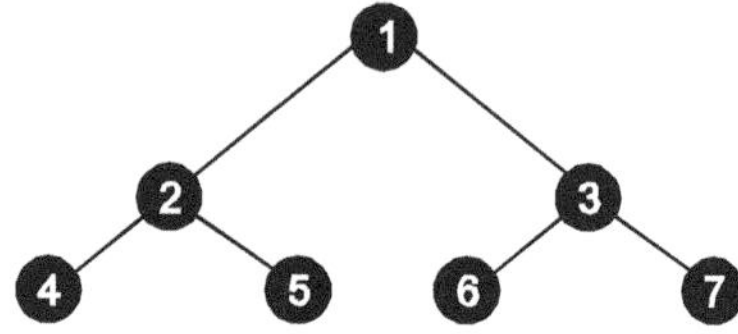

If the post order traversal gives ab − cd * + then the label of the nodes 1, 2, 3... will be

(a) +, −, *, a, b, c, d   (b) a, −, b, +, c, *, d

(c) a, b, c, d, −, *, +   (d) −, a, b, +, *, c, d

51. What is the output of the following program?

```
main ()
{
    int a = 10;
    if (fork() ==0))
    a++;
    printf("%d\n", a);
}
```

(a) 10 and 11   (b) 10

(c) 11   (d) 11 and 11

52. Given reference to the following pages by a program

 0,9,0,1,8,1,8,7,8,7,1,2,8,2,7,8,2,3,8,3

How many page faults will occur if the program has three page frames available to it and uses an optimal replacement?

(a) 7   (b) 8

(c) 9   (d) None of the above

53. In a doubly linked list the number of pointers affected for an insertion operation will be

(a) 4

(b) 0

(c) 1

(d) Depends on the nodes of doubly linked list

54. Consider the following function

```
void swap (int a, int b)
{
    int temp;
    temp = a;
    a = b;
    b = temp;
}
```

In order to exchange the values of two variables x and y

(a) call swap (x, y)

(b) call swap $(\& x, \& y)$

(c) swap (x, y) cannot be used as it does not return any value

(d) swap (x, y) cannot be used as the parameters are passed by value

55. What does the following C-statement declare?

int (*f) (int *);

(a) A function that takes an integer pointer as argument and returns an integer

(b) A function that takes an integer as argument and returns an integer pointer

(c) A pointer to a function that takes an integer pointer as argument and returns an integer

(d) A function that takes an integer pointer as argument and returns a function pointer

56. Mutual exclusion problem occurs

(a) between two disjoint processes that do not interact

(b) among processes that share resources

(c) among processes that do not use the same resource

(d) between two processes that uses different resources of different machine

57. $(1217)_8$ is equivalent to

(a) $(1217)_{16}$ (b) $(028F)_{16}$

(c) $(2297)_{10}$ (d) $(0B17)_{16}$

58. Which of the following is not a life cycle model?

(a) Spiral model

(b) Prototyping model

(c) Waterfall model

(d) Capability maturity model

59. The best data structure to check whether an arithmetic expression has balanced parenthesis is a:

(a) Queue

(b) Stack

(c) Tree

(d) List

60. The cyclomatic complexity of each of the modules A and B shown below is 10. What is the cyclo-matic complexity of the sequential integration shown on the right hand side?

(a) 19

(b) 21

(c) 20

(d) 10

61. In software maintenance tackling the changes in the hardware or software environment where the software works, is

(a) Corrective maintenance

(b) Perfective maintenance

(c) Adaptive maintenance

(d) Preventive maintenance

62. What will be the output of the following C code?

```c
#include <stdio. h>
main()
{
    int i;
    for (i=0; i<5; 1++)
    {
        int i=10;
        printf("%d" , i);
        i++;
    }
    return 0;
}
```

(a) 10 11 12 13 14

(b) 10 10 10 10 10

(c) 0 1 2 3 4

(d) Compilation error

63. What does the following program do when the input is unsigned 16 bit integer?

```c
#include <stdio.h>
main () {
    unsigned int num;
    int i;
    scanf("%u", &num);
    for (i = 0; i < 16 ; i++) {
    printf ("%d", (num <<i & 1 << 15) ? 1 : 0);
    }
}
```

(a) It prints all even bits from num

(b) It prints all odd bits from num

(c) It prints binary equivalent of num

(d) None of above

64. What is the output of the following program?

```c
#include < stdio.h>
int (tmp = 20;
main ()
{
    printf ("%d", tmp);
    func();
    printf (" %d", tep);
}
func ()
{
    static int tmp = 10;
    printf ("%d", tmp);
}
```

(a) 20 10 10   (b) 20 10 20

(c) 20 20 20   (d) 10 10 10

65. Which product metric gives the measure of the average length of words and sentence in documents?

(a) SCI number   (b) Cyclomatic complexity

(c) LOC   (d) Fog index

66. Consider the disk system with 100 cylinders. The request to access the cylinders occur in the following sequence.

4, 37, 10, 7, 19, 73, 2, 15, 6, 20

Assuming the head is currently at cylinder 50 what is the time taken to satisfy all requests if it takes 1 ms to move from one cylinder to adjacent one and shortest seek ime first algorithm is used.

(a) 95 ms   (b) 19 ms

(c) 233 ms   (d) 276 ms

67. A B-Tree used as an index for a large database table has four levels including the root node. If a new key is inserted in this index, then the maximum number of nodes that could be newly created in the process are

(a) 5   (b) 4

(c) 3   (d) 2

68. A critical region

(a) is apiece of code which only one process executes at a time

(b) is a region prone to deadlock

(c) is a piece of code which only a finite number of processes execute

(d) is found only in windows NT operating system

69. Choose the equivalent prefix form of the following expression

(a+(b-c))*((d-e)/(f+g-h))

(a) *+a-bc/-de-+fgh   (b) *+a-bc-/de-+fgh

(c) *+a-bc/-ed-+fgh   (d) *+ab-c/-de-+fgh

70. We use malloc and calloc for:
   (a) Dynamic memory allocation
   (b) Static memory allocation
   (c) Both dynamic memory allocation and static memory allocation
   (d) None of these

71. At a particular time the value of counting semaphore is 10. It will become 7 after:
   (a) 3 V operations
   (b) 3 P operations
   (c) 5 V operations and 2 P operations
   (d) 2 V operations and 5 P operations

72. The Linux command mknod myfifo b 4 16
   (a) will create a character device if user is root
   (b) will create a named pipe FIFO if user is root
   (c) will create a block device if user is root
   (d) None of these

73. Which of the following statement is true?
   (a) Hard real time OS has less jitter than soft real time OS
   (b) Hard real time OS has more jitter than soft real time OS
   (c) Hard real time OS has equal jitter as soft real time OS
   (d) None of the above

74. Which of these is a super class of all errors and exceptions in the Java language?
   (a) Runtime Exceptions
   (b) Throwable
   (c) Catchable
   (d) None of the above

75. Choose the most appropriate HTML tag in the following to create a numbered list
   (a) <dl}   (b) <list>
   (c) <ul>   (d) <ol>

76. Which of the following algorithms solves the all pair shortest path problem?
   (a) Prim's algorithm
   (b) Dijkstra's algorithm
   (c) Bellman ford algorithm
   (d) Floyd warshalls algorithm

77. If L and P are two recursively enumerable languages then they are not closed under
   (a) Kleene star L* of L
   (b) Intersection $L \cap P$
   (c) Union $L \cup P$
   (d) Set difference

78. In the context of modular software design, which one of the following combinations is desirable?
   (a) High cohesion and high coupling
   (b) High cohesion and low coupling
   (c) Low cohesion and high coupling
   (d) Low cohesion and low coupling

79. The output of a lexical analyzer is
   (a) A parse tree
   (b) Intermediate code
   (c) Machine code
   (d) A stream of tokens

80. The time complexity of computing the transitive closure of a binary relation on a set of n elements is known to be
   (a) $O(n \log n)$ (b) $O(n^{3/2})$
   (c) $O(n^3)$ (d) $O(n)$

ANSWERS

1. (d)	**2.** (d)	**3.** (c)	**4.** (d)	**5.** (a)	**6.** (b)	**7.** (b)	**8.** (b)	**9.** (b)	**10.** (c)
11. (d)	**12.** (d)	**13.** (c)	**14.** (b)	**15.** (d)	**16.** (b)	**17.** (b)	**18.** (b)	**19.** (b)	**20.** (c)
21. (a)	**22.** (b)	**23.** (c)	**24.** (d)	**25.** (d)	**26.** (b)	**27.** (b)	**28.** (c)	**29.** (d)	**30.** (a)
31. (d)	**32.** (b)	**33.** (d)	**34.** (a)	**35.** (b)	**36.** (a)	**37.** (c)	**38.** (b)	**39.** (c)	**40.** (b)
41. (c)	**42.** (d)	**43.** (b)	**44.** (d)	**45.** (d)	**46.** (a)	**47.** (a)	**48.** (c)	**49.** (d)	**50.** (a)
51. (a)	**52.** (a)	**53.** (*)	**54.** (d)	**55.** (c)	**56.** (b)	**57.** (b)	**58.** (d)	**59.** (b)	**60.** (a)
61. (c)	**62.** (b)	**63.** (c)	**64.** (b)	**65.** (d)	**66.** (b)	**67.** (a)	**68.** (a)	**69.** (a)	**70.** (a)
71. (*)	**72.** (c)	**73.** (a)	**74.** (b)	**75.** (d)	**76.** (d)	**77.** (d)	**78.** (b)	**79.** (d)	**80.** (c)

EXPLANATIONS

1. For symmetric matrix, the condition : $A^t = A$ where t= transpose of matrix

   For skew Symmetric matrix , the condition: $A^t = -A$

2. It is true if events are independent;

   In general, $P(A \cap B) = P(A|B) * P(B)$.

   If A and B are independent, then knowing B doesn't affect probability of A, hence $P(A|B) = P(A)$

   So $P(A \cap B) = P(A) * P(B)$ when A and B are independent

   It is true only if events are mutually exclusive i.e. $P(A \cap B) = 0$

   It is false everywhere

   It is always true as

   $$P(A \cup B) = P(A) + P(B) - P(A \cap B)$$

   Since, $P(A \cup B) \geq 0, P(A \cup B) \leq P(A) + P(B)$

3. $f(x) = x^3 - 3x - 5$ and $f'(x) = 3x^2 - 3$, beginning with $x_0 = 3$, the iterates are given in Table 2 which shows a stop at iteration no. 5 since the error is $x_5 - x_4 < 10^{-5}$ resulting in a root of $x^* = 2.27902$, see Figure 2.

Table 2: Interations for Example–2				
Interation no.	$x_n = 3$	$f(x_n)$	$f'(x_n)$	x_{n+1} using (1)
1	$x_n = 0$	13	24	2.45833
2	2.4583	2.48165	15.13016	2.29431
3	2.2943	0.19399	12.79158	2.27914
4	2.2791	0.00153	12.58344	2.27902
5	2.279	1.5E-05	12.5818	2.27902

   Here, $\qquad f(x) = x^3 - 3x - 5$

   $\therefore \qquad\qquad f'(x) = 3x^2 - 3$

   Newton- Raphson method formula is

   $$x_{n+1} = x_n - \frac{f(xn)}{f'(xn)}$$

   $$x_{n+1} = x_n - \frac{x_n^3 - 3x_n - 5}{3x_n^2 - 2}$$

   $$n = 0, 1, 2 \qquad\qquad ...(1)$$

   Let $\qquad\qquad x_0 = 3$

   $\qquad\qquad f(x_0) = f(3)$

   $\qquad\qquad\qquad = (3)^3 - 3(3) - 5$

   $\qquad\qquad\qquad = 27 - 9 - 5$

   $\qquad\qquad\qquad = 13$

   and $\qquad\qquad f'(x_0) = f'(3)$

   $\qquad\qquad\qquad = 3(3)^2 - 3 = 27 - 3 = 24$

   Putting n = 0 in (1); we get

   $$x_1 = 3 - \left(\frac{13}{24}\right)$$

   $$= \frac{59}{24} = 2.458$$

4. A data dictionary is a file or a set of files that contains a database's metadata. The data dictionary contains records about other objects in the database, such as data ownership, data relationships to other objects, and other data. The data dictionary is a crucial component of any relational database.

   This typically includes the names and descriptions of various tables (records or Entities) and their contents (fields) plus additional details, like the type and length of each data element.

5. Time stamp and 2PL both ensure CS, but only timestamp is deadlock free

   Timestamp based Protocol ensures freedom from Deadlock as no transaction ever waits, transitions are simply rolled back and started afresh with new Timestamp.

6. To maintain integrity of the database , the transactions follow ACID properties:

   A - Atomicity, the Recovery management component of DBMS software is responsible for atomicity.

   C - Consistency, the Database Administrator or Database Creator takes care of consistency.

   I - Isolation, taken care by the concurrency control component of DBMS software.

   D - Durability, again the Recovery management component of DBMS software responsible for this.

7. Select Emp, Dept from overtime – Allowance;

Emp	Dept	Dept	OT
RAMA	Mechanical	Mechanical	5000
GOPI	Electrical	Electrical	2000
SINDHU	Computer	Computer	4000
MAHESH	Civil	Civil	1500

   Same table will be printed after Applying Notural Join No. of Rows by count f^n will return = 4 (B) will be correct.

8.

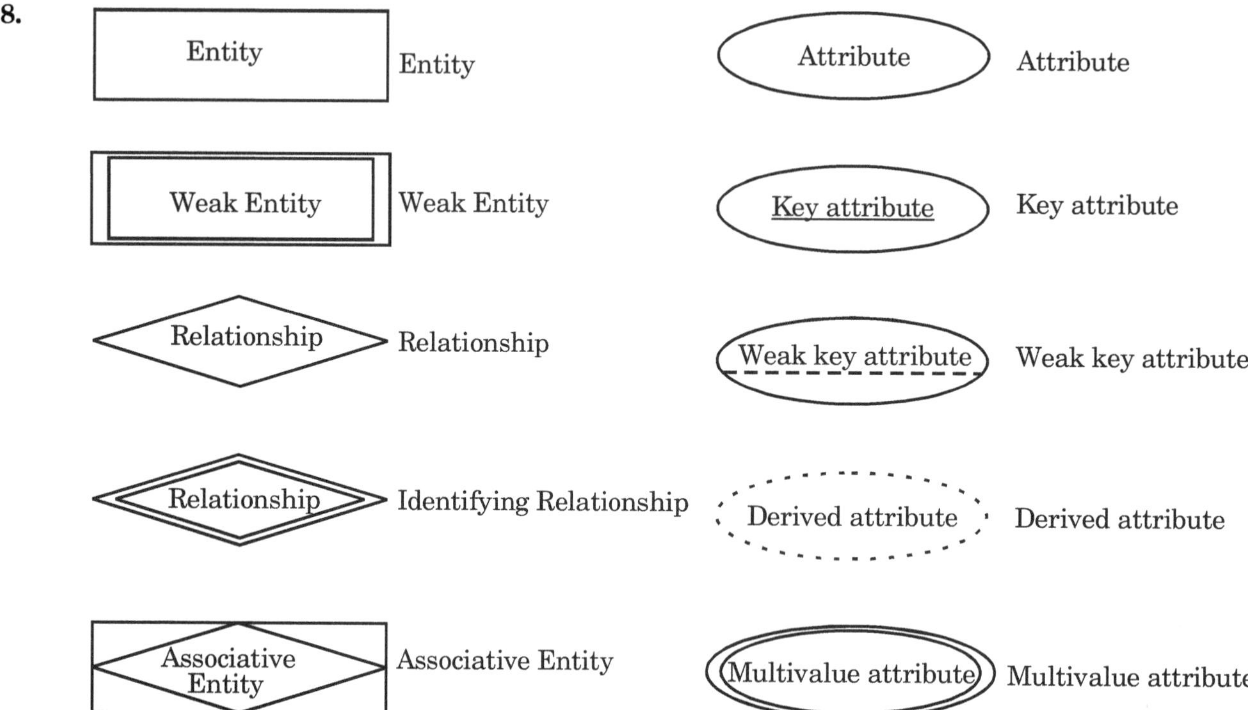

9. A = {1,2, 3,4, 5, 6, 7, 8} **And** B = {1, 3, 5, 6, 7,8,9}

A (symmetric difference) B = Elements which are in A but not in B ∪∪ Elements which are in B but not in A

$$= (A - B) \cup \cup (B - A)$$

$$= \{2, 4\} \cup \cup \{9\} = \{2, 4, 9\}$$

Option B is correct.

10. With 2-SAT, one can only express implications of the form a ⇒ b, where a and b are literals. That is, every 2-clause $I_1 V l_2$ can be understood as a pair of implications: $\neg l_1 \Rightarrow l_2$ and $\neg l_2 \Rightarrow l_1$.

If a is set to true, b must be true as well.

If b is set to false, a must be false as well.

Such implications are straightforward:

There is only 1 possibility, there is no room for case-multiplication.

Every possible implication chain can be followed to check if one ever derive both ¬l from l and l from ¬l : if it is done for some l, then the 2-SAT formula is unsatisfiable, otherwise it is satisfiable. It is the case that the number of possible implication chains is polynomially bounded in the size of the input formula.

With 3-SAT, implications of the form a ⇒ bVc can be expressed, where a, b and c are literals. Now;: if a is set to true, then either b or c must be true, but which one?

There are 2 possibilities, so case-multiplication becomes possible, and the combinatorial explosion arises.

In other words, 3-SAT is able to express the presence of more than one possibility, while 2-SAT doesn't have such ability. It is precisely such presence of more than one possibility (2 possibilities in case of 3-SAT, k–1 possibilities in case of k-SAT) that causes the typical combinatorial explosion of NP-complete problems.

11. Both are correct since context sensitive is a proper subset of recursive languages.

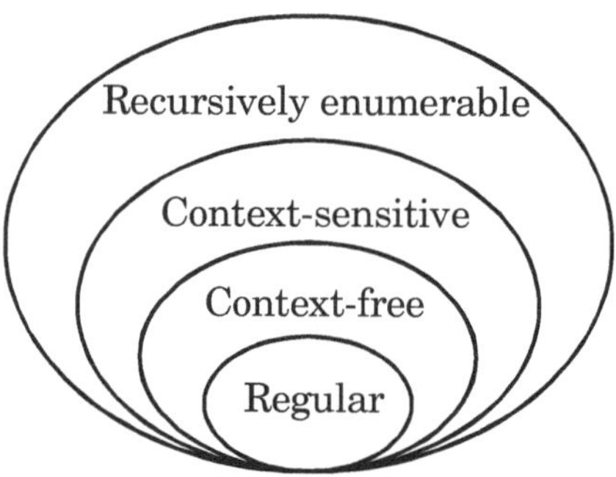

12. Deterministic PDA cannot handle languages or grammars with ambiguity, but NDPDA can handle languages with ambiguity and any context-free grammar. Also, The Power of NPDA is greater than DPDA

So every nondeterministic PDA cannot be converted to an equivalent deterministic PDA.

13. It has to be started by a letter followed by any number of letters (or) digits.

L(L + D)*

14. It is B. searching for only one half of the list. leading to T(n/2)+ constant time in comparing and finding mid element.

The time complexity of Binary Search can be written as: T(n) = T(n/2) + constant

15. Selection sort because in selection the maximum swaps which can take place are O(n) because we pick up an element an find the minimum (in case of forward sorting) from the next index till the end of array and then perform the swap hence O(n) whereas in all other algos the swaps are greater (considering Worst-Case scenario)

16. Here both statements are correct only when they don't mention the word " should be " in question.

Just they ask those 2 operations should be done at respective positions make both statements false,

"Insertion of an element should be done at the last node of the circular list = = True , it can be possible at last node .

"Deletion of an element should be done at the last node of the circular list = = True , it can also be possible at last node

That makes B is correct option

17. Breadth-first search uses a Queue data structure. Queue is used to implement traversal in Breadth First Search.

Stack is used to implement traversal in Depth First Search.

18. Number of RAM = (32 * K * 32) / 128 * 8

$$= 2^5 * 2^{10} * 2^5 / 2^7 * 2^3$$

$$= 2^{20} / 2^{10}$$

$$= 1024$$

19. In **Indirect addressing mode** the instruction does not have the address of the data to be operated on,but the instruction points where the address is stored(it is indirectly specifying the address of memory location where the data is stored or to be stored)

In **immediate addressing mode** the data is to be used is immediately given in instruction itself;so it deals with constant data.

In **Autodecrement addressing mode**, Before determining the effective address, the value in the base register is decremented by the size of the data item which is to be accessed.

Within a loop, this addressing mode can be used to step backwards through all the elements of an array or vector.

20. There are five interrupt input TRAP,RST 75,SRT 65,RST 55 and IWTR.

TRAP is a non maskable interrupt, that is, it cannot be disabled by an instruction

RST75,65,55 and INTR are maskable interrupt i.e. they can be enabled or disabled by software.

21. Effective Memory Access Time

$$= \text{Cache hit} * \text{Cache access time}$$
$$+ \text{Cache miss (Cache miss Penalty}$$
$$+ \text{memory Access time)}$$
$$= 0.8(30) + (1 - 0.8)(30 + 150) \text{ ns}$$
$$= 24 + 0.2(180) \text{ ns}$$
$$= 24 + 36 \text{ ns} = 60 \text{ ns.}$$

22. A. $((a \to b) \wedge (b \to c)) \to (a \to c)$

$\equiv ((\sim a \vee b) \wedge (\sim b \vee c)) \vee (\sim a \vee c)$

$\equiv \sim ((\sim a \vee b) \wedge (\sim b \vee c)) \vee (\sim a \vee c)$

$\equiv ((a \wedge \sim b) \vee (b \wedge \sim c)) \vee (\sim a \vee c)$

$\equiv (\sim a \vee (a \wedge \sim b)) \vee ((b \wedge \sim c) \vee c)$

$\equiv ((\sim a \vee a) \wedge (\sim a \vee \sim b)) \vee ((b \vee c) \wedge (\sim c \vee c))$

$\equiv (T \wedge (\sim a \vee \sim b)) \vee ((b \vee c) \wedge T)$

$\equiv \sim a \vee (\sim b \vee b) \vee c$

$\equiv \sim a \vee T \vee c$

$\equiv T$

B. $(a \leftrightarrow c) \to (b \to (a \wedge c))$

$\equiv ((a \to c) \wedge (c \to a)) \to ((\sim b \to (a \wedge c))$

$\equiv \sim ((\sim a \vee c) \wedge (\sim c \vee a)) \vee ((b \vee (a \wedge c))$

$\equiv \sim ((a \wedge c)(\sim a \wedge \sim c)) \vee ((b \vee (a \wedge c))$

$\equiv ((a \wedge \sim c) \vee (\sim a \wedge c)) \vee ((b \vee (a \wedge c))$

$\equiv ((a \wedge \sim c) \vee c(\sim a \wedge a)) \vee b$

$\equiv ((a \wedge \sim c) \vee c \vee b$

$\equiv a \vee b \vee c$

C. $(a \wedge b \wedge c) \to (c \vee a)$

$\equiv \sim (a \wedge b \wedge c) \vee (c \vee a)$

$\equiv \sim a \sim b \sim c \vee c \vee a$

$\equiv (a \vee \sim a) \vee \sim b \vee (\sim c \vee c)$

$\equiv T \vee \sim b \vee T$

$\equiv T$

D. $a \to (b \to a)$

$\equiv \sim a \vee (\sim b \vee a)$

$\equiv (\sim a \vee a) \vee \sim b$

$\equiv T \vee \sim b$

$\equiv T$

23. Need only 3 NAND Gate : A+B = ((A + B)')'
= (A' .B')'

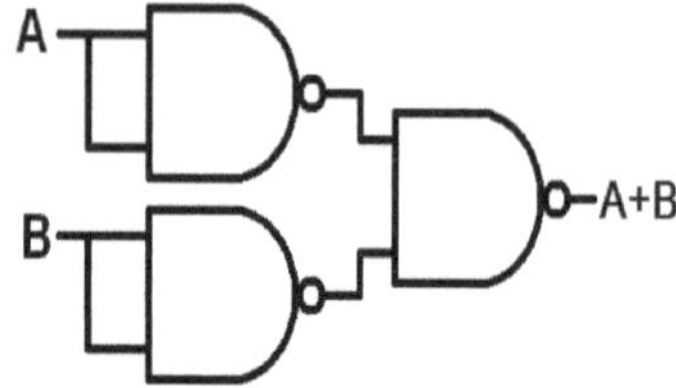

24. At some point in addition of two n-bit numbers when two bit are added we inurn add three bits.

First bit is the bit from the first operand, the second bit is the bit from the second operand and then third bit is the carry bit resulted due to addition of bits at previous place value.

Let the nth bit of operands including the carry bit (obtained from addition of bits at previous place value) be 11 so as to get the maximum sum. In such a case the nth bit addition will give 11, where the most significant bit is carry bit but ultimately become the most significant bit of final result. Thereby increasing the number of bit of result by just one.

Also, the result of addition will not have more than $(n+1)$ bits. For some value of n perform addition with $2n - 1$(largest n-bit binary number) as its both the operands and see if the result you get is of $(n+1)$ bits or not.

25.

Inputs		Outputs
X	Y	Z
0	0	0
0	1	1
1	0	1
1	1	0

Here High output is attained when X and Y are Different.

27. Fiber distributed data interface (FDDI), which is an optical data communication standard used for long distance networks provides communication with fiber optic lines up to 200 kilometers at a speed of 100 megabit per second (Mbps). FDDI has dual primary and secondary communication rings. The primary ring works alongside the network, and the secondary ring remains idle and available for backup.

28. UTP means Unshielded Twisted Pair: Unshielded twisted pair (UTP) is a ubiquitous type of copper cabling used in telephone wiring and local area networks (LANs). There are five types of UTP cables -- identified with the prefix CAT, as in category.By -- each supporting a different amount of bandwidth.

29. (There are total 4 octets which contains network and hosts)

Network and host are divided according to IPV4 classes:

Classes are : A,B,C, D(MULTICAST/BROADCAST), E(RESERVE FOR EXPERIMENTAL PURPOSE)

N:H:H:H ---A

N:N:H:H---B

N:N:N:H---C

30. Mesh topology: every computer in the network has a connection to each of the other computers in that network. This specific topology uses the most cables, however it is the system that is less likely to fail or experience any faults.

The number of connections in this network can be calculated using the following formula (n is the number of computers in the network): n(n–1)/2

Star Topology: This is the only system that uses a central hub to connect to all the computers. The cables provided will travel from each computer to the hub and the network will be powered from the central device.

1 node is connected to remaining nodes and the are (n–1) remaining nodes which required : (n–1) cables

31. SMTP : simple mail transfer protocol

SMTP (Simple Mail Transfer Protocol) is a TCP/IP protocol used in sending and receiving e-mail. However, since it is limited in its ability to queue messages at the receiving end, it is usually used with one of two other protocols, POP3 or IMAP, that let the user save messages in a server mailbox and download them periodically from the server.

Users use a program that uses SMTP for sending e-mail and either POP3 or IMAP for receiving e-mail.

32. The IEEE 802.11 MAC protocol is a carrier sense multiple access protocol with collision avoidance (CSMA/CA).

CSMA/CA can optionally be supplemented by the exchange of a Request to Send (RTS) packet sent by the sender S, and a Clear to Send (CTS) packet sent by the intended receiver R. Thus alerting all nodes within range of the sender, receiver or both, to not transmit for the duration of the main transmission. This is known as the IEEE 802.11 RTS/CTS exchange. Implementation of RTS/CTS helps to partially solve the hidden node problem that is often found in wireless networking

33. A runt frame is an Ethernet frame that is less than the IEEE 802.3's minimum length of 64 octets. Runt frames are most commonly caused by collisions; other possible causes are a malfunctioning network card, buffer underrun, duplex mismatch or software issues.

34. (A) Multicast group membership IGMP

(B) Interior gateway protocol OSPF

(C) Exterior gateway protocol BGP

(D) RIP Distance vector routing

The **Internet Group Management Protocol (IGMP)** is a communications protocol used by hosts and adjacent routers on IPv4 networks to establish multicast group memberships. IGMP is an integral part of IP multicast.

An **IGP (Interior Gateway Protocol)** is a protocol for exchanging routing information between gateways (hosts with routers) within an autonomous network (for example, a system of corporate local area networks). The routing information can then be used by the Internet Protocol (IP) or other network protocols to specify how to route transmissions.

There are two commonly used IGPs: the Routing Information Protocol (RIP) and the Open Shortest Path First (OSPF) protocol

Exterior Gateway Protocol (EGP) is a protocol for exchanging routing information between two neighbor gateway hosts (each with its own router) in a network of autonomous systems. EGP is commonly used between hosts on the Internet to exchange routing table information. The routing table contains a list of known routers, the addresses they can reach, and a cost metric associated with the path to each router so that the best available route is chosen. Each router polls its neighbor at intervals between 120 to 480 seconds and the neighbor responds by sending its complete routing table. EGP-2 is the latest version of EGP. A more recent exterior gateway protocol, the Border Gateway Protocol (BGP), provides additional capabilities.

RIP (Routing Information Protocol) is a dynamic, distance vector routing protocol based around the Berkely BSD application routed and was developed for smaller IP based networks.

35. The MD5 algorithm is a widely used hash function producing a 128-bit hash value. Although MD5 was initially designed to be used as a cryptographic hash function, it has been found to suffer from extensive vulnerabilities. ... The abbreviation "MD" stands for "Message Digest."

36. In computing, Internet Protocol Security (IPsec) is a network protocol suite that authenticates and encrypts the packets of data sent over a network. IPsec includes protocols for establishing mutual authentication between agents at the beginning of the session and negotiation of cryptographic keys for use during the session.

IPsec is an end-to-end security scheme operating in the Internet Layer of the Internet Protocol Suite, while some other Internet security systems in widespread use, such as Transport Layer Security (TLS) and Secure Shell (SSH), operate in the upper layers at the Transport Layer (TLS) and the Application layer (SSH). Hence, only IPsec protects all application traffic over an IP network. IPsec can automatically secure applications at the IP layer.

37. Pretty Good Privacy (PGP) encryption program provides cryptographic privacy and authentication for data communication. PGP is used for signing, encrypting, and decrypting texts, e-mails, files, directories, and whole disk partitions and to increase the security of e-mail communications

38. Wi-Fi Protected Access (WPA) and Wi-Fi Protected Access II (WPA2) are two security protocols and security certification programs developed by the Wi-Fi Alliance to secure wireless computer networks.

39. Basic COCOMO model takes the form:

$$E = a_b (KLOC)^{b_b}$$

$D = c_b (E)^{d_b}$ where E is effort applied in Person-Months, and D is the development time in months

Software Project	a_b	b_b	c_b	d_b
Organic	2	1.05	2.5	0.38
Semidetached	3.0	1.12	2.5	0.35
Embedded	3.6	1.20	2.5	0.32

(i) Organic mode:

E = 2.4 (KLOC) 1.05 PM

40. XPath is defined as XML path language. It is a syntax or language for finding any element on the web page using XML path expression.

41. Due to function overloading concept support in C++, it will call the 2nd square function.

Moreover, it is passed by reference So $30 \times 29 = 870$ will reflect in the main function

42. A ternary operator has the following form,

exp1 ? exp2 : exp3

The expression exp1 will be evaluated always. Execution of exp2 and exp3 depends on the outcome of exp1. If the outcome of exp1 is non-zero exp2 will be evaluated, otherwise exp3 will be evaluated.

Side Effects:

Any side effects of exp1 will be evaluated and updated immediately before executing exp2 or exp3. In other words, there is sequence point after the evaluation of condition in the ternary expression. If either exp2 or exp3 have side effects, only one of them will be evaluated.

Return Type:

It is another interesting fact. The ternary operator has return type. The return type depends on exp2, and convertibility of exp3 into exp2 as per usual\overloaded conversion rules. If they are not convertible, the compiler throws an error. See the examples below,

The following program compiles without any error. The return type of ternary expression is expected to be float (as that of exp2) and exp3 (i.e. literal zero - int type) is implicitly convertible to float.

```
#include <iostream>
using namespace std;
int main()
{
    int test = 0;
    float fvalue = 3.111f;
    cout << (test ? fvalue : 0) << endl;
    return 0;
}
```

43. UML 2.0 diagrams capture behavioral aspects of a system :

1. Activity diagram
2. Communication Diagram
3. Interaction diagram
4. state machine diagram
5. Timing diagram
6. use case diagram

44. An entity that has state and behavior is known as an object e.g. chair, bike, marker, pen, table, car etc. It can be physical or logical (tangible and intangible). The example of intangible object is banking system.

An object has three characteristics:

O state: represents data (value) of an object.

O behavior: represents the behavior (functionality) of an object such as deposit, withdraw etc.

O identity: Object identity is typically implemented via a unique ID. The value of the ID is not visible to the external user. But, it is used internally by the JVM to identify each object uniquely.

45. The parity data are not written to a fixed drive, they are spread across all drives. Using the parity data, the computer can recalculate the data of one of the other data blocks, should those data no longer be available. That means a RAID 5 array can withstand a single drive failure without losing data or access to data

46. Serial Advanced Technology Attachment Serial ATA (Serial Advanced Technology Attachment or SATA) is a standard for connecting and transferring data from hard disk drives (HDDs) to computer systems. As its name implies, SATA is based on serial signaling technology, unlike Integrated Drive Electronics (IDE) hard drives that use parallel signaling.

47. The SEI capability maturity model initiative is an attempt to improve software quality by improving the process by which software is developed.

The Capability Maturity Model (CMM) is a methodology used to develop and refine an organization's software development process. The model describes a five-level evolutionary path of increasingly organized and systematically more mature processes

48. The Banker's algorithm, sometimes referred to as avoidance algorithm and Deadlock algorithm, was developed by Edsger Dijkstra (another of Dijkstra's algorithms!). It tests the safety of allocation of predetermined maximum possible resources and then makes states to check the deadlock condition

For the banker's algorithm to work, it should know three things:

1. How much of each resource each person could maximum request [MAX]
2. How much of each resource each person currently holds [Allocated]
3. How much of each resource is available in the system for each person [Available]

So we need MAX and REQUEST.

If REQUEST is given MAX = ALLOCATED + REQUEST

NEED = MAX - ALLOCATED

A resource can be allocated only for a condition.

REQUEST<= AVAILABLE or else it waits until resources are available.

Let 'n' be the number of processes in the system and 'm' be the number of resource types.

- Available - It is a 1D array of size 'm'. Available [j] = k means there are k occurrences of resource type Rj.
- Maximum - It is a 2D array of size 'm*n' which represents maximum demand of a section. Max[i,j] = k means that a process i can maximum demand 'k' amount of resources.
- Allocated - It is a 2D array of size 'm*n' which represents the number of resources allocated to each process. Allocation [i,j] =k means that a process is allocated 'k' amount of resources.
- Need - 2D array of size 'm*n'. Need [i,j] = k means a maximum resource that could be allocated.

$$\text{Need } [i,j] = \text{Max } [i,j] - \text{Allocation}[i,j]$$

49. Answer is 10. All swaps are in following order:

8,7,22,9,31,5,13
8,7,9,22,31,5,13
8,7,9,22,5,31,13
8,7,9,22,5,13,31
7,8,9,22,5,13,31
7,8,9,5,22,13,31
7,8,9,5,13,22,31
7,8,5,9,13,22,31
7,5,8,9,13,22,31
5,7,8,9,13,22,31

50. PostOrder Traversal of the given tree gives the output: 4 5 2 6 7 3 1.

Comparing the output with a b - c d * + , and making one-to-one correspondence with 4 5 2 6 7 3 1 , we get

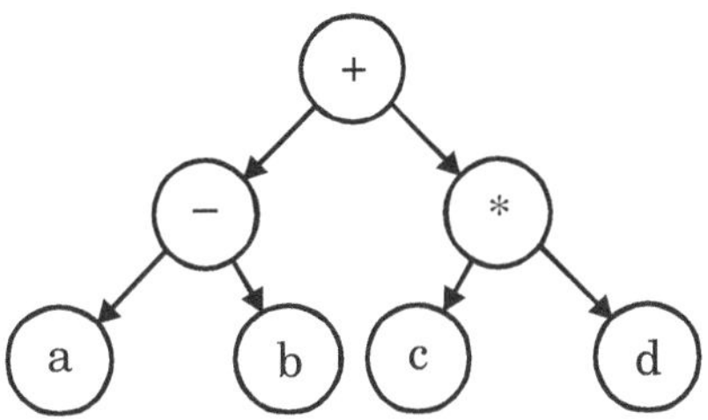

51. call fork() is used to create processes. It takes no arguments and returns a process ID. The purpose of fork() is to create a new process, which becomes the child process of the caller. After a new child process is created, both processes will execute the next instruction following the fork() system call.

In given question, for parent process fork call will return pid which will make if condition false. Hence parent process will print 10

Child process will execute next instruction i.e. a++ because in child process if-condition is not tested. Execution starts from next instruction. So it will print 11

Answer should be A

52.

0	9	0	1	8	1	8	7	8	7	1	2	8	2	7	8	2	3	8	3
			1	1	1	1	1	1	1	1	2	2	2	2	2	2	2	2	2
	9	9	9	9	9	9	7	7	7	7	7	7	7	7	7	7	3	3	3
0	0	0	0	8	8	8	8	8	8	8	8	8	8	8	8	8	8	8	8
F	F	H	F	F	H	H	F	H	H	F	H	H	H	H	H	H	F	H	H

so total no. Of page fault = 7

53. For insertions in the middle of the list, to splice in a new node as follows:

A --- B

^^ splice M in here

A.next = M

M.prev = A

B.prev = M

M.next = B

Hence four pointer assignments take place. However, if the insertion be at the head or tail, then only two pointer assignments would be needed:

TAIL (insert M afterward)

TAIL.next = M

M.prev = TAIL

54. **Option A** will not swap the values because it is passed by value...

Option B will not swap the value

void swap(int a, int b) in which arguments will not take address because its value not pointer

Option C is false, given reason is wrong

Option D is correct. We can't use swap(x,y) swap(x,y) because it is pass value function call which will not swap the values

55. int (*a) (int) in C, is as a variable of a pointer for a function.

If it is preceded with typedef it's a function pointer type:

Typedef int (*my_function_type)(int);

An equivalent definition may be on other languages something like:

a: (int) => int

56. A mutual exclusion (mutex) is a program object that prevents simultaneous access to a shared resource. This concept is used in concurrent programming with a critical section, a piece of code in which processes or threads access a shared resource.

Hence, option B is correct.

57. $(1217)_8 = (1 \times 8^3 + 2 \times 8^2 + 7 \times 8^0)_{10} = (655)_{10}$

$(655)_{10} = (28F)_{16}$

Alternative Method:

$(1217)_8 = (001\ 010\ 001\ 111)_8$

Grouping by 4 bits

$(0010\ 1000\ 1111)_{16} = (28F)_{16}$

58. CMM is not a software life cycle model. Instead, it is a strategy for improving the software process.

59. Balanced Parenthesis is one of the applications of Stack

Algorithm:

(1) Declare a character stack S.

(2) Now traverse the expression string exp.

  (a) If the current character is a starting bracket ('(' or '{' or '[') then push it to stack.

  (b) If the current character is a closing bracket (')' or '}' or ']') then pop from stack and if the popped character is the matching starting bracket then fine else parenthesis are not balanced.

(3) After complete traversal, if there is some starting bracket left in stack then "not balanced"

60. Cyclomatic Complexity of module

$$= \text{Number of decision points} + 1$$

Number of decision points in A = 10 – 1 = 9

Number of decision points in B = 10 – 1 = 9

Cyclomatic Complexity of the integration = Number of decision points + 1

$$= (9 + 9) + 1 = 19$$

61. Adaptive maintenance is concerned with the change in the software that takes place to make the software adaptable to new environment such as to run the software on a new operating system. It consists of adapting software to changes in the environment such as the hardware or the operating system. The term environment in this context refers to the conditions and the influences which act (from outside) on the system. For example, business rules, work patterns, and government policies have a significant impact on the software system.

62. for every time loop condition check with outer declare i and dor every outer declared i every time new variable i is declared and assign 10 to it .

so output will be 10, 10, 10, 10, 10,

At last vlaue of outer i = 5 and inner i = 11

63.
```c
#include <stdio.h>
int main() {
    unsigned short int num; // num is 16 bit
    unsigned integer
    int i;
    scanf("%u",&num);
    for(i=0;i<16;i++) {
      printf("%d",(num<<i & 1<<15)?1:0);
      // ( (num<<i) & (1<<15) )?1:0
      // << has higher precedence than &
    }
}
```

// num << i == ith bit from MSB in the actual num is at the MSB position now

// 1 << 15 == 1000000000000000

// (num<<i)&(1<<15) check each bits of num starting from MSB and prints one by one

SO The program **prints binary equivalent of num**

64. Since tmp is a global variable. So, line: 1 will print 20.

then on calling the function "func() " in Line:2, control of program will go to Line 4 then under which new local variable "tmp=10" is defined statically, So, on executing line:6 gives output 10

On executing Line: 3, again global variable comes into the picture, Since C language follows static scoping so free variable refers to global variable. so it prints value:20

so final output will be : 20 10 20

65. The Fog Index and Readability Formulas

"Readability formulas" determine if documents are written at the correct reading audience.

Gunnings's Fog Index is one of the best known and measures the level of reading difficulty of any document.

The formula for the index is as follows:

((average number of words per sentence) + (number of words of 3 syllables or more)) × 0.4

= Fog index

The Fog Index level 'translates' the number of years education a reader needs to understand the material. The "ideal" score is 7 or 8; anything above 12 is too hard for most people to read.

The Fog Index does not determine if the writing is too basic or too advanced for a particular audience; instead, it helps you decide whether a document could benefit from editing or using "plain language" techniques.

66. As shortest seek time algorithm is used and the head starts from cylinder 50, the order followed is :

$$50{\rightarrow}37{\rightarrow}20{\rightarrow}19{\rightarrow}15{\rightarrow}10{\rightarrow}7{\rightarrow}6{\rightarrow}4{\rightarrow}2{\rightarrow}7350$$
$${\rightarrow}37{\rightarrow}20{\rightarrow}19{\rightarrow}15{\rightarrow}10{\rightarrow}7{\rightarrow}6{\rightarrow}4{\rightarrow}2{\rightarrow}73$$

So, as it takes 1 ms to move to adjacent cylinder, the time taken is:

$$13+17+1+4+5+3+1+2+2+71 = 119 \text{ ms}$$

Hence option (B) is right answer.

67. All levels and all nodes are completely filled with keys.

Another key came.

It went down to leaf.

Overflow happened at the leaf.

The leaf is broken into two parts and one key moved to the upper level.

Again overflow. That node is broken into two parts and one key moved to the upper level.

Same thing will happen till we reach the root.

The root itself is broken into two parts + we have a new root.

So in all 'n' levels, we got one extra node and we got a new root too.

So total n+1 extra nodes. Hence answer is 4+1 = 5.

68. That part of the program where the shared memory is accessed is called critical section.

To avoid race condition we need mutual exclusion.

Mutual Exclusion: It is some way of making sure that if one process is using a shared variable or file, the other process will be excluded from doing the somethings.

The difficulty in printer spooler occurs because process B started using one of the shared variables before process A was finished with it. If we could arrange matter such that no two processes were ever in there critical regions at the same time, we could avoid race conditions

69. $(a + (b - c)) \times ((d - e)/(f + g - h)$

$(a + (-bc)) \times ((-de)/(-+fgh)$

$(+a-bc) \times (/-de-+fgh)$

$\times +a - bc/-de - +fgh.$

(a) Option answer.

70. The name **malloc** and calloc() are library functions that allocate memory dynamically. It means that memory is allocated during runtime(execution of the program) from heap segment.

71. (1) wait : It is denoted by P, It is used when some process enter into the critical section by decreasing semaphore value by 1.

(2) signal :It is denoted by V, It is used when some process exit into the critical section by increasing semaphore value by 1.

So, in the question they are asking about value is decreasing from 10 to 7 so, there would be 3 P operations used.

72. The Linux command mknod myfifo b 4 16 Will create a block device if the user is root.

73. Jitter MEANS timing error in task

Hard real time OS is a type of OS we can predict the deadline, they will respond at a time t=0. Hard real time systems are constrained to predicted time constraints, deadlines and latency.

So A hard real-time operating system has less jitter than a soft real-time operating system

74. The Throwable class is the superclass of all errors and exceptions in the Java language.

75. <ul>unordered list without numbering

<ol>ordered list with numbering

<dl>description list

<ol>numbered list

76. The all-pairs shortest path problem is the determination of the shortest graph distances between every pair of vertices in a given graph.

The Floyd Warshall Algorithm is for solving the All Pairs Shortest Path problem. The problem is to find shortest distances between every pair of vertices in a given edge weighted directed Graph.

77. Option (a) Kleene Star L * of L :

Statement: R.E languages are closed under concatenation and Kleene closure.

Proof. Given TMs M_1 and M_2 recognizing L_1 and L_2

- A TM to recognize L_1L_2: On input x, do in parallel, for each of the $|x| + 1$ ways to divide x as yz: run M_1 on y and M_2 on z, and accept if both accept. Else reject.

- A TM to recognize L_1^* : On input x, if x = ε accept. Else, do in parallel, for each of the $2^{|x|-1}$ ways to divide x as $w_1 \ldots w_k$ ($w_i \neq ε$): run M_1 on each w_i and accept if M_1 accepts all. Else reject.

Option (b) Intersection L   P (c) Union L   P:

Statement: R.E. languages are closed under union, and intersection.

Proof. Given TMs M1, M2 that recognize languages L1, L2

- A TM that recognizes L1 ∪ L2: on input x, run M1 and M2 on x in parallel, and accept iff either accepts. (Similarly for intersection; but no need for parallel simulation)

Option (d) Set difference : L–P = L P^C

statement: R.E. languages are not closed under complementation.

Proof. A_{TM} is R.E. but $\overline{A_{TM}}$ is not.

Since recursively enumerable languages are not closed under complement. So Set difference of these two language is not closed.

78. Cohesion is a measure of internal strength within a module, whereas coupling is a measure of inter dependency among the modules.

Ideal software design requires less interaction between modules so that any module can be easily modified/replaced as the requirements change

So in the context of modular software design there should be high cohesion and low coupling

79. A lexical analyzer coverts character sequences to set of tokens. A lexical analyzer coverts character sequences to set of tokens.

A lexical token is a sequence of characters that can be treated as a unit in the grammar of the programming languages.

80. Binary relation can be represented as a directed graph. Now for a directed graph transitive closure means we have to find a matrix in which if there is path between two nodes directly or indirectly then there should be one(1) otherwise 0 & all diagonals are always 1's ,since there is no direct path between node 1 and 2 but still in matrix there is 1 from node 2 to node 1 because there is indirect path from node 2 to 4 then to 1.

To find such matrix we use Warshall's algorithm to find the transitive closure here we start with adjacency matrix with all diagonals matrix as 1

T(0)=

(1 0 0 0

0 1 1 1

0 1 1 0

1 0 1 1)

then modify the matrix by checking is there any indirect path between all the pairs of nodes using node 1 as intermediate node .

T(1)=

(1 0 0 0

0 1 1 1

0 1 1 0

1 0 1 1)

so Then again modify the matrix by checking is there any indirect path between all the pairs nodes using node 2 as intermediate node . so we keep on doing this to all the nodes we are having here we are going to repeat the process upto n no of times (since n nodes)

To modify one matrix it takes order of O(n^2) time complexity because there are n^2 elements in the matrix . And we are modifying matrix n no of times so Total time complexity = n * O(n^2) = O(n^3).

1. Suppose A is a finite set with n elements. The number of elements and the rank of the largest equivalence relation on A are
   - (a) {n, 1}
   - (b) {n, n}
   - (c) {n2, 1}
   - (d) {1, n2}

2. Consider the set of integers I. Let D denote "divides with an integer quotient" (e.g. 4D8 but 4Đ7). Then D is
   - (a) Reflexive, not symmetric, transitive
   - (b) Not reflexive, not antisymmetric, transitive
   - (c) Reflexive, antisymmetric, transitive
   - (d) Not reflexive, not antisymmetric, not transitive

3. A bag contains 19 red balls and 19 black balls. Two balls are removed at a time repeatedly and discarded if they are of the same colour, but if they are different, black ball is discarded and red ball is returned to the bag. The probability that this process will terminate with one red ball is
   - (a) 1
   - (b) $\dfrac{1}{21}$
   - (c) 0
   - (d) 0.5

4. If $x = -1$ and $x = 2$ are extreme points of $f(x) = \alpha \log |x| \beta x^2 + x$ then
   - (a) $\alpha = -6, \beta = -\dfrac{1}{2}$
   - (b) $\alpha = 2, \beta = -\dfrac{1}{2}$
   - (c) $\alpha = 2, \beta = \dfrac{1}{2}$
   - (d) $\alpha = -6 \ \beta = \dfrac{1}{2}$

5. Let $f(x) = \log |x|$ and $g(x) = \sin x$. If A is the range of $f(g(x))$ and B is the range of $g(f(x))$ then $A \cap B$ is
   - (a) $[-1, 0]$
   - (b) $[-1, 0)$
   - (c) $[-\infty, 0]$
   - (d) $[-\infty, 1]$

6. The proposition $(P \Rightarrow Q) \wedge (Q \Rightarrow P)$ is a
   - (a) tautology
   - (b) contradiction
   - (c) contingency
   - (d) absurdity

7. If T(x) denotes x is a trigonometric function, P(x) denotes x is a periodic function and C(x) denotes x is a continuous function then the statement "It is not the case that some trigonometric functions are not periodic" can be logically represented as
   - (a) $\neg \exists x \left[T(x) \wedge \neg P(x) \right]$
   - (b) $\neg \exists x \left[T(x) \vee \neg P(x) \right]$
   - (c) $\neg \exists x \left[\neg T(x) \wedge \neg P(x) \right]$
   - (d) $\neg \exists x \left[T(x) \wedge P(x) \right]$

8. The number of elements in the power set of $\{\{1, 2\}, \{2, 1, 1\}, \{2, 1, 1, 2\}\}$ is
   - (a) 3
   - (b) 8
   - (c) 4
   - (d) 2

9. The function $f : [0, 3] \to [1, 29]$ defined by $f(x) = 2x^3 - 15x^2 + 36x + 1$ is
   - (a) injective and surjective
   - (b) surjective but not injective
   - (c) injective but not surjective
   - (d) neither injective nor surjective

10. If vectors $\vec{a} = 2\hat{i} + \lambda\hat{j} + \hat{k}$ and $\vec{b} = \hat{i} - 2\hat{j} + 3\hat{k}$ are perpendicular to each other, then value of λ is
    - (a) $\dfrac{2}{5}$
    - (b) 2
    - (c) 3
    - (d) $\dfrac{5}{2}$

11. Consider the schema

    Sailors(sid,sname,rating,age) with the following data

sid	sname	rating	age
22	Dustin	7	45
29	Borg	1	33
31	Pathy	8	55
32	Robert	8	25
58	Raghu	10	17
64	Herald	7	35
71	Vishnu	10	16
74	King	9	35
85	Archer	3	26
84	Bob	3	64
96	Flinch	3	17

For the query

SELECT S.rating, AVG(S.age) AS avgage FROM Sailors S

Where S.age > = 18

GROUP BY S.rating

HAVING 1 < (SELECT COUNT(*) FROM Sailors S2 where S.rating = S2.rating)

The number of rows returned is

(a) 6

(b) 5

(c) 4

(d) 3

12. Consider a table that describes the customers :

Customers(custid, name, gender, rating)

The rating value is an integer in the range 1 to 5 and only two values (male and female) are recorded for gender. Consider the query "how many male customers have a rating of 5"? The best indexing mechanism appropriate for the query is

(a) Linear hashing

(b) Extendible hashing

(c) B + tree

(d) Bit-mapped index

13. Consider the following schema :

Sailors(sid,sname,rating,age) Boats(bid,bname, colour)

Reserves(sid,bid,day)

Two boats can have the same name but the colour differentiates them.

The two relations

$\rho(\text{Tempsids}, (\pi_{\text{sid, bid}} \text{ Reserves})/(\pi_{\text{bid}} (\sigma_{\text{bname = 'Ganga'}} \text{Boats})))$,

$\pi_{\text{sname}} (\text{Tempsids} \bowtie \text{Sailors})$

If / is division operation, the above set of relations represents the query

(a) Names of sailors who have reserved all boats called Ganga

(b) Names of sailors who have not reserved any Ganga boat

(c) Names of sailors who have reserved at least one Ganga boat

(d) Names of sailors who have reserved at most one Ganga boat

14. Type IV JDBC driver is a driver

(a) which is written in C++

(b) which requires an intermediate layer

(c) which communicates through Java sockets

(d) which translates JDBC function calls into API not native to DBMS

15. Consider the following table : Faculty(facName, dept, office, rank, dateHired)

facName	dept	office	rank	dateHired
Ravi	Art	A101	Professor	1975
Murali	Math	M201	Assistant	2000
Narayanan	Art	A101	Associate	1992
Lakshmi	Math	M201	Professor	1982
Mohan	CSC	C101	Professor	1980
Sreeni	Math	M203	Associate	1990
Tanuj	CSC	C101	Instructor	2001
Ganesh	CSC	C105	Associate	1995

(Assume that no faculty member within a single department has same name. Each faculty member has only one office identified in office). 3NF refers to third normal form and BNCF refers to Boyce-Codd normal form Then Faculty is

(a) Not in 3NF, in BCNF

(b) In 3NF, not in BCNF

(c) In 3NF, in BCNF

(d) Not in 3NF, not in BCNF

16. Consider the following query :

SELECT E.eno, COUNT(*)

FROM Employees E

GROUP BY E.eno

If an index on eno is available, the query can be answered by scanning only the index if

(a) the index is only hash and clustered

(b) the index is only B+ tree and clustered

(c) index can be hash or B+ tree and clustered or non-clustered

(d) index can be hash or B+ tree and clustered

17. If C is a skew-symmetric matrix of order n and X is n × 1 column matrix, then $X^T CX$ is a

(a) scalar matrix

(b) null matrix

(c) unit matrix

(d) matrix will all elements 1

18. Consider the recurrence equation

$$T(n) = \begin{cases} 2T(n-1), & \text{if } n > 0 \\ 1 & \text{otherwise} \end{cases}$$

Then T(n) is (in big O order)

(a) O(n)   (b) $O(2^n)$

(c) O(1)   (d) O(log n)

19. Consider the program

```
void function(int  n)    {
int i, j, count=0;
for (i=n/2; i <= n; i++)
for (j = 1; j <= n; j = j*2)
          count++;
}
```

The complexity of the program is

(a) O(log n)   (b) $O(n^2)$

(c) $O(n^2 \log n)$ (d) O(n log n)

20. Match the following and choose the correct answer for the order A,B,C,D

A. Strassen matrix multiplication	p. Decrease and Conquer
B. Insertion sort	q. Dynamic Programming
C. Guassian Elimination	r. Divide and Conquer
D. Floyd shortest path algorithm	s. Transform and Conquer

(a) r, s, p, q

(b) r, p, s, q

(c) q, s, p, r

(d) s, p, q, r

21. For $\sum\{a,b\}$ the regular expression

$r = (aa)*(bb)*b$ denotes

(a) Set of strings with 2 a's and 2 b's

(b) Set of strings with 2 a's 2 b's followed by b

(c) Set of strings with 2 a's followed by b's which is a multiple of 3

(d) Set of strings with even number of a's followed by odd number of b's

22. Consider the grammar with productions

$$S \rightarrow aSb|SS|\varepsilon$$

This grammar is

(a) not context-free, not linear

(b) not context-free, linear

(c) context-free, not linear

(d) context free, linear

23. Identify the language generated by the following grammar

$S \rightarrow AB$

$A \rightarrow aAb|\varepsilon$

$B \rightarrow bB|b$

(a) $\left\{a^m b^n \,|\, n \geq m, m > 0\right\}$

(b) $\left\{a^m b^n \,|\, n \geq m, m \geq 0\right\}$

(c) $\left\{a^m b^n \,|\, n > m, m > 0\right\}$

(d) $\left\{a^m b^m \,|\, n > m, m \geq 0\right\}$

24. Let L1 be regular language, L_2 be a deterministic context free language and L_3 a recursively enumerable language, but not recursive. Which one of the following statements is false?

(a) $L_3 \cap L_1$ is recursive

(b) $L_1 \cap L_2 \cap L_3$ is recursively enumerable

(c) $L_1 \cup L_2$ is context free

(d) $L_1 \cap L_2$ is context free

25. Let $L = \left\{a^p \,|\, p \text{ is a prime}\right\}$. Then which of the following is true

(a) It is not accepted by a Turing Machine

(b) It is regular but not context free

(c) It is context free but not regular

(d) It is neither regular nor context free, but accepted by a Turing Machine

26. Which of the following are context free?

$$A = \left\{a^n b^n a^m b^m \,|\, m, n \geq 0\right\}$$

$$B = \left\{a^n b^n a^m b^n \,|\, m, n \geq 0\right\}$$

$$C = \left\{a^m b^n \,|\, m \neq 2n, m, n \geq 0\right\}$$

(a A and B only   (b) A and C only

(c) B and C only   (d) C only

27. Let S be an NP-complete problem. Q and R are other two problems not known to be NP. Q is polynomial time reducible to S and S is polynomial time reducible to R. Which of the following statements is true?

(a) R is NP-complete   (b) R is NP-hard

(c) Q is NP-complete   (d) Q is NP-hard

28. The number of structurally different possible binary trees with 4 nodes is

(a) 14   (b) 12

(c) 336   (d) 168

29. Using public key cryptography, X adds a digital signature s to a message M, encrypts $\langle M, \sigma \rangle$ and sends it to Y, where it is decrypted. Which one of the following sequence of keys is used for operations?

(a) Encryption : X's private key followed by Y's private key. Decryption : X's public key followed by Y's public key

(b) Encryption : X's private key followed by Y's public key; Decryption : X's public key followed by Y's private key

(c) Encryption : X's private key followed by Y's public key; Decryption : Y's private key followed by X's public key.

(d) Encryption : X's public key followed by Y's private key; Decryption : Y's public key followed by X's private key.

30. Which of the following are used to generate a message digest by the network security protocols?

(P) SHA-256   (Q) AES

(R) DES   (S) MD5

(a) P and S only   (b) P and Q only

(c) R and S only   (d) P and R only

31. In the IPv4 addressing format, the number of networks allowed under Class C addresses is

(a) 220   (b) 224

(c) 214   (d) 221

32. An Internet Service Provider (ISP) has the following chunk of CIDR-based IP addresses available with it: 245.248.128.0/20. The ISP wants to give half of this chunk of addresses to Organization A, and a quarter to Organization B, while retaining the remaining with itself. Which of the following is a valid allocation of addresses to A and B?

(a) 245.248.136.0/21 and 245.248.128.0/22

(b) 245.248.128.0/21 and 245.248.128.0/22

(c) 245.248.132.0/22 and 245.248.132.0/21

(d) 245.248.136.0/24 and 245.248.132.0/21

33. Assume that Source S and Destination D are connected through an intermediate router R.

How many times a packet has to visit the network layer and data link layer during a transmission from S to D?

(a) Network layer – 4 times, Data link layer – 4 times

(b) Network layer – 4 times, Data link layer – 6 times

(c) Network layer – 2 times, Data link layer – 4 times

(d) Network layer – 3 times, Data link layer – 4 times

34. Generally TCP is reliable and UDP is not reliable. DNS which has to be reliable uses UDP because

(a) UDP is slower

(b) DNS servers has to keep connections

(c) DNS requests are generally very small and fit well within UDP segments

(d) None of these

35. Consider the set of activities related to e-mail

A : Send an e-mail from a mail client to mail server

B : Download e-mail headers from mail box and retrieve mails from server to a cache

C : Checking e-mail through a web browser

The application level protocol used for each activity in the same sequence is

(a) SMTP, HTTPS, IMAP

(b) SMTP, POP, IMAP

(c) SMTP, IMAP, HTTPS

(d) SMT

36. Station A uses 32 byte packets to transmit messages to Station B using a sliding window protocol. The round trip time delay between A and B is 40 ms and the bottleneck bandwidth on the path A and B is 64 kbps. What is the optimal window size that A should use?

(a) 5   (b) 10

(c) 40   (d) 80

37. A two way set associative cache memory unit with a capacity of 16 KB is built using a block size of 8 words. The word length is 32 bits. The physical address space is 4 GB. The number of bits in the TAG, SET fields are

(a) 20, 7   (b) 19, 8

(c) 20, 8   (d) 21, 9

38. A CPU has a 32 KB direct mapped cache with 128 byte block size. Suppose A is a 2 dimensional array of size 512×512 with elements that occupy 8 bytes each. Consider the code segment

```
for (i =0; i < 512; i++) {
for (j =0; j < 512; j++) {
x += A[i][j];
      }
}
```

Assuming that array is stored in order A[0][0], A[0][1], A[0][2]......, the number of cache misses is

(a) 16384   (b) 512

(c) 2048   (d) 1024

39. A computer with 32 bit word size uses 2s compliment to represent numbers. The range of integers that can be represented by this computer is

(a) -2^{32} to 2^{32} (b) -2^{31} to $2^{32}-1$

(c) -2^{31} to $2^{31}-1$ (d) $-2^{31}-1$ to $2^{32}-1$

40. Let A = 1111 1010 and B = 0000 1010 be two 8-bit 2's complement numbers. Their product in 2's complement is

(*a*) 1100 0100   (*b*) 1001 1100

(*c*) 1010 0101   (*d*) 1101 0101

41. For a pipelines CPU with a single ALU, consider the following :

A. The $j + 1^{st}$ instruction uses the result of jth instruction as an operand

B. Conditional jump instruction

C. j^{th} and $j + 1^{st}$ instructions require ALU at the same time

Which one of the above causes a hazard?

(a) A and B only   (b) B and C only

(c) B onl   (d) A, B, C

42. In designing a computer's cache system, the cache block (or cache line) size is an important parameter. Which one of the following statements is correct in this context?

(a) Smaller block size incurs lower cache miss penalty

(b) Smaller block size implies better spatial locality

(c) Smaller block size implies smaller cache tag

(d) Smaller block size implies lower cache hit time

43. Consider an instruction of the type LW R1, 20(R2) which during execution reads a 32 bit word from memory and stores it in a 32 bit register R1. The effective address of the memory location is obtained by adding a constant 20 and contents of R2. Which one best reflects the source operand

(a) Immediate addressing

(b) Register addressing

(c) Register Indirect addressing

(d) Indexed addressing

44. A sorting technique is called stable if

(a) If it takes O(n log n) time

(b) It uses divide and conquer technique

(c) Relative order of occurrence of non-distinct elements is maintained

(d) It takes O(n) space

45. Match the following and choose the correct answer in the order A, B, C

A. Heap Construction	p. O(n log n)
B. Hash table construction with linear probing	q. O(n²)
	r. O(n)
C. AVL Tree construction	

(Bounds given may or may not be asymptotically tight)

(a) q, r, p   (b) p, q, r

(c) q, p, r   (d) r, q, p

46. In a compact one dimensional array representation for lower triangular matrix (all elements above diagonal are zero) of size n × n, non zero elements of each row are stored one after another, starting from first row, the index of $(i, j)^{th}$ element in this new representation is

(a) $i + j$ (b) $j + \dfrac{i(i-1)}{2}$

(c) $i + j - 1$ (d) $i + \dfrac{j(j-1)}{2}$

47. Which of the following permutation can be obtained in the same order using a stack assuming that input is the sequence 5, 6, 7, 8, 9 in that order?

(a) 7, 8, 9, 5, 6   (b) 5, 9, 6, 7, 8

(c) 7, 8, 9, 6, 5   (d) 9, 8, 7, 5, 6

48. Quick sort is run on 2 inputs shown below to sort in ascending order

A. 1, 2, 3......n

B. n, n – 1, n – 2 1

Let C1 and C2 be the number of comparisons made for A and B respectively.

Then

(a) C1 > C2

(b) C1 = C2

(c) C1 < C2

(d) Cannot say anything for arbitrary n

49. A binary search tree is used to locate the number 43. Which one of the following probe sequence is not possible?

(a) 61, 52, 14, 17, 40, 43

(b) 10, 65, 31, 48, 37, 43

(c) 81, 61, 52, 14, 41, 43

(d) 17, 77, 27, 66, 18, 43

50. The characters of the string K R P C S N Y T J M are inserted into a hash table of size of size 10 using hash function

$h(x) = (ord(x) - ord(A) + 1)$

If linear probing is used to resolve collisions, then the following insertion causes collision

(a) Y

(b) C

(c) M

(d) P

51. Suppose the numbers 7, 5, 1, 8, 3, 6, 0, 9, 4, 2 are inserted in that order into an initially empty binary search tree. The binary search tree uses the reversal ordering on natural numbers i.e. 9 is assumed to be smallest and 0 is assumed to be largest. The in-order traversal of the resultant binary search tree is

(a) 9, 8, 6, 4, 2, 3, 0, 1, 5, 7

(b) 0, 1, 2, 3, 4, 5, 6, 7, 8, 9

(c) 0, 2, 4, 3, 1, 6, 5, 9, 8, 7

(d) 9, 8, 7, 6, 5, 4, 3, 2, 1, 0

52. A priority queue is implemented as a Max-heap. Initially it has 5 elements. The level order traversal of the heap is 10, 8, 5, 3, 2. Two new elements '1' and '7' are inserted into the heap in that order. The level order traversal of the heap after the insertion of the elements is

(a) 10, 8, 7, 5, 3, 2,

(b) 10, 8, 7, 2, 3, 1, 5

(c) 10, 8, 7, 1, 2, 3, 5

(d) 10, 8, 7, 3, 2, 1, 5

53. The minimum number of stacks needed to implement a queue is

(a) 3

(b) 1

(c) 2

(d) 4

54. A strictly binary tree with 10 leaves

(a) cannot have more than 19 nodes

(b) has exactly 19 nodes

(c) has exactly 17 nodes

(d) has exactly 20 nodes

55. What is the maximum height of any AVL tree with 7 nodes? Assume that height of tree with single node is 0.

(a) 2

(b) 3

(c) 4

(d) 5

56. Which one of the following property is correct for a red-black tree?

(a) Every simple path from a node to a descendant leaf contains the same number of black nodes

(b) If a node is red, then one children is red and another is black

(c) If a node is red, then both its children are red

(d) Every leaf node (sentinel node) is red

57. The in-order and pre-order traversal of a binary tree are d b e a f c g and a b d e f g respectively. The post order traversal of a binary tree is

(a) e d b g f c a

(b) e d b f g c a

(c) d e b f g c a

(d) d e f g b c a

58. A virtual memory system uses FIFO page replacement policy and allocates a fixed number of frames to the process. Consider the following statements

M : Increasing the number of page frames allocated to a process sometimes increases the page fault rate

N : Some programs do not exhibit locality of reference

Which one of the following is true?

(a) Both M and N are true and N is the reason for M

(b) Both M and N are true but N is not the reason for M

(c) Both M and N are false

(d) M is false, but N is true

59. Consider three CPU intensive processes, which require 10, 20, 30 units and arrive at times 0,2,6 respectively. How many context switches are needed if shortest remaining time first is implemented? Context switch at 0 is included but context switch at end is ignored

(a) 1

(b) 2

(c) 3

(d) 4

60. A process executes the following code

for (i = 0; i < n; i ++) fork( );

The total number of child processes created is

(a) n^2

(b) $2^{n+1} - 1$

(c) 2^n

(d) $2^n - 1$

61. Consider the following scheduling :

A.	Gang scheduling	s.	Guaranteed scheduling
B.	Rate Monotonic scheduling	t.	Thread scheduling
C.	Fair share scheduling	u.	Real time scheduling

Matching the table in the order A, B, C gives

(a) t, u,   (b) s, t, u

(c) u, s, t   (d) u, t, s

62. A system uses FIFO policy for page replacement. It has 4 page frames with no pages loaded to begin with. The system first accesses 50 distinct pages in some order and then accesses

the same 50 pages in reverse order. How many page faults will occur?

(a) 96   (b) 100

(c) 97   (d) 92

63. Which of the following is false?

(a) User level threads are not scheduled by the kernel

(b) Context switching between user level threads is faster than context switching between kernel level threads

(c) When a user thread is blocked all other threads of its processes are blocked

(d) Kernel level threads cannot utilize multiprocessor systems by splitting threads on different processors or cores

64. Which of the following is not true with respect to deadlock prevention and deadlock avoidance schemes?

(a) In deadlock prevention, the request for resources is always granted if resulting state is safe

(b) In deadlock avoidance, the request for resources is always granted, if the resulting state is safe

(c) Deadlock avoidance requires knowledge of resource requirements a priori

(d) Deadlock prevention is more restrictive than deadlock avoidance

65. Which one of the following are essential features of object oriented language?

A. Abstraction and encapsulation

B. Strictly-typed

C. Type-safe property coupled with sub-type rule

D. Polymorphism in the presence of inheritance

(a) A and B only (b) A, D and B only

(c) A and D only (d) A, C and D only

66. Which languages necessarily need heap allocation in the run time environment?

(a) Those that support recursion

(b) Those that use dynamic scoping

(c) Those that use global variables

(d) Those that allow dynamic data structures

67. Consider the code segment

```
int i, j, x, y, m, n;
n=20;
for (i = 0, i < n; i++)
{
for (j = 0; j < n; j++)
{
if (i % 2)
{
x + = ((4*j) + 5*i);
y += (7 + 4*j);
}
}
}
m = x + y;
```

Which one of the following is false?

(a) The code contains loop invariant computation

(b) There is scope of common sub-expression elimination in this code

(c) There is scope of strength reduction in this code

(d) There is scope of dead code elimination in this code

68. Consider the following table :

A.	Activation record	p.	Linking loader
B.	Location counter	q.	Garbage
C.	Reference counts		collection
D.	Address relocation	r.	Subroutine call
		s.	Assembler

Matching A, B, C, D in the same order gives :

(a) p, q, r, s   (b) q, r, s, p

(c) r, s, q, p   (d r, s, p, q

69. Consider a disk sequence with 100 cylinders. The request to access the cylinder occur in the following sequence :

4, 34, 10, 7, 19, 73, 2, 15, 6, 20

Assuming that the head is currently at cylinder 50, what is the time taken to satisfy all requests if it takes 2 ms to move from one cylinder to adjacent one and shortest seek time first policy is used?

(a) 190   (b) 238

(c) 233   (d) 276

70. A counting semaphore was initialised to 7. Then 20 P (wait) operations and x V (signal) operations were completed on this semaphore. If the final value of semaphore is 5, then the value x will be

(a) 0   (b) 13

(c) 18   (d) 5

71. A 32 bit adder is formed by cascading 4 bit CLA adder. The gate delays (latency) for getting the sum bits is
   - (a) 16
   - (b) 18
   - (c) 17
   - (d) 19

72. We consider the addition of two 2's compliment numbers $b_{n-1} b_{n-2} .... b_0$ and $a_{n-1} a_{n-2} ... a_0$.

   A binary adder for adding two unsigned binary numbers is used to add two binary numbers.

   The sum is denoted by $c_{n-1} c_{n-2} ... c_0$. The carry out is denoted by c_{out}. The overflow condition is identified by

   - (a) $c_{out} \left(\overline{a_{n-1} \oplus b_{n-1}} \right)$

   - (b) $\overline{a_{n-1}} \overline{b_{n-1}} \overline{c_{n-1}} + \overline{a_{n-1}} \overline{b_{n-1}} c_{n-1}$

   - (c) $c_{out} \oplus c_{n-1}$

   - (d) $a_{n-1} \oplus b_{n-1} \oplus c_{n-1}$

73. Consider the function
   int fun(x: integer)
   {
   If x > 100 then fun = x – 10;
      else
   fun = fun(fun(x + 11));
   }
   For the input x = 95, the function will return
   - (a) 89
   - (b) 90
   - (c) 91
   - (d) 92

74. Consider the function

   ```
   int func(int num) {
   int count = 0;
   while(num) {
   count++;
   num >>= 1;
   }
   return(count) ;
   }
   ```

   For func(435) the value returned is
   - (a) 9
   - (b) 8
   - (c) 0
   - (d) 10

75. In IEEE floating point representation, the hexadecimal number 0xC0000000 corresponds to
   - (a) –3.0
   - (b) –1.0
   - (c) –4.0
   - (d) –2.0

76. Which of the following set of components is sufficient to implement any arbitrary Boolean function?
   - (a) XOR gates, NOT gates
   - (b) AND gates, XOR gates and 1
   - (c) 2 to 1 multiplexer
   - (d) Three input gates that output (A.B) + C for the inputs A, B, C

77. Consider the following :

A.	Condition Coverage	p.	Black box testing
		q.	System testing
B.	Equivalence Class partitioning	r.	White box testing
		s.	Performance testing
C.	Volume Testing		
D.	Beta Testing		

   Matching A, B, C, D in the same order gives.
   - (a) r, p, s, q
   - (b) p, r, q, s
   - (c) s, r, q, p
   - (d) q, r, s, p

78. Consider the results of a medical experiment that aims to predict whether someone is going to develop myopia based on some physical measurements and heredity. In this case, the input dataset consists of the person's medical characteristics and the target variable is binary: 1 for those who are likely to develop myopia and 0 for those who aren't. This can be best classified as
   - (a) Regression
   - (b) Decision Tree
   - (c) Clustering
   - (d) Association Rules

79. Which of the following related to snowflake schema is true?
   - (a) Each dimension is represented by a single dimensional table
   - (b) Maintenance efforts are less
   - (c) Dimension tables are normalised
   - (d) It is not an extension of star schema

80. Consider the following C function

   ```c
   #include <stdio.h>
   int main(void)
   {
   char c[ ] = "ICRBCSIT17";
   char *p=c;
   printf("%s", c+2[p] – 6[p] – 1);
   return 0;
   }
   ```

   The output of the program is
   - (a) SI
   - (b) IT
   - (c) T1
   - (d) 17

ANSWERS

1. (c)	**2.** (b)	**3.** (a)	**4.** (b)	**5.** (a)	**6.** (c)	**7.** (a)	**8.** (b)	**9.** (b)	**10.** (d)
11. (d)	**12.** (d)	**13.** (a)	**14.** (c)	**15.** (b)	**16.** (c)	**17.** (b)	**18.** (c)	**19.** (d)	**20.** (b)
21. (d)	**22.** (c)	**23.** (d)	**24.** (a)	**25.** (d)	**26.** (b)	**27.** (a)	**28.** (a)	**29.** (c)	**30.** (a)
31. (d)	**32.** (a)	**33.** (d)	**34.** (c)	**35.** (c)	**36.** (b)	**37.** (b)	**38.** (a)	**39.** (c)	**40.** (a)
41. (d)	**42.** (a)	**43.** (c)	**44.** (c)	**45.** (d)	**46.** (b)	**47.** (c)	**48.** (a)	**49.** (d)	**50.** (c)
51. (d)	**52.** (d)	**53.** (c)	**54.** (b)	**55.** (b)	**56.** (a)	**57.** (c)	**58.** (b)	**59.** (c)	**60.** (d)
61. (a)	**62.** (a)	**63.** (d)	**64.** (a)	**65.** (c)	**66.** (d)	**67.** (d)	**68.** (c)	**69.** (b)	**70.** (b)
71. (b)	**72.** (c)	**73.** (c)	**74.** (a)	**75.** (d)	**76.** (b)	**77.** (a)	**78.** (b)	**79.** (c)	**80.** (d)

EXPLANATIONS

1. An Equivalence relation is always Reflexive, Symmetric and Transitive, so for a set of size 'n' elements the largest Equivalence relation will always contain n2 elements whereas the smallest Equivalence relation on a set of 'n' elements contain n elements itself.

   The Rank of an Equivalence relation is equal to the number of induced Equivalence classes. Since we have maximum number of ordered pairs(which are reflexive, symmetric and transitive) in largest Equivalence relation, its rank is always 1. So option C is correct.

2. Reflexibility: for all $x \in I$, $R(x, x)$ is reflexive but here $R(0, 0)$ is a violation as 0 belongs to the set of integers but does not satisfy this relation.

   Symmetric: for all $x \in I$, $R(x, y)$ and $R(y, x)$ is symmetric and clearly the above relation cannot be symmetric. Consider the example

   $S = \{1, 2\}$.

   For this to be symmetric $(1, 2)(2, 1)$ both ordered pair should be present but it is also a violation as 2 can be divided by 1 but 1 cannot be divided by 2 to give an integer quotient.

   Antisymmetric: for all $x \in I$, $R(x, y)$ and $R(y, x)$ then $x = y$ is antisymmetric. We can easily make a violation as $R(-2, 2)$ and $R(2, -2)$ are not antisymmetric.

   Transitivity:for all $x \in I$, $R(x, y)$, $R(y, z)$ then $R(x, z)$. This is always true for the above divides relation. So the relation is not-reflexive, not-antisymmetric but transitive.

3. Possible outcomes will be RR, BB, RB and BR. If two same coloured balls appear then both are discarded whereas if different coloured balls appear then only black ball is discarded. Black balls will always be used up and 1 red ball will remain at the end regardless of the outcome of the experiment. The probability that this process will terminate with one red ball is always 1. Therefore option (a) is correct.

4. $f(x) = \alpha \log |x| + \beta x^2 + x$

   for extreme points $f'(x)=0$

   $f'(x) = \dfrac{\alpha}{x} + 2\beta x + 1 = 0$

   for $x = -1$: $-\alpha - 2\beta = -1$

   for $x = 2$: $\dfrac{\alpha}{2} + 4\beta = -1$

   from here we get the value of $\alpha = 2$ and $\beta = -\dfrac{1}{2}$

5. Given, $f(x) = \log|x|$ and $g(x) = \sin(x)$

   Now,

   $f(g(x)) = \log|g(x)| = \log|\sin(x)|$

   So, A = range of $\log|\sin(x)| = (-\infty, 0]$

   And

   $g(f(x)) = \sin(f(x)) = \sin(\log|x|)$

   So, B = range of $\sin(\log|x|) = [-1, 1]$

   Therefore, $A \cap B = [-1, 0]$

   Note that $-1 \le \sin(x) \le 1$ and $-\infty \le \log|x| \le \infty$

   So, option (a) is correct.

6. $(P \Rightarrow Q) \wedge (Q \Rightarrow P) = (\neg P + Q)(\neg Q + P) = (\neg P \neg Q + \neg PP + \neg QQ + PQ) = (\neg P \neg Q + PQ)$

   Therefore it is a contingency.

7. Some trigonometric functions are not periodic

   $= \exists (x) [T(x) \wedge \neg P(x)]$

   And it's negation is = $\neg \exists (x) [T(x) \wedge \neg P(x)]$

   Which is equivalent to "It is not the case that some trigonometric functions are not periodic" is equivalent to "All trigonometric functions are periodic" can be expression as

   $= \forall (x) [T(x) \rightarrow P(x)] = \forall (x) [\neg T(x) \vee P(x)] = \forall (x) \neg [T(x) \wedge \neg P(x)] = \neg \exists (x) [T(x) \wedge \neg P(x)]$

   Option (a) is correct.

8. Total number of elements in given set (n) = 3

So, total number of elements in power set of given set = $2^n = 2^3 = 8$

So, option (b) is correct.

9. Given,

$f(x) = 2x^3 - 15x^2 + 36x + 1$

$\Rightarrow f'(x) = 6(x^2 - 5x + 6) = 6(x - 2)(x - 3)$

Since f(x) is non monotonic in $\in [0,3]$

$\Rightarrow$ f(x) is not one-one

And, f(x) is increasing in $x \in [0,2)$ and decreasing in $\in (0,2]$

$f(0) = 1, f(2) = 29 \ \& \ f(3) = 28$

Therefore Range of f(x) is [1, 29]

$\Rightarrow$ f(x) is onto.

So, option (b) is correct.

10. Given, vectors $\vec{a} = 2\hat{i} + \lambda\hat{j} + \hat{k}$ and $\vec{b} = \hat{i} - 2\hat{j} + 3\hat{k}$

are perpendicular to each other, so

$$\overrightarrow{ab} = 0$$

$$\overrightarrow{ab} = 2 \times 1 - 2 \times \lambda + 3 \times 1 = 0$$
$$-2\lambda = -5$$

$$\Rightarrow \qquad \lambda = \frac{5}{2}$$

11. The qiven query would run like:

First of all where statement would be executed and all the tuples with age less than 18 would be eliminated.

Now with Group By the remaining tuples will be grouped according to rating:

rating	sid	sname	age
1	29	Borg	33
	85	Archer	26
3	84	Bob	64
	22	Dustin	45
7	64	Herald	35
	31	Pathy	55
8	32	Robert	25
9	74	King	35

After this, all the group-by tuples having their count more than 1 will be selected and their ratings and average age will be given as output.

rating	average Degee
3	45
7	40
8	40

So, the correct option is d.

12. We require only 2 bits 0 and 1 to record gender of customers, we can easily implement it using bit-mapped index.

The correct answer is (d)

13. According to Division operator, Tempsids gives sid and bid of who have reserved all boats called Ganga

And π_{sname}(Tempsids $\bowtie$ Sailors) will return sname of sailors who have reserved all boats called Ganga

So, option (a) is correct.

14. JDBC type 4 driver,works directly by connecting to the database server through socket connections and converts JDBC calls to vendor-specific database protocols.These drivers don't require any intermediate layer.

So, option (c) is correct.

15. There are two non-trivial functional dependencies (FD) in given table:

facName $\rightarrow$ dept, office, rank, datehired

office $\rightarrow$ dept

Given, Eachfaculty member has only one office identified in office, that means facName is the primary key (so superkey).

Therefore, FD facName $\rightarrow$ dept, office, rank, datehired is in 3 NF as well as in BCNF, because facName is the primary key. But FD office$\rightarrow$ dept is not in BCNF because office is not superkey but dept is in 3 NF as dept is the prime attribute because {dept, rank} is super key.

So, overall relation Faculty is in 3 NF but not in BCNF.

Option (b) is correct.

17. A is skew symmetric of order n × n,order of X = n × 1 and order of X' = 1 x n, then order of

X'AX = ((1 × n)(n × n))(n × 1)

= (1 × n)(n × 1) = 1

Let X'AX = Y

(X'AX)' = Y'

X' A' X" = Y' (since (AB)' = B'A')

As A is a skew-symmetric matrix, A' = –A

X'(–A)X" = Y'

–X'AX) = Y

–Y = Y

Y = 0

So, option (b) is correct.

18. Using sbustitution method,

$$T(n) = 2T(n-1)$$
$$= 2(2T(n-2))$$
$$= 2^2T(n-2)$$
$$= 2(2^2T(n-2)) = 2^3T(n-3)....$$
$$= 2(2^{n-3}T(n-(n-1)))$$
$$= 2^{n-2}T(n-(n-2))$$
$$= 2(2^{n-2}T(n-(n-1)))$$
$$= 2^{n-1}T(n-(n-1))$$
$$= 2^{n-1}T(1)$$
$$= 2(2^{n-1}T(n-(n)))$$
$$= 2^nT(n-(n)) = 2^nT(O)$$
$$T(n) = O(2^n).$$

19. The outer loop runs $\dfrac{n}{2}$ times

The inner loop runs logn times

Therefore the total time complexity of the program is O(nlogn) which is option (d)

20. Strassen matrix multiplication uses Divide and Conquer technique to reduce the complexity of matrix multiplication. For details refer: Strassen's Matrix Multiplication

Insertion sort uses decrease and conquer approach as its loop invariant condition is at each step, $A[1..j-1]$ contains the first $j-1$ elements in sorted order. Refer Decrease and Conquer

Gaussian elimination uses transform and conquer approach to solve set of equations. Refer Gaussian Elimination to Solve Linear Equations

Floyd Warshall shortest path algorithm is an all-pair shortest path algorithm which uses Dynamic Programming to compute the result. Refer Floyd Warshall Algorithm

21. We can approach this question by making refutations for wrong options:

Option 1: Set of strings with 2 a's and 2 b's :

clearly it is wrong as the given regular expression can accept aaaabbb.

Option 2: Set of strings with 2 a's 2 b's followed by b

Again it is wrong as aaaabbb is a violation in this case also.

Option 3: Set of strings with 2 a's followed by b's which is a multiple of 3

It is wrong as aaaab is accepted by the expression.

Option 4: Set of strings with even number of a's followed by odd number of b

Clearly it is correct as no violation exists in this case.

So, correct option is (d).

22. According to Chomsky Hierarchy, context free grammar (CFG) are with each productions follows production rules $A \to B$, where A singal non-terminal and B is the set of terminal and non-terminal. Therefore, given grammar is Context Free.

According to linear grammar is a context-free grammar that has at most one non-terminal in the right hand side of each of its productions. So, given grammar can not be linear because of $S \to SS$ production.

So, option (c) is correct.

23. $S \to AB$

$A \to aAb \,|\, \in$

$B \to bB \,|\, b$

strings generated by the the language:

b, bb, abb, abbb, aabbb and so on.

Alternative way -

The production rule $B \to bB \,|\, b$ will generate b^p, $p \geq 1$

The production rule $A \to aAb \,|\,$ will generate $a^m b^m$, $n \geq 0$

The production rule $S \to AB$ will generate $a^m b^{(m+p)}$, i.e.,

{ambn | n > m, m > =0}

So option (d) is correct.

25. $L = \{a^p \,|\, p \text{ is a prime}\}$

L can only be accepted by a turing machine. So option (d) is correct.

28. The total number of structurally different possible binary trees can be found out using the Catalon

number which is $\dfrac{(2n)!}{\left(n! * (n+1)!\right)}$.

Here n = 4, so, answer is 14.

29. **Given:** X encrypts a message and send it to Y.

To find: Correction encryption - decryption order

Analysis: To make sure that Y receives the message & is able to decrypt it and no one else is able to X. The message over the network should be encrypted by Y's public key.

So, order of encryption is X's private key, Y's public key. On receiving the encrypted message, Y will have to decrypt it using its private key & then use X's public key for signature. So, order of decryption is Y's private key followed by X's public key.

So, the answer is (*d*)

33. Router is a network layer device. See the following diagram source S and destination D have 1 network layer and 1 datalink layer each whereas intermediate router R has 2 datalink layers and 1 network layer.

So, Network layer - 3 times, Data link layer - 4 times

Correct answer is (d).

34. Generally DNS requests are smaller and need to be faster so they use UDP datagrams which has a size of 512 Bytes but when the response data either exceeds 512 Bytes in size or requires to be secure, it also uses TCP.

So option (c) is correct.

35. Option (c) is correct.

Simple Mail Transfer Protocol (SMTP) is typically used by user clients for sending mails.

IMAP is an application level protocol that stores email messages on a mail server and allows the end user to view and customize the messages as if they are readily stored on the end user's device.

Checking mails in web browser is a simple HTTP process.

36. Round Trip propagation delay = 40ms

Frame size = 32*8 bits

Bandwidth = 64kbps

$$\text{Transmission Time} = \frac{32*8}{(64)} \text{ ms}$$

$$= 4 \text{ ms}$$

Let n be the window size.

$$\text{UtiliZation} = \frac{n}{(1+2a)} \text{ where a}$$

$$= \text{Propagation time /transmission time}$$

$$= \frac{n}{\left(\frac{1+40}{4}\right)}$$

For maximum utilization: n = 11

which is close to option (b)

37. Offset field(block size) = 8 words * size of each word

$$= 8 * 4 \text{ Bytes}$$

$$= 32 \text{ Bytes}$$

Number of blocks = size of cache/ block size

$$= \frac{16\text{KB}}{32\text{B}} = 512$$

Number of sets $= \dfrac{512}{2} = 256$

Bits required for set field $= \log_2(256) = 8$ bits

Tag bits $= 32 - 5 - 8 = 19$ bits

38. Block size = 128 Byte

Number of elements in 1 block

$$= \frac{128}{8} = 16$$

Block 0: A[0][0] to A[0][15]

Block 1: A[0][16] to A[0][31] and so on

For i = 0: A[0][0] is not present in the cache, so there will be a miss but for the next 15 elements (j = 1 to j = 15), there will be no miss.

j runs from 0 to 512 and there will be a miss after every 16 elements. So total number of misses for

i=0 is $\left(\dfrac{512}{16}\right) = 32$.

The outer loop of i runs from 0 to 512 so the total number of misses will be

$$512 * 16 = 16384$$

39. (c) Range of 'n' bit 2's compliment binary number is always $-2^{(n-1)}$ to $2^{(n-1)} - 1$.

So, option (c) is correct

40. M = 11111010

$$= -2^7 + 2^6 + 2^5 + 2^4 + 2^3 + 2^1$$

$$= -6 \text{ (since number. is stored in two's}$$
$$\text{complement format)}$$

N $= 2^3 + 2^1$

$$= 8 + 2 = 10$$

MN $= -60$, which is 11000100

44. (c) Refer Stability in sorting algorithms

Option (c) is correct.

47. The sequence given in option (c) is one of the only possible sequence which can be obtained.

We can obtain the sequence by performing operations in the manner:

Push 5

Push 6

Push 7

Pop 7

Push 8

Pop 8

Push 9

Pop 9

Pop 6

Pop 5.

hence the sequence will be 7, 8, 9, 6, 5.

48. Both case A and case B will yield worst case comparisons if the pivot chosen is either first or last element.

50. The hash table with size 10 will have index from 0 to 9.

hash function = h(x)

$$= ((ord(x) - ord(a) + 1)) \bmod 10$$

So for string K R P C S N Y T J M:

K will be inserted at index : $(11-1+1) \bmod 10 = 1$

R at index: $(18 - 1 + 1) \bmod 10 = 7$

P at index: $(16 - 1 + 1) \bmod 10 = 5$

C at index: $(3 - 1 + 1) \bmod 10 = 2$

S at index: $(19 - 1 + 1) \bmod 10 = 8$

N at index: $(14 - 1 + 1) \bmod 10 = 3$

Y at index $(25 - 1 + 1) \bmod 10 = 4$

T at index $(20 - 1 + 1) \bmod 10 = 9$

J at index $(10 - 1 + 1) \bmod 10 = 9$ // first collision occurs.

M at index $(13 - 1 + 1) \bmod 10 = 2$ //second collision occurs.

So, option (c) is correct.

51. Inorder traversal of a binary search tree always produces the keys in increasing order. In this question Reverse ordering of natural numbers are used i.e. 9 is assumed to be the smallest and 0 to be the largest. So the sequence in increasing order will be 9, 8, 7, 6, 5, 4, 3, 2, 1, 0.

So, option (d) is correct.

54. A strict binary tree with 'n' nodes always have '2n-1' intermediate nodes. With 10 leaf nodes a strict binary tree will have exactly 19 nodes.

So, option (b) is correct.

57. From given inorder and preorder traversal, the binary tree can be formed.

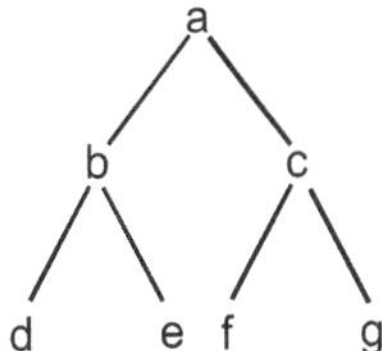

Since a is first node traversed in preorder, so it will be root of tree elements (nodes) left to a and right to a in inorder traversal will be left subtree and right subtree respectively of the tree. In left subtree elements d, b, e since bcomes first in preorder, so b will be root of left subtree d is left to b in inorder, so it will be left child of d and e will be right child of d. Tree will be like

58. Both M and N are true But N is not the reason for P because page fault is concerned with pages present in frame not with pages nearly the page accessed recently.

59. Let three process be P0, P1 and P2 with arrival times 0, 2 and 6 respectively and CPU burst times 10, 20 and 30 respectively. At time 0, P0 is the only available process so it runs. At time 2, P1 arrives, but P0 has the shortest remaining time, so it continues. At time 6, P2 also arrives, but P0 still has the shortest remaining time, so it continues. At time 10, P1 is scheduled as it is the shortest remaining time process. At time 30, P2 is scheduled.

So option (c) is correct.

Let three process be P0, P1 and P2 with arrival times 0, 2 and 6 respectively and CPU burst times 10, 20 and 30 respectively. At time 0, P0 is the only available process so it runs. At time 2, P1 arrives, but P0 has the shortest remaining time, so it continues. At time 6, P2 also arrives, but P0 still has the shortest remaining time, so it continues. At time 10, P1 is scheduled as it is the shortest remaining time process. At time 30, P2 is scheduled

So option (c) is correct.

60.
```
        F0          //  There will be 1 child process
      /   \             created by first fork
    F1      F1      //  There will be 2 child processes
   / \    / \           created by second fork
  F2 F2  F2  F2     //  There will be 4 child processes
 /\  /\  /\  /\         created by third fork
    ..............  //  and so on
```

If we sum all levels of above tree for i = 0 to n-1, we get $2^n - 1$. So there will be $2^n - 1$ child processes.

64. Deadlock Prevention: Deadlocks can be prevented by preventing at least one of the four required conditions:

1. Mutual Exclusion – not required for sharable resources; must hold for non-sharable resources.

2. Hold and Wait – must guarantee that whenever a process requests a resource, it does not hold any other resources. Require process to request and be allocated all its sources before it begins execution, or allow process to request resources only when the process has none. Low resource utilization; starvation possible. Restrain the ways request can be made.

3. No Pre-emption – If a process that is holding some resources requests another resource that cannot be immediately allocated to it, and then all resources currently being held are released. Pre-empted resources are added to the list of resources for which the process is waiting. Process will be restarted only when it can regain its old resources, as well as the new ones that it is requesting.

4. Circular Wait – impose a total ordering of all resource types, and require that each process requests resources in an increasing order of enumeration.

Deadlock Avoidance:

When a scheduler sees that starting a process or granting resource requests may lead to future deadlocks, then that process is just not started or the request is not granted. The deadlock-avoidance algorithm dynamically examines the resource-allocation state to ensure that there can never be a circular-wait condition. Resource-allocation state is defined by the number of available and allocated resources, and the maximum demands of the processes.

65. Abstraction, Encapsulation, Polymorphism and Inheritance are the essential features of a OOP Language.

66. Heap allocation is needed for dynamic data structures like tree, linked list, etc.

67. int i,j,x,y,m,n;

n=20;

for(i=0;i<n;i++)

{

    for(j=0;j<n;j++)

    {

        if(i%2)

        {

            x+=((4*j[4<<j] strength reduction)+5*i (loop invarient place after 1st for loop));

            y+=(7+4*j);

        }

    }

}

m=x+y;

I mean D is correct ! It is false among all

69. 4, 34, 10, 7, 19, 73, 2, 15, 6, 20

Since shortest seek time first policy is used, head will first move to 34. This move will cause 16*2 ms. After 34, head will move to 20 which will cause 14*1 ms. And so on. So cylinders are accessed in following order 34, 20, 19, 15, 10, 7, 6, 4, 2, 73 and total time will be $(16 + 14 + 1 + 4 + 15 + 3 + 1 + 1 + 1 + 71)*2 = 238$ ms.

So option (b) is correct.

70. In semaphores, P operation means wait operation and it decrements the value of the counting semaphore by 1 whereas V operation means signal operation and it increments the value of the counting semaphore..

Here a counting semaphore S = 7

After 20 P operations , s = $7 - 20 = -13$

After 'x' V operations value of S = 5, So $-13 + xV$

$$= 5 \text{ and } S = 18 .$$

Option C is correct.

71. There will be eight 4 bits CLA added in cascaded manner.

Each CLA will have bits (A31, A30 ....A0, B31, B30.............B0) available to it. so in 1 cycle each will compute EXOR operation on its 4 bits, now each CLA will take 2 cycles to pass on carry-out to next CLA, and at then end one more cycle is needed to get the SUM output from 8th CLA.

So total gate delays will be,

$1 + 2 * 8 + 1 = 18$ gate delays.

72. $f(95) \rightarrow f(f(106)) = f(96) \rightarrow f(f(107))$

$$= f(97) \rightarrow f(f(108))$$

$$= f(98) \rightarrow f(f(109))$$

$$= f(99) \rightarrow f(f(110))$$

$$= f(100) \rightarrow f(f(111))$$

$$= f(101) = 91$$

So the correct option is (c)

75. $0 \times C0000000$

$= 1100\ 0000\ 0000\ 0000\ 0000\ 0000\ 0000\ 0000$

In IEEE Floating point representation: First MSB bit is the sign bit for Mantissa, next 8 bits represents Exponent value and the last 23 bits represents the value of Mantissa. Also it is a biased exponent system where biased value = $2^{(\text{exp bits-1})} - 1 = 127$

So number = $(-1)\ 1.M \times 2^{(128-127)} = -1.0 \times 2 = -2.0$

So option (d) is correct.

76. See: implimentation of logic gates using 2×1 Multiplexers. So 2×1 Multiplexers are sufficient to implement any Boolean function.

Similarly, we can also use $\{\wedge, \oplus, T\}$ (i.e., AND, XOR, and 1) to implement any Boolean functions.

So, option (b) is correct.

77. Regression: It is a statistical analysis which is used to establish relation between a response and a predictor variable. It is mainly used in finance related applications.

Decision Tree: Decision tree is a computational method which works on descriptive data and records the observations of each object to reach to a result.

Clustering: It is a method of grouping more similar objects in a group and the non-similar objects to other groups.

Association Rules: It uses if-then reasoning method using the support-confidence technique to give a result.

According to the question Decision Tree is the most suitable technique that can be used to get best result of the experiment.

79. (c) Snowflake schema is an arrangement of tables in a multidimensional database system. It contains Fact Tables connected to multi-dimension tables.

Third statement is true as it is the most important feature of snowflake schema. Normalization of dimension tables are done to remove data redundancy and thereby reducing the space required to hold data.

80. (d) Given String = "ICRBCSIT17"

Index of I=0, C=1, R=2, B=3 and so on. Now we are making a pointer p point to character array c.

Here 2[p] = p[2] ='R' and 6[p] = p[6] ='I'

'R'-'I' = 9 and c + 2[p] – 6[p] – 1 = c + 9 – 1 = c + 8

So "17" is printed as the string.

1. Consider the following program

```
main()
{
int x = l;
printf("%d", (*char(char *) & x));
}
```

Assuming required header files are included and if the machine in which this program is executed is little endian, then the output will be-

(a) 0   (b) 99999999

(c) 1   (d) unpredictable

2. Consider the following **declaration :**

```
structaddr {
    char city[10];
    char street[30];
    int pin ;
};
struct {
    char name[30];
    int gender;
    struct addr locate ;
} person, *kd = &person ;
```

Then *(kd -> name +2) can be used instead of

(a) person.name+2

(b) kd->(name+2)

(c) *((*kd).name + 2)

(d) either (a) or (b), but not (c)

3. If a variable can take only integral values from 0 to n, where n is an integer, then the variable can be represented as a bit-field whose width is (the log in the answers are to the base 2, and [log n] means the floor of log n)

(a) [log(n)] + 1 bits   (b) [log (n-1)] + 1 bits

(c) [log (n+1)] +1 bits   (d) None of the above

4. The following C program

```
main()
{
    fork() ; fork(); printf("yes");
}
```

If we execute this core segment, how many times the string yes will be printed?

(a) Only once   (b) 2 times

(c) 4 times   (d) 8 times

5. **Consider the following table in a relational database**

Last Name	Rank	Room	Shift
Smith	Manager	214	Morning
Jones	Custodian	33	Afternoon
Smith	Custodian	33	Evening
Doe	Clerical	777	Morning

According to the data shown In the table, which of the following could be a candidate key of the table?

(a) {Last Name}   (b) {Room}

(c) {Shift}   (d) {Room, Shift}

6. A data driven machine is one that executes an instruction if the needed data is available. The physical ordering of the code listing does not dictate the course of execution. Consider the following **pseudo-code**

(A) Multiply E by 0.5 to get F

(B) Add A and **B** to get E

(C) Add B with 0.5 to get D

(D) Add E and **F** to get G

(E) Add A with 10.5 to get C

Assume A, B, C are already assigned values and the desired output is G. Which of the following sequence of execution is valid?

(a) B, C, D, A, E   (b) C, B, E, A, D

(c) A, B,C, D,E   (d) E, D, C, B, A

7. Assume A and B are non zero positive integers. The following code segment

```
while (A != B){
    If (A > B )
    A -= B;
    else
    B -= A;
}
cout <<A; //printing the value of A
```

(a) Computes the LCM of two numbers

(b) Divides the larger number by the smaller number

(c) Computes the GCD of two numbers

(d) Finds the smaller of two numbers

8. A language with string manipulation facilities uses the following operations.

   head(s)- returns the first character of the string s

   tail(s) - returns all but the first character of the string s

   concat(s1, s2)- concatenates string S1 with s2.

   The output of concat(head(s), head(tail(tail(s)))), **where** s **is** acbc **is**

   (a) ab
   (b) ba
   (c) ac
   (d) aa

9. 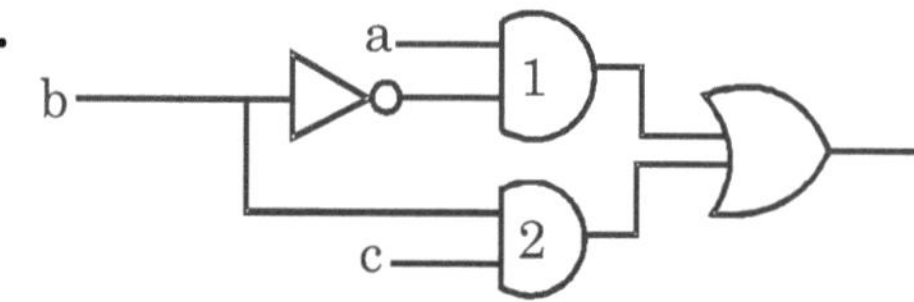

   In the diagram above, the inverter (NOT gate) and the AND-gates labeled 1 and 2 have delays of 9,10 and 12 nanoseconds(ns), respectively. Wire delays are negligible. For certain values of a and c, together with certain transition of b, a glitch (spurious output) is generated for a short time, after which the output assumes its correct value. The duration of the glitch is

   (a) 7 ns
   (b) 9 ns
   (c) 11ns
   (d) 13 ns

10. Which of the following comparisons between static and dynamic type checking is incorrect.

    (a) Dynamic type checking slows down the execution

    (b) Dynamic type checking offers more flexibility to the programmers

    (c) In contrast to Static type checking, dynamic type checking may cause failure in runtime due to type errors

    (d) Unlike static type checking, dynamic type checking is done during compilation

11. ________can detect burst error of length less than or equal to degree of the polynomial and detects burst errors that affect odd number of bits.

    (a) Hamming Code
    (b) CRC
    (c) VRC
    (d) None of the above

12. An array A consists of n integers in locations A[0], A[1] ....A[n – 1], It is required to shift the elements of the array cyclically to the left by k places, where $1 <= k <= (n-1)$. An incomplete algorithm for doing this in linear time, without using another array is given below. Complete the algorithm by filling in the blanks.

    Assume all the variables are suitably declared.

    ```
    min = n; i = 0;
    while (________) {
    ```

    ```
    temp = A[i] ;j = i;
    while (________) {
    A[j] = ________;
    j = (j + k) mod n;
    If (j < min ) then
    min = j;
    }
    A[(n+ i-k) mod n] = ___________;
    i = ________;
    }
    ```

    (a) i > min; j !=(n+i) mod n ; A[j + k]; temp;i + 1;
    (b) i < min; j ! =(n + i) mod n ; A[j + k]; temp; i + 1;
    (c) i > min; j! =(n + i + k) mod n; A[j + k]; temp; i + 1;
    (d) i < min; j ! =(n + i – k) mod n ; A[(j + k) mod n]; temp; i + 1 ;

13. The difference between a named pipe and a regular file in Unix is that

    (a) Unlike a regular file, named pipe is a special file

    (b) The data in a pipe is transient, unlike the content of a regular file

    (c) Pipes forbid random accessing, while regular files do allow this.

    (d) All of the above

14. A class of 30 students occupy a classroom containing 5 rows of seats, with 8 seats in each row. If the students seat themselves at random, the probability that the sixth seat in the fifth row will be empty is

    (a) $\dfrac{1}{5}$
    (b) $\dfrac{1}{3}$
    (c) $\dfrac{1}{4}$
    (d) $\dfrac{2}{5}$

15. The domain of the function log(log sin(x)) is

    (a) $0 < x < \pi$
    (b) $2n\pi < x < (2n + 1)\,\pi,$ for n in N
    (c) Empty set
    (d) None of the above

16. The following paradigm can be used to find the solution of the problem in minimum time:

    Given a set of non-negative integer, and a value K, determine if there is a subset of the given set with sum equal to K:

    (a) Divide arid Conquer
    (b) Dynamic Programming
    (c) Greedy Algorithm
    (d) Branch and Bound

17. (G, *) is an abelian group. Then
    (a) $x = x^{-1}$, for any x belonging to G
    (b) $x = x^2$, for any x belonging to G
    (c) $(x \times y)^2 = x^2 \times y^2$, for any x, y belonging to G
    (d) G is of finite order

18. Consider the following C code segment:

```
#include <stdio.h>

main()
{
    int i, j , x;
    scanf("%d", &x);
    i = 1 ; j = 1;
    while (i< 10) {
    j = j * i;
    i = i + 1;
    if (i = =x ) break;
    }
}
```

    For the program fragment above, which of the following statements about the variables i and j must be true after execution of this program? [! exclamation) sign denotes factorial in the answer]
    (a) $(j = (x-1)!)$ ^ $(i \geq x)$
    (b) $(j = 9!)$ ^ $(i = 10)$
    (c) $((j = 10!)$ ^ $(i = 10))V((j = (x - 1)!)^{\wedge}(i = x))$
    (d) $((j = 9!)$ ^ $(i \geq 10))$ V $((j = (x - 1)!)$ ^ $(i = x))$

19. Given $\sqrt{224_r} = 13_r$ the value of radix r is
    (a) 10
    (b) 8
    (c) 6
    (d) 5

20. Determine the number of page faults when references to pages occur in the order - 1, 2, 4, 5, 2, 1, 2, 4. Assume that the main memory can accommodate 3 pages and the main memory already has the pages 1 and 2, with page 1 having brought earlier than page 2. (assume LRU i.e. Least-Recently-Used algorithm is applied)
    (a) 3
    (b) 4
    (c) 5
    (d) None of the above

21. Consider a system having m resources of the same type. These resources are shared by 3 processes A, B, C, which have peak time demands of 3, 4, 6 respectively. The minimum value of m that ensures that deadlock will never occur is
    (a) 11
    (b) 12
    (c) 13
    (d) 14

22. A computer has 1000K of main memory. The jobs arrive and finish in the following sequence.
    Job 1 requiring 200 K arrives
    Job 2 requiring 350 K arrives
    Job 3 requiring 300 K arrives
    Job 1 finishes
    Job 4 requiring 120 K arrives
    Job5 requiring 150 K arrives
    Job 6 requiring 80 K arrives
    Among best fit and first fit, which performs better for this sequence?
    (a) First fit
    (b) Best fit
    (c) Both perform the same
    (d) None of the above

23. Disk requests come to a disk driver for cylinders in the order 10, 22, 20, 2, 40, 6 and 38, at a time when the disk drive is reading from cylinder 20. The seek time is 6 ms /cylinder. The total seek total, if the disk arm scheduling algorithms is first-come-first-served is
    (a) 360 ms
    (c) 900 ms
    (b) 850 ms
    (d) None of the above

24. Choose the correct statement -
    (a) $A = \{a^n b^n \mid n = 1,2,3,....\}$ is a regular language
    (b) The set B, consisting of all strings made up of only a's and b's having equal number of a's and bs defines a regular language
    (c) $L(A * B) \cap B$ gives the set A
    (d) None of the above

25. CFG (Context Free Grammar) is not closed under
    (a) Union
    (b) Complementation
    (c) Kleene star
    (d) Product

26.

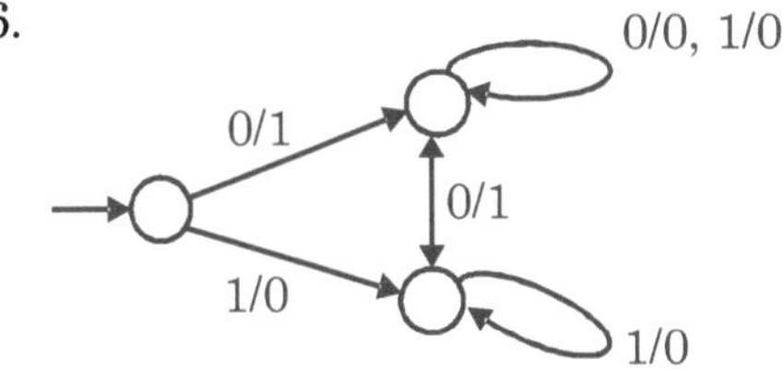

    The FSM (Finite State Machine) machine pictured in the figure above
    (a) Complements a given bit pattern
    (b) Finds 2's complement of a given bit pattern
    (c) Increments a given bit pattern by 1
    (d) Changes the sign bit

27. A CFG(Context Free Grammar) is said to be in Chomsky Normal Form (CNF), if all the productions are of the form A -> BC or A -> a. Let G be a CFG in CNF. To derive a string of terminals of length x, the number of products to be used is
   (a) $2x - 1$ (b) $2x$
   (c) $2x + 1$ (d) 2^x

28. Incremental-Compiler is a compiler
   (a) which is written in a language that is different from the source language
   (b) compiles the whole source code to generate object code afresh
   (c) compiles only those portion of source code that have been modified.
   (d) that runs on one machine but produces object code for another machine

29. DU-chains(Definition-Use) in compiler design
   (a) consist of a definition of a variable and all its uses, reachable from that definition
   (b) are created using a form of static code analysis
   (c) are prerequisite for many compiler optimization including constant propagation and common sub expression elimination
   (d) All of the above

30. Which of the following comment about peep-hole optimization is true?
   (a) It is applied to small part of the code and applied repeatedly
   (b) It can be used to optimize intermediate code
   (c) It can be applied to a portion of the code that is not contiguous
   (d) It is applied in symbol table to optimize the memory requirements.

31. A byte addressable computer has a memory capacity of 2^m KB(kbytes) and can perform 2^n operations. An instruction involving 3 operands and one operator needs maximum of
   (a) $3m$ bits
   (b) $3m + n$ bits
   (c) $m + n$ bits
   (d) None of the above

32. A computer uses ternary system instead of the traditional binary system. An n bit string in the binary system will occupy
   (a) $3 + n$ ternary digits
   (b) $2n/3$ ternary digits .
   (c) $n(\log_2 3)$ ternary digits
   (d) $n(\log_3 2)$ ternary digits

33. Which of the following is application of Breath First Search on the graph?
   (a) Finding diameter of the graph
   (b) Finding bipartite graph
   (c) Both (a) and (b)
   (d) None of the above

34. Micro program is
   (a) the name of a source program in micro computers
   (b) set of microinstructions that defines the individual operations in response to a machine-language instruction
   (c) a primitive form of macros used in assembly language programming
   (d) a very small segment of machine code

35. Given two sorted list of size m and n respectively. The number of comparisons needed the worst case by the merge sort algorithm will be
   (a) mxn
   (b) maximum of m and n
   (c) minimum of m and n
   (d) $m + n - 1$

36. A has table with 10 buckets with one slot per bucket is depicted here. The symbols, SI to S7 are initially entered using a hashing function with linear probing. The maximum number of comparisons needed in searching an item that is not present is

0	S7
1	SI
2	
3	S4
4	S2
5	
6	SS
7	
8	S6
9	S3

   (a) 4   (b) 5
   (c) 6   (d) 3

37. The running time of an algorithm is given by
   $$T(n) = T(n - 1) + T(n - 2) - T(n - 3), \text{ if } n > 3$$
   $$= n, \text{ otherwise}$$
   Then what should be the relation between T(1), T(2) and T(3), so that the order of the algorithm is constant ?
   (a) $T(1) = T(2) = T(3)$ (c) $T(1) - T(3) = 2*T(2)$
   (b) $T(1) - T(3) = T(2)$ (b) $T(1) + T(2) = T(3)$

38. The number of edges in a regular graph of degree d and n vertices is
    (a) maximum of n and d
    (b) n+d
    (c) nd
    (d) $\dfrac{nd}{2}$

39. Perform window to viewport transformation for the point (20, 15). Assume that $(X_{w\,min}, Y_{w\,min}$ is $(0,0)$; (Xwmax, Ywmax) is $(100,100)$; (X_{vmin}, Y_{vmin}) is $(5,5)$; (X_{vmax}, Y_{vmax}) is $(20,20)$. The value of x and y in the viewport is
    (a) x = 4,y = 4   (b) x = 3,y =3
    (b) x = 8, y = 7.25   (d) x = 3,y = 4

40. Given relations R(w, x) and S(y, z), the result of
    SELECT DISTINCT w, x
    FROM R, S
    is guaranteed to be same as R, if
    (a) R has no duplicates and S is non-empty
    (b) R and S have no duplicates
    (c) S has no duplicates and R is non-empty
    (d) R and S have the same number of tuples

41. For a database relation R(a,b,c,d) where the domains of a, b, c and d include only atomic values, only the following functional dependencies and those that can be inferred from them hold
    a -> c
    b -> d
    The relation is in
    (a) First normal form but not in second normal form
    (b) Second normal form but not in third normal form
    (c) Third normal form
    (d) None of the above

42. Consider the set of relations given below and the SQL query that follows:
    Students : (Roll_number, Name, Date_of_birth)
    Courses: (Course_number, Course_name, Instructor)
    Grades:(Roll_number, Course_number, Grade)
    SELECT DISTINCT Name
    FROM Students, Courses, Grades
    WHERE Students.Roll_number
    = Grades.Roll_number
    AND Courses.Instructor =Sriram
    AND Courses.Course_number
    = Grades.Course_number
    AND_Grades.Grade = A

Which of the following sets is computed by the above query?
    (a) Names of Students who have got an A grade in all courses taught by Sriram
    (b) Names of Students who have got an A grade in all courses
    (c) Names of Students who have got an A grade in at least one of the courses taught by Sriram
    (d) None of the above

43. Consider the following C++ program

```cpp
int a (int m)
{return ++m ;}
int b(int&m)
{return ++m;}
intc(char &m)
{return ++m ; }
void main ()
{
    int p = 0, q=0, r = 0;
p + = a(b(p));
q+ = b(a(q));
r+ = a(c(r));
cout«p«q « r;
}
```

Assuming the required header files are already included, the above program
    (a) results in compilation error
    (b) print 123
    (c) print 111
    (d) print 322

44. Station A uses 32 byte packets to transmit messages to Station B using a sliding window protocol. The round trip delay between A and B is 80 ms and the bottleneck bandwidth on the path between A and B is 128 kbps. What is the optimal window size that A should use?
    (a) 20   (c) 160
    (b) 40   (d) 320

45. Assuming that for a given network layer implementation, connection establishment overhead is 100 bytes and disconnection overhead is 28 bytes. What would be the minimum size of the packet the transport layer needs to keep up, if it wishes to implement a datagram service above the network layer and needs to keep its overhead to a minimum of 12.5%. (Ignore transport layer overhead)
    (a) 512 bytes   (b) 768 bytes
    (c) 1152 bytes   (d) 1024 bytes

46. In cryptography, the following uses transposition ciphers and the keyword is LAVER. Encrypt the following message. (Spaces are omitted during encryption)

    WELCOME TO NETWORK SECURITY !

    (a) WMEKREETSILTWETCOOCYONRU!
    (b) EETSICOOCYWMEKRONRU!LTWET
    (c) LTWETONRUIWMEKRCOOCYEETSI
    (d) ONRUICOOCYLTWETEETSIWMEKR

47. In a particular program, it is found that 1% of the code accounts for 50% of the execution time. To code a program in C++, it takes 100 man-days. Coding in assembly language is 10 times harder than coding in C++, but runs 5 times faster. Converting an existing C++ program into an assembly language program is 4 times faster.

    To completely write the program in C++ and rewrite the 1% code in assembly language, if a project team needs 13 days, the team consists of

    (a) 13 programmers
    (b) 10 programmers
    (c) 8 programmers
    (d) 100/13 programmers

48. in unit testing of a module, it is found that for a set of test data, at the maximum 90% of the code alone were tested with the probability of success 0.9. The reliability of the module is

    (a) Greater than 0.9   (b) Equal to 0.9
    (c) At most 0.81   (d) At least 0.81

49. In a file which contains 1 million records and the order of the tree is 100, then what is the maxim number of nodes to be accessed if B+ tree index is used?

    (a) 5   (b) 4
    (c) 3   (d) 10

50. A particular disk unit uses a bit string to record the occupancy or vacancy of its tracks, with 0 denoting vacant and 1 for occupied. A 32-bit segment of this string has hexadecimal value D4FE2003 The percentage of occupied tracks for the corresponding part of the disk, to the nearest percentage is

    (a) 12   (b) 25
    (c) 38   (d) 44

51. Which of the following is dense index?

    (a) Primary index
    (b) Clusters index
    (c) Secondary index
    (d) Secondary non key index

52. In E-R model, Y is the dominant entity and X is subordinate entity

    (a) If X is deleted, then Y is also deleted
    (b) If Y is deleted, then X is also deleted
    (c) If Y is deleted, then X is not deleted
    (d) None of the above

53. Immunity of the external schemas (or application programs) to changes in the conceptual schema is referred to as:

    (a) Physical Data Independence
    (b) Logical Data Independence
    (c) Both (a) and (b)
    (d) None of the above

54. The set of attributes X will be fully functionally dependent on the set of attributes Y if the following conditions are satisfied.

    (a) X is functionally dependent on Y
    (b) X is not functionally dependent on any subset of Y
    (c) Both (a) and (b)
    (d) None of these

55. Let us assume that transaction T1 has arrived before transaction T2. Consider the schedule S = rl(A); r2(B); w2(A); wl(B)

    Which of the following is true?

    (a) Allowed under basic timestamp protocol.
    (b) Not allowed under basic timestamp protocols because Tl is rolled back.
    (c) Not allowed under basic timestamp protocols because T2 is rolled back.
    (d) None of these

56. The time complexity of computing the transitive closure of binary relation on a set of n elements is known to be

    (a) $O(n)$ (b) $O(n*\log(n))$
    (c) $O\left(n^{\frac{3}{2}}\right)$ (d) $O(n^3)$

57. Given a binary-max heap. The elements are stored in an arrays as 25, 14, 16, 13, 10, 8, 12. What content of the array after two delete operations?

    (a) 14, 13, 8, 12, 10   (b) 14,12,13,10,8
    (c) 14,13,12,8,10   (d) 14,13,12,10,8

58. The Functions Point (FP) metric is

    (a) Calculated from user requirement
    (b) Calculated from lines of code
    (c) Calculated from software complexity assessment
    (d) None of the above

59. The lower degree of cohesion is kind of
    (a) Logical Cohesion
    (b) Coincidental Cohesion
    (c) Procedural Cohesion
    (d) Communicational Cohesion

60. What is the output of the following program?

```
main (){
int x = 2, y = 5;
if(x <y) return (x = x+y);
else print ("zl");
printf("z2");
}
```

    (a) z2   (b) zlz2
    (c) Compilation error (d) None of these

61. The Operating System of a computer may periodically collect all the free memory space to form contiguous block of free space. This is called
    (a) Concatenation
    (b) Garbage collection
    (c) Collision
    (d) Dynamic Memory Allocation

62. Any set of Boolean operators that is sufficient to represent all Boolean expressions is said to be complete. Which of the following is not complete?
    (a) {AND, OR}   (b) (AND, NOT}
    (c) { NOT, OR }   (d) {NOR}

63. Consider a singly linked list of the form where F is a pointer to the first element in the linked list and L is the pointer to the last element in the list. The time of which of the following operations depends on the length of the list?

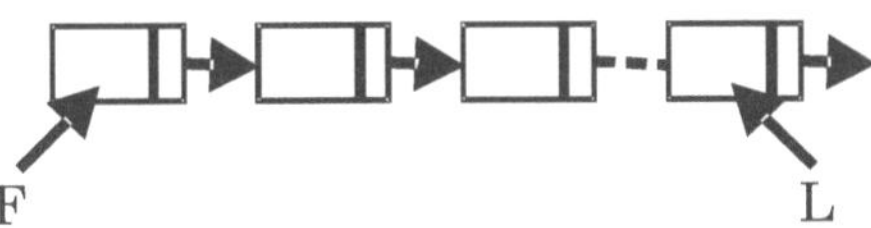

    (a) Delete the last element of the list
    (b) Delete the first element of the list
    (c) Add an element after the last element of the list
    (d) Interchange the first two elements of the list

64. A particular BNF definition for a "word" is given by the following rules.

```
<word> :: = <letter> | <lettercharpair> | <letterintpair>
<charpair> :: = <letterletter> | <charpairxletterletter>
<intpair> :: = <integerinteger> | <intpairintegerinteger>
<letter> :: = a | b | c | ....| y | z
<integer> :: = 0 | 1 | 2 | .... | 9
```

Which of the following lexical entries can be derived from < word > ?
I. pick
II. picks
III. c44
    (a) I, II and III   (b) I and II only
    (c) I and III only   (d) II and III only

65. Of the following, which best characterizes computers that use memory mapped I/O.
    (a) The computer provides special instructions for manipulating I/O ports
    (b) I/O ports are placed at addresses on the bus and are accessed just like other memory locations
    (c) To perform I/O operations, it is sufficient to place the data in an address register and call channel to perform the operation
    (d) I/O can be performed only when memory management hardware is turne on

66. Of the following sorting algorithms, which has a running time that is least dependent on the initial ordering of the input?
    (a) Merge Sort   (b) Insertion Sort
    (c) Selection Sort   (d) Quick Sort

67. Processes PI and P2 have a producer-consumer relationship, communicating by the use of a set of share buffers.

PI: repeat
      Obtain an empty buffer
      Fill it
      Return a full buffer
      forever
P2: repeat
      Obtain a full buffer
      Empty it
      Return an empty buffer
forever

Increasing the number of buffers is likely to do which of the following?
I. Increase the rate at which requests are satisfied (throughput)
II. Decrease the likelihood of deadlock
III. Increase the ease of achieving a correct implementation
    (a) III only   (b) II only
    (c) I only   (d) II and III only

68. In multi-programmed systems, it is advantageous if some programs such as editors and compilers can be shared by several users.

    Which of the following must be true of multi-programmed systems in order that a single copy of a program can be shared by several users?

    I.   The program is a macro

    II. The program is recursive

    III. The program is reentrant

    (a) I only   (b) II only

    (c) III only   (d) I, II and III

69. Let P be a procedure that for some inputs calls itself (i.e. is recursive). If P is guaranteed to terminate, which of the following statement(s) must be true?

    I.   P has a local variable

    II. P has an execution path where it does not call itself

    III. P either refers to a global variable or has at least one parameter

    (a) I only   (b) II only

    (c) III only   (d) II and III only

70. Consider the following C program

```
#include <stdio.h>
main()
{
float sum = 0.0, j = 1.0, i = 2.0; ,
while (i/j > 0.001){
    j = j + l;
    sum = sum + i/j;
    printf("%f\n", sum);
}
}
```

    How many lines of output does this program produce?

    (a) 0-9 lines of output

    (b) 10-19 lines out output

    (c) 20-29 lines of output

    (d) More than 29lines of output.

71. A particular parallel program computation requires 100 sec when executed on a single processor. If 40% of this computation is inherently sequential (i.e. will not benefit from additional processors), then theoretically best possible elapsed times of this program running with 2 and 4 processors, respectively, are

    (a) 20 sec and 10 sec

    (b) 30 sec and 15 sec

    (c) 50 sec and 25 sec

    (d) 70 sec and 55 sec

72. Consider the following C code segment

```
int f(intx)
{
if(x < l) return 1;
else return ( f(x − l) + g(x) ) ;
int g (int x )
{
    if ( x < 2 ) return 2 ;
    else return (f(x − l) + g(x/2));
}
```

    Of the following, which best describes the growth of f(x) as a function of x ?

    (a) Linear

    (b) Exponential

    (c) Quadratic

    (d) Cubic

73. For a multi-processor architecture, In which protocol a write transaction is forwarded to only those processors that are known to possess a copy of newly altered cache line ?

    (a) Snoopy bus protocol

    (b) Cache coherency protocol

    (c) Directory based protocol

    (d) None of the above

74. Avalanche effect in cryptography

    (a) Is desirable property of cryptographic algorithm

    (b) Is undesirable property of cryptographic algorithm

    (c) Has no effect on encryption algorithm

    (d) None of the above

75. In neural network, the network capacity is defined as

    (a) The traffic carry capacity of the network

    (b) The total number of nodes in the network

    (c) The number of patterns that can be stored and recalled in a network

    (d) None of the above

76. Cloaking is a search engine optimization (SEO) technique. During cloaking

    (a) Content presented to search engine spider is different from that presented to user's browser

    (b) Content present to search engine spider and browser is same

    (c) Contents of user's requested website are changed

    (d) None of the above

77. What is one advantage of setting up a DMZ(Demilitarized Zone) with two firewalls?
   (a) You can control where traffic goes in the three networks
   (b) You can do stateful packet filtering
   (c) You can do load balancing
   (d) Improve network performance

78. Which one of the following algorithm is not used in asymmetric key cryptography?
   (a) RSA Algorithm
   (b) Diffie-Hellman Algorithm
   (c) Electronic Code Book Algorithm
   (d) None of the above

79. A doubly linked list is declared as

```
struct Node {
    int Value ;
    struct Node *Fwd ;
    struct Node *Bwd ;
};
```

Where Fwd and Bwd represent forward and backward link to the adjacent elements of the list. Which of the following segments of code deletes the node pointed to by X from the doubly linked list, if it is assumed that X points to neither the first nor the last node of the list?

(a) X->Bwd->Fwd = X->Fwd; X->Fwd->Bwd = X->Bwd ;

(b) X->Bwd.Fwd = X->Fwd ; X.Fwd->Bwd = X->Bwd ;

(c) X.Bwd->Fwd = X.Bwd ; X->Fwd.Bwd = X.Bwd;

(d) X->Bwd->Fwd = X->Bwd ; X->Fwd->Bwd = X->Fwd ;

80. If Tree-1 and Tree-2 are the trees indicated below:

Tree-1   Tree-2

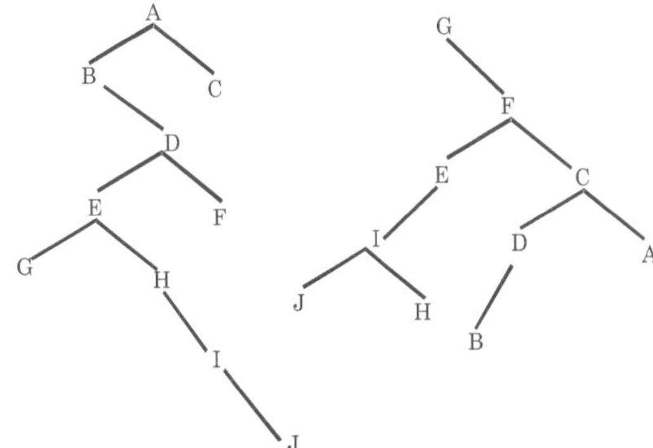

Which traversals of Tree-1 and Tree-2, respectively, will produce the same sequence?
(a) Preorder, postorder
(b) Postorder, inorder,
(c) Postorder, preorder
(d) Inorder, preorder

ANSWERS

1. (c)	2. (c)	3. (a)	4. (c)	5. (d)	6. (c)	7. (c)	8. (a)	9. (a)	10. (d)
11. (b)	12. (d)	13. (d)	14. (c)	15. (c)	16. (b)	17. (d)	18. (d)	19. (d)	20. (b)
21. (a)	22. (a)	23. (d)	24. (d)	25. (b)	26. (c)	27. (a)	28. (c)	29. (d)	30. (a)
31. (d)	32. (d)	33. (c)	34. (b)	35. (d)	36. (b)	37. (a)	38. (d)	39. (c)	40. (a)
41. (a)	42. (c)	43. (a)	44. (b)	45. (d)	46. (b)	47. (c)	48. (c)	49. (b)	50. (d)
51. (c)	52. (b)	53. (b)	54. (b)	55. (b)	56. (d)	57. (c)	58. (c)	59. (b)	60. (d)
61. (b)	62. (a)	63. (a)	64. (d)	65. (b)	66. (a)	67. (c)	68. (c)	69. (d)	70. (d)
71. (d)	72. (b)	73. (c)	74. (a)	75. (c)	76. (a)	77. (a)	78. (c)	79. (a)	80. (b)

EXPLANATIONS

1.
```
main()
{
int x=1;
printf("%d",(*char(char*)&x));
}
```
Here, we will get a compilation error because 'char' is extra.

If the code is :
```
main()
{
int x=1;
printf("%d",(*(char*)&x));
}
```
Note: We don't need to typecast it(again) to get the value stored at the char pointer.

Option C is correct.

2. A and B points to the address of the location whereas we require to access the value at that location, which is the third character of name.

Option C is correct.

3. Here we have to choose a variable from the interval (0, n]

A number of the form 2^m has $m + 1$ bits.

If $2^m \leq n \leq 2^{(m+1)}$; then n should also have $m + 1$ bits.

Thus any number chosen in between (0, n] should have $[\log (n)] + 1$ bits.

option A correct.

4. code can be re-written as
```
main {
fork();
fork();
printf("yes");
}
```
First fork() will create a child process,which is going to execute the next instruction i.e 2nd fork() and parent process also going to execute 2nd fork.

So, 2 more process will be created. so in system now there are 4 process and they are going to execute printf statement. so total no. of yes will be 4

Total number of times yes will be printed = 4

Therefore option C is correct.

5. Candidate key:- must be able to uniquely determine every other attribute. i.e., whenever a candidate key value is repeated, all other values must repeat or in a set, candidate key cannot be repeated.

option
a. Last Name cannot be key as smith value are repeated.
b. Room:- 33 value is repeated
c. shift:- morning repeated
d. Composite key Room+ shift $\Rightarrow$ Every tuple is now unique

234 + morning

33 + afternoon

33 + evening

222 + morning.

Option D Correct

6. E * 0.5 = F

A + B = E

B + 0.5 = D

E + F = G

A + 10.5 = C

As execution is based on availability values for variables (A, B, C, D, E): G is the output. So, E + F = G (requires the E and F computed before this operation)

E and F computed in step (B) and (A) of the execution list (E and F are not assigned any values at start of the execution).

So, Step (B) and step (A) should be completed before step (D).

Option C Correct

7. This is Euclidean algorithm for determining HCF of two numbers which works in this way :

If we subtract smaller number from larger (we reduce larger number), GCD doesn't change. So if we keep subtracting repeatedly the larger of two, we end up with GCD

Therefore option C is correct.

8.
```
s = acbc
concat(head(s), head(tail(tail(s))))
concat(head(s), head(tail(cbc)))
concat(head(s), head(bc))
concat(head(s), b)
concat(a,b)
ab
```
Therefore option A is correct.

9. The output of AND gate 1 will be available at the input of OR gate after 9 + 10 = 19 nanoseconds but Output of AND gate 2 will be available after 12 nanoseconds only.

So a glitch will be generated for 19 − 12 = 7 nanoseconds after which the output assumes its correct value.

Option A is correct.

10. Static Type Checking

A language is statically-typed if the type of a variable is known at compile time instead of at runtime. Common examples of statically-typed languages include Ada, C, C++, C#, JADE, Java, Fortran, Haskell, ML, Pascal, and Scala.

Dynamic Type Checking

Dynamic type checking is the process of verifying the type safety of a program at runtime. Common dynamically-typed languages include Groovy, JavaScript, Lisp, Lua, Objective-C, PHP, Prolog, Python, Ruby, Smalltalk and Tcl.

So, dynamic type checking offers more flexibility to the programmers at the expense of runtime type checking overhead and possible runtime type errors.

Therefore option D is correct.

11. CRC performance

All burst errors of length equal to the polynomial's degree are detected

All burst errors affecting an odd number of bits are detected

Burst errors of length greater than the degree of polynomials are detected with high probability 32-bit CRC used in Ethernet, Token Ring

Therefore option B correct.

12. In the five blanks given in the question the last two blanks must be temp and i + 1 because all the given options for the fourth and fifth blanks has temp and i + 1.

Now, for the first blank it must be i < min because if it is i > min then the control goes out of the while loop in the initial case when i = 0 and min = n

So, the first blank is i < min which implies either option B or option D is correct.

Assume option B is correct then in the bracket of while we have j! = (n + i) mod n

That means whenever j becomes equal to (n + i)mod n then control goes out of the while loop.

Now (n + i)mod n = i and j is always equal to i because in the line 3 of the code we are assining the value of i to j.

So, if option B is true control never enters the second while loop but it has to enter the second while loop to shift the nos. K places left.

Hence, option D is correct.

13. All of the Above

14. No. of ways will be $= {}^{40}C_{30}$ ways

Probability of sixth seat in row no. 5 will be

empty is $= \dfrac{{}^{39}C_{30}}{{}^{40}C_{30}}$

$${}^{39}C_{30} = \dfrac{39 \times 38 \times ----- \times 1}{(39 \times 29 \times --- \times 1) \times (9 \times 8 \times ----- \times 1)}$$

$$= \dfrac{39 \times 38 \times ----- \times 31}{(9 \times 8 \times ----- \times 1)}$$

$${}^{40}C_{30} = \dfrac{40 \times 39 \times ----- \times 1}{(30 \times 29 \times ----- \times 1) \times (10 \times 9 \times 8 --- \times 1)}$$

$$= \dfrac{40 \times 39 \times --- \times 31}{10 \times 9 \times 8 \times --- \times 1} = \dfrac{10}{40} = \dfrac{1}{4}$$

option c is correct.

15. log(log sin(x))

$-1 \le \sin x \le +1$

log a is defined for positive values of a

log sin(x) is defined for sin(x) = (0,1]

Possible values for log sin(x) = $(-\infty, 0]$

Domain of log(log sin(x) = Not defined

Therefore, Answer (c) Empty Set

16. It's a subset sum problem which requires dynamic programming to solve.

so option B is correct.

17. A. False : if every element in the group has its own inverse i.e. x = x–1 for all x ∈ G ⇒ G is abelian but the converse is not true.

(z, +) is an infinite abelian group its own but the following are not true for it; e = 0

$x = x^{-1}$: inverse of $1 \ne 1$ but $= -1$

B. False : $1^2 = 1 + 1 \ne 1$ but $= 2$

True : G is abelian if and only if $(xy)^2 = x^2 y^2$ for all x and y in G

$\Rightarrow$ Let x, y ∈ G then (xy)2 = xyxy

= xxy xy sin c y is

abelian (commutative); xxyy = $x^2 y^2$.

Thus $(xy)^2 = x^2 y^2$.

Assume $(xy)^2 = x^2 y^2 \ \forall \ x, y \in y$

then $(xy)^2 = x^2 y^2$

xy xy = xxyy

x–1 xy xy = x^{-1} xx yy

yxy = xyy

yx yy^{-1} = $xyyy^{-1}$.

yx = xy

Hence G is abelian.

(D) False : since (z, +) is an infinite abelian group

18. When value of x $\geq$ 10 then value of j will be 9! because condition of while loop is (i < 10). so i will run till 9 and j value will be computed as 9! and if x < 10 then loop will terminate when i will be incremented up to x.So that time j value will be computed as (x −1)!

Option D Correct

19. Given $\sqrt{(224)_r} = 13r$

$2r^2 + 2r + 4 = (r + 3)^2$

$2r^2 + 2r + 4 = r^2 + 9 + 6r$

$r^2 = 4r − 5 = 0$

$r = 5, − 1$

Option d is correct.

20. 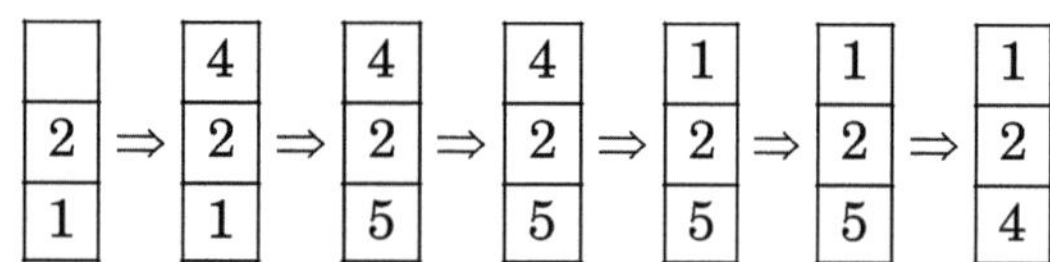

Pf = 1 Pf = 2 Pf = 3 Pf = 4

21. The sufficient condition for ensuring that deadlock doesn't occur:

Si < n + m

where Si = Total request resource of its process

 n = Total number of process

 m = Total number of resource

if above condition is false then DL may occur, if the condition is true then-No DL.

for the above problem, total demand is: 3 + 4 + 6 = 13

13 < 3 + m

10 < m, the minimum value of m that ensure deadlock is never occurring is 11.

22. Initialty there is 1000k main memory available ...

Then, job 1 arrive ..and occupied 200k, then

job 2 arrive ,occupy 350k, after that

job3 arrive and occupy 300k (assume continuous allocation) now free memory is 1000 - 850 (200 + 350 + 300) = 150k ...(till these jobs first fit and best fit are same now job1 is finished . so that space is also free... so here 200k slot and 150k slot are free .now job 4 arrive which is 120k

case 1: first fit, so it will be in 200 k slot (free slot) and now free is = 200 − 120 = 80k, now 150k arrive which will be in 150 k slot.

Then 80k arrive which will occupy in 80k slot (200-120) so all jobs will be allocated successfully.

case 2: best fit, 120 k job will occupy best fit free space which is 150k so now remaining 150 −120 = 30k, then 150k job arrive it will be occupied in 200k slot.

Which is best fit for this job , so free space = 200 − 150 = 50, now job 80k arrive , but there is no continuous 80k memory free ...so it will not be allocated successfully ... so first fit is better .

Option A Correct

23. FCFS

Total seek time

= 10*6 + 12*6 + 2*6 + 18*6 + 38 * 6 + 34*6 + 32*6

= 146*6

= 876 ms

none of the above

24. (a) A={$a^n b^n$ | n = 1, 2..} is DCFL. So, (a) is False

 (b) The set B, consisting of all strings made up of only a's and b's having equal number of a's and b's is a DCFL. So,(b) is False.

 (c) L(A*B) $\cap$ B

A= {$a^n b^n$ | n = 1, 2..}

B = consisting of all strings made up of only a's and b's having equal number of a's and b's

L(A*B) = L({ B + AB + AAB + ...})

Now, L(A*B) $\cap$ B = B

So,(c) is False.

Option D Correct

25. CFG are not closed under intersection and complement. so (B).

The context-free languages are closed under union, concatenation and Kleene closure.

26. 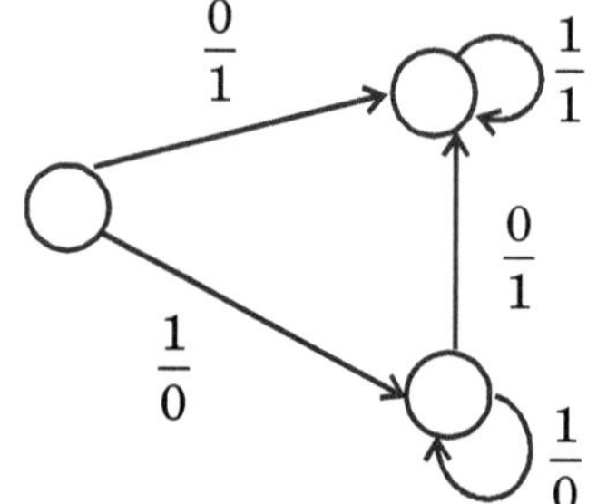

option c correct

fairmont a given bit pattern by 1.

27. Chomsky Normal Form (If all of its production rules are of the form):

A $\rightarrow$ BC or

A$\rightarrow$ a or S $\rightarrow$ ε

where A, B and C are nonterminal symbols, a is a terminal symbol (a symbol that represents a constant value), S is the start symbol, and ε is the empty string. Also, neither B nor C may be the start symbol, and the third production rule can only appear if ε is in L(G), namely, the language produced by the context-free grammar G.

Applying productions of the first form will increase the number of nonterminals from k to k + 1, since you replace one nonterminal (–1) with two non-terminals (+2) for a net gain of +1 nonterminal. Since you start with one nonterminal, this means you need to do l – 1 productions of the first form. You then need l more of the second form to convert the nonterminals to terminals, giving a total of l + (l – 1) = 2l – 1 productions.

Option A Coorect

28. An incremental compiler is a kind of incremental computation applied to the field of compilation. Quite naturally, whereas ordinary compilers make so called clean build, that is, (re) build all program modules, incremental compiler recompiles only those portions of a program that have been modified.

Option C Correct

29. A Use-Definition Chain (UD Chain) is a data structure that consists of a use, U, of a variable, and all the definitions, D, of that variable that can reach that use without any other intervening definitions.

A definition can have many forms, but is generally taken to mean the assignment of some value to a variable (which is different from the use of the term that refers to the language construct involving a data type and allocating storage).

A counterpart of a UD Chain is a Definition-Use Chain (DU Chain), which consists of a definition, D, of a variable and all the uses, U, reachable from that definition without any other intervening definitions.

Both UD and DU chains are created by using a form of static code analysis known as data flow analysis. Knowing the use-def and def-use chains for a program or subprogram is a prerequisite for many compiler optimizations, including constant propagation and common sub expression elimination.

Option D Correct

30. According to Aho Ullman book, PeepHole Optimization is done by examining a sliding window of target instructions (called the peephole) and replacing instruction sequences within the peephole by a faster sequence. It can be applied directly after Intermediate Code Generation to improve the intermediate representation. The code in the peephole need not be contiguous, although some implementations do require this.

So, options A, B and C are true. Only D is false.

31. Memory capacity = 2^mKB = 2^{m+10} B

Since byte addressable memory is given 1 word = 1 byte

Memory capacity = 2^{m+10} words

No. of bits required to point 1 memory location = m + 10 bits

Total no. of operations = 2n

No. of bits to define 1 operation = nbits

Given an instruction have 3 operands and 1operator.

No. of bits needed by instructions

$\qquad$ = 3 * (m + 10) + n = 3m + n + 30 bits

Option (d) is the correct answer

32. Maximum No. possible using n-bit in Binary:- 2n – 1

Maximum no. possible using x bit in Ternary:- 3x –1

Both will take different no. of bits to represent same number.

$3^x - 1 = 2n - 1$

$3^x = 2n$

taking log on both side:;-

$X = \log_3 (2^n)$

$X = n * \log_3 2$.

Option D Correct

33. to find diameter of graph

- Run BFS on any arbitrary vertex and remember the last node visited (say t)
- Run BFS from t and remember the last node visited (say t')
- Shortest distance between t and t' will be the diameter of the graph.

Following is a simple algorithm to find out whether a given graph is Bipartite or not using Breadth First Search (BFS) :-

Assign RED color to the source vertex (putting into set U).

Color all the neighbors with BLUE color (putting into set V).

Color all neighbors' neighbor with RED color (putting into set U).

This way, assign color to all vertices such that it satisfies all the constraints of m way coloring problem where m = 2.

While assigning colors, if we find a neighbor which is colored with same color as current vertex, then the graph cannot be colored with 2 vertices (or graph is not Bipartite).

Option C

34. In micro programmed control unit, the logic of the control unit is specified by a microprogram.

A microprogram consists of a sequence of instructions in a microprogramming language. These are instructions that specify microoperations.

A microprogrammed control unit is a relatively simple logic circuit that is capable of (1) sequencing through microinstructions and (2) generating control signals to execute each microinstruction.

The concept of microprogram is similar to computer program. In computer program the complete instructions of the program is stored in main memory and during execution it fetches the instructions from main memory one after another. The sequence of instruction fetch is controlled by program counter (PC)

Microprogram are stored in microprogram memory and the execution is controlled by microprogram counter (PC).

Option B Correct

35. The number of comparisons needed in the worst case by the merge sort algorithm will be m + n – 1 i.e. only last element will not be compare only.

Option D Correct

36. No of comparison in worst case for an element not in hash table is size of largest cluster +1. This is because the probe stops as soon as an empty slot is found

Size of largest cluster is 4 (S6, S3, S7, S1)

No of comparison is 4 +1= 5

Option B Correct

37. For sufficiently large n,

T(n) = Tn – 1) + T(n – 2) – T(n–3).

If the order of the algorithm for which above recurrence is applicable for the time complexity, is a constant,

T(n) = T(n – 1).

$\Rightarrow$ T(n) = T(n) + T(n – 2) –T(n – 3)

$\Rightarrow$ T(n – 2) = T(n – 3)

Going like this, we must have T(1) = T(2) = T(3)

Option A Correct

38. As every vertex has degree d, so sum of degrees is n*d.

we know 2* number of edges = sum of degrees

so, 2*E = nd

$$\Rightarrow E = \frac{nd}{2}$$

Option D Correct

39. Following information is given:-

(xwmin, ywmin) = (0, 0)

Point (xw, yw) = (20, 15)

(xwmax, ywmax) = (100, 100)

(xvmin, yvmin) = (5, 5)

(xvmax, yvmax) = (20, 20). We have to find the value of (xv, yv).

The following formula is used:-

xv-xvmin / xvmax-xvmin = xw-xwmin / xwmax-xwmin (for xv coordinate)

yv-yvmin / yvmax-yvmin = yw-ywmin / ywmax-ywmin (for yv coordinate)

Now substitute the values in the equation (xv, yv) = (8, 7.25)

Option C Correct

40. This question is about SQL, in SQL Relations are MULTISET, not SET. So R or S can have duplicated.

A. If R has duplicates, in that case, due to distinct keyword those duplicates will be eliminated in final result. So R can not have duplicates. If S is empty RXS becomes empty, so S must be non empty. This is true.

B. Here assume that S is empty. (No duplicates.) Then R X S will be empty. SO this is false.

C. Same argument as B.

D. Assume that R has duplicates. Then Distinct keyword will remove duplicates. So Result of query ! = R, so This is false.

Option A Correct .

41. Candidate Key is ab.

Since all a, b, c, d are atomic so the relation is in 1 NF.

Checking the FDs :

a → c (Prime derives Non-Prime.)

b → d (Prime derives Non-Prime.)

Since there are partial dependencies it is not in 2NF.

Option A Correct

42. The query gives the name of all the students who have scored "A" grade in any of the courses that are taught by sriram

Option C Correct

43. The statements q + = b(a(q)) and r + = a(c(r)) will result in compilation error.

Option A Correct

44. Round trip delay = 80 ms. the round-trip delay time (RTD) or round-trip time (RTT) is the length of time it takes for a signal to be sent plus the length of time it takes for an acknowledgment of that signal to be received.

44. Window size = $\dfrac{RTT * BW}{frame\ size}$

$$= \dfrac{80 \times 10^{-3} * 128 \times 10^3}{32 \times 8} = 4p$$

option b correct

45. Since tcp is byte oriented protocol, the overheads are = 100 + 28 = 128 bytes

what is the total value for which 12.5 percentage = 128

so, $X * \dfrac{12.5}{100} = 128$

$X = \left(\dfrac{128 * 100}{12.5}\right) = 1024$

Option D Correct

46. Write the plaintext in rows of width l(length of Key) and read it off by columns. Take the columns in a order defined by a key.

Here, l = 5,

Keyword = L A Y E R

Key = 3 1 5 2 4

Plaintext = W E L C O

    M E T O N

    E T W O R

    K S E C U

    R I T Y !

Cipher text: EETSI C0OCY WMEKR ONRU! LTWET

Option B Correct

47. At first 100% work can be done in 100 days means 1% work in a man day. Now writing code in assembly language is 10 times harder means 10 times more time consuming.

Also converting existing code form c++ is 4 times easier i.e less time consuming so overall by this scenario we can say 100% work can be done in 100*10/4 man days = 250 days.

So, 1% work will be done in 2.5 days.

NOW, 99% work in C++ + 1% rewriting code will take = 99*1 + 1*2.5 = 101.5 man days.

But we are given 13 days to complete so $\dfrac{101.5}{13} = 18$ programmer we need.

Option C Correct

48. In Unit testing of the module, at the max 90% of the code was tested (0.9)

Probability of success = 0.9

Reliability = 0.9 * 0.9 = 0.81

Answer is at the most 0.81 since it is given that at the max 90% code was tested .

Option C Correct

49. We need to find the maximum no. of nodes to be accessed so consider the minimum fill factor.

Here,order of b+tree= #ptrs per node=p=100

Mini. ptrs per node = p2=50

#Nodes in last leve l= $\dfrac{106}{50}$ = 2 * 104

#Nodes in Second last level = $2 * \dfrac{104}{50}$ = 400

#Nodes in Third last leve l= $\dfrac{400}{50}$ = 8

#Nodes in Forth last level = $\dfrac{8}{50}$ = 1

The maximum no. of nodes to be accessed

    = #B+ tree levels = 4

Option B Correct

50. Bit String: D4FE2003:1101 0100 1111 1110 0010 0000 0000 0011

Number of vacant tracks: 18

Number of occupied tracks:14

Percentage occupied tracks: 1432 100 = 43.75% 44%

Option D correct

51. A. Primary index is maintain for the anchor value of block i,e one key value per block maintained in Index file.

B. Clustering index is basically mixed sort of Indexing i,e Dense as it is maintained for unique value (key) and Sparse as it is not maintained for every value.

C. Index is maintained for every key value so dense index.

Option C Correct

52. Y is dominant entity : Strong entity

X is Subordinate entity : Weak entity

Strong entity connects weak entity by using identifying relationship so we generally prefer cascading effect.

If anything happens in dominant entity that is also reflected in Subordiante entity but vice versa is not true.

Employee $\leftrightarrow$ Dependent (Relationship << is dependent >>)

If employee deleted its depedent tuple must be deleted.

Answer B

53. Immunity here means if we make certain changes in the one level of database design it will not affect other part of database design.

Physical data independence:- if we make any change in the physical storage of schema that it will not affect our logical schema / conceputal schema like relation table.

Logical data indepedence:- if we make any change in the conceputal schema it will not affect external schema or end software using this database.

So ans B.

54. Full functional dependency (FFD)

The term full functional dependency (FFD) is used to indicate the minimum set of attributes in of a functional dependency (FD). In other words, the set of attributes X will be functionally dependent on the set of attributes Y if the following conditions are satisfied:

X is functionally dependent on Y and

X is not functionally dependent on any subset of Y.

55. According to basic timestamp ordering protocol conflicting operation should be executed in the timestamp order.

Here T2 performing read on B, than its timestamp will be newer and when older transaction perform Write on B i.e. T1 than it violated our condition. so option B Correct

56. The matrix of transitive closure of a relation on a set of n elements can be found using

$n^2(2n-1)(n-1)+(n-1)n^2$ bit operations

Which gives time of $O(n^4)$

But using warshall's alogrithm (Transitive closure) it can be done in $O(n^3)$ bit operations

option d is correct.

57.

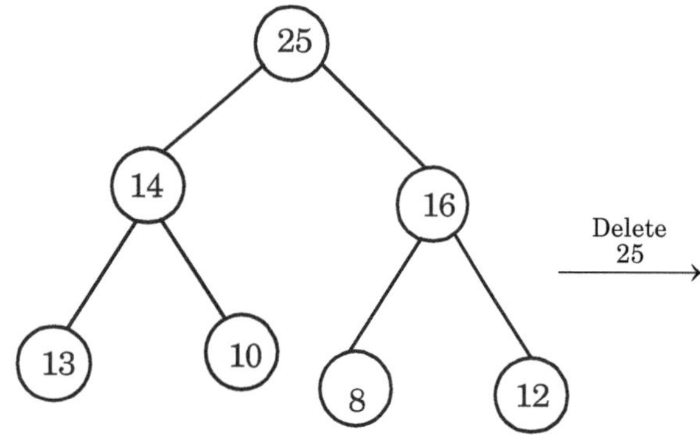

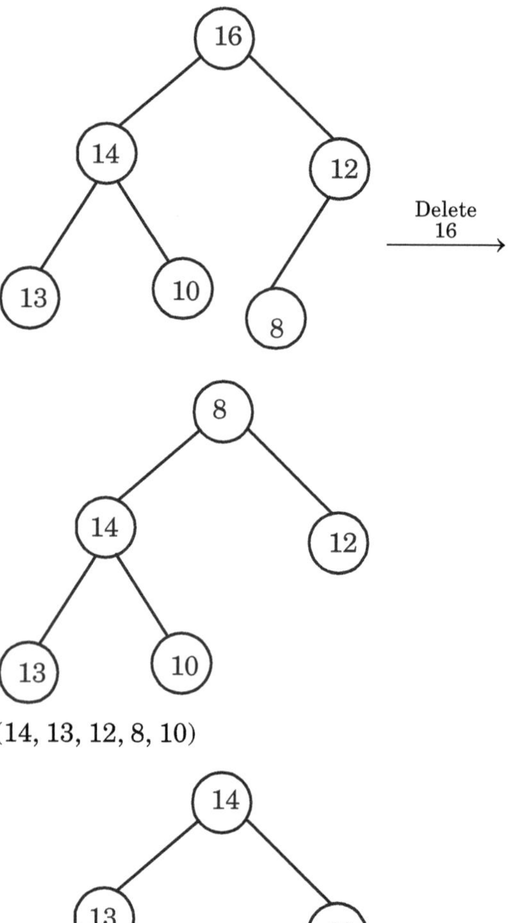

(14, 13, 12, 8, 10)

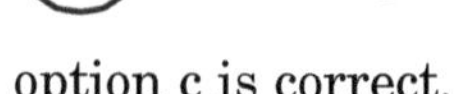

option c is correct.

58. Function Oriented Metrics

In 1977, A. J. Albrecht of IBM developed a method of software metrics based on the functionality of the software delivered by an application as a normalization value. He called it the Function Points (FPs). They are derived using an empirical relationship based on direct measures of software's information domain and assessments of software complexity.

Option C Correct

59. A class exhibits coincidental cohesion if the tasks its methods perform are totally unrelated:

```
class MyFuns {
void initPrinter() { ... }
double calcInterest() { ... }
Date getDate() { ... }
}
```

A class exhibits logical cohesion if the tasks its methods perform are conceptually related. For example, the methods of the following class are related by the mathematical concept of area:

```
class AreaFuns {
double circleArea() { ... }
double rectangleArea() { ... }
double triangleArea() { ... }
}
```

A logically cohesive class also exhibits temporal cohesion if the tasks its methods perform are invoked at or near the same time. For example, the methods of the following class are related by the device initialization concept, and they are all invoked at system boot time:

```
class InitFuns {
void initDisk() { ... }
void initPrinter() { ... }
void initMonitor() { ... }
}
```

One reason why coincidental, logical, and temporal cohesion are at the low end of our cohesion scale is because instances of such classes are unrelated to objects in the application domain. For example, suppose x and y are instances of the InitFuns class:

InitFuns x = InitFuns(), y = new InitFuns();

procedural cohesion, the next step up in our cohesion scale, if the tasks its methods perform are steps in the same application domain process. For example, if the application domain is a kitchen, then cake making is an important application domain process. Each cake we bake is the product of an instance of a Make Cake class:

```
class Make Cake {
void addIngredients() { ... }
void mix() { ... }
void bake() { ... }
}
```

A class exhibits informational cohesion if the tasks its methods perform operate on the same in-formation or data. In object oriented pro-gramming this information would be the information contained in the variables of an object.

For example, the Airplane class exhibits informational cohesion because its methods all work on the same information: the speed and altitude of some airplane object.

```
class Airplane {
double speed, altitude;
void takeoff() { ... }
void fly() { ... }
void land() { ... }
}
```

Option B Correct

60. This code will first replace value of variable x by (5 + 2) = 7 because x < y. Then x will return it's current value 7.

So no output will be printed.

Option D correct

61. It is job of Garbage collector to collect all free memory space at one place.

Garbage collection is the systematic recovery of pooled computer storage that is being used by a program when that program no longer needs the storage. This frees the storage for use by other programs (or processes within a program). It also ensures that a program using increasing amounts of pooled storage does not reach its quota (in which case it may no longer be able to function).

Option B Correct

62. {AND,OR,NOT}

{AND,NOT}

{OR,NOT}

{NAND}

{NOR} all are functionally complete set . and not gate must be present in the set.

option A is not functionally complete.

63. A. as we need to traverse (n − 1) element to delete nth element. time taken to do so depends on length of linked list $\Rightarrow$ O(n)

B. Temp = F.

F = F $\rightarrow$ NEXT

FREE(TEMP)

O(1) and it doesnt depend on the length of list

C. F $\rightarrow$ NEXT = TEMP;

F = TEMP; WHERE TEMP is our new element

D. CONSTANT TIME OPERATION

Option A Correct

64. <word> = <letter> <chirpier>

= <letter> <charpair> letter> <letter> <letter>

= Picks

<word> = <letter> <intpair>

= <letter> = <integer> <integer>

= c44

Picks c44

option D is correct

65. Microprocessors normally use two methods to connect external devices: memory mapped or port mapped I/O. However, as far as the peripheral is concerned, both methods are really identical.

Memory mapped I/O is mapped into the same address space as program memory and/or user memory, and is accessed in the same way.

Port mapped I/O uses a separate, dedicated address space and is accessed via a dedicated set of microprocessor instructions.

The difference between the two schemes occurs within the microprocessor. Intel has, for the most part, used the port mapped scheme for their microprocessors and Motorola has used the memory mapped scheme.

As 16-bit processors have become obsolete and replaced with 32-bit and 64-bit in general use, reserving ranges of memory address space for I/O is less of a problem, as the memory address space of the processor is usually much larger than the required space for all memory and I/O devices in a system.

Therefore, it has become more frequently practical to take advantage of the benefits of memory-mapped I/O. However, even with address space being no longer a major concern, neither I/O mapping method is universally superior to the other, and there will be cases where using port-mapped I/O is still preferable.

Option B Correct

66. In merge sort we divide the array in 2 subarrays, then again divide it in 2 subarrays, like that it divide entire array

And time of merging, we merge 2 subarrays, again merge next two sub arrays

So, here input hardly matters to sort the array

But if we consider quick sort , here initial ordering matters. Because if the array is increasing or decreasing order, quick sort takes maximum running time to find, is the array is sorted or not

Similarly, for insertion sort and selection sort, for sorted and unsorted input running time differs in every case.

Option A Correct

67. Increasing the memory size increases the rate at which requests are satisfied but can not alter the possibility of deadlock and neither does it play any role in implementation.

Option C -I Only Correct

68. Macro (which stands for "macroinstruction") is a programmable pattern which translates a certain sequence of input into a preset sequence of output. Macros can be used to make tasks less repetitive by representing a complicated sequence of keystrokes, mouse movements, commands, or other types of input.

In computer programming, macros are a tool which allow a developer to re-use code. For instance,

#define square(x) ((x) * (x))

After being defined like this, our macro can be used in the code body to find the square of a number. When the code is preprocessed before compilation, the macro will be expanded each time it occurs. For instance, using our macro like this:

int num = square(5);

is the same as writing:

int num = ((5) * (5));

Recursive describes a function or method that repeatedly calculates a smaller part of itself to arrive at the final result.

Example:

function factorial(n) {

return (n === 0) ? 1 : n * factorial(n – 1);

}

Reentrant is an adjective that describes a computer program or routine that is written so that the same copy in memory can be shared by multiple users. A programmer writes a reentrant program by making sure that no instructions modify the contents of variable values in other instructions within the program. Each time the program is entered for a user, a data area is obtained in which to keep all the variable values for that user. The data area is in another part of memory from the program itself. When the program is interrupted to give another user a turn to use the program, information about the data area associated with that user is saved. When the interrupted user of the program is once again given control of the program, information in the saved data area is recovered and the program can be reentered without concern that the previous user has changed some instruction within the program.

Option C Correct

69. It is said that the recursive procedure p will terminate ultimately. If p don't have any parameter or don't refer to any global variable then p will consist of only local variables. So each time when p will recursively be called then a new copy of local variables will be created in the stack. In this case we can't track how many times p is called till now. So p have to refer at least one global variable or take at least one parameter.

Along with that we have to use the global variable or the parameter by imposing a condition that when p will not call itself. At that time only p will terminate.

Option D correct

70. Here while loop runs till $\left(\dfrac{i}{j}\right)$ becomes equal to 0.001.

Now, $0.001 = \left(\dfrac{1}{1000}\right)$

So, the while loop runs till $\left(\dfrac{i}{j}\right) = \left(\dfrac{1}{1000}\right)$

$\Rightarrow$ i*1000 = j

Now i = 2 and j = 1

So, the while loop runs till j becomes equal to 2000.

So, the output will have more or less 2000 lines.

option D correct.

71. 40% sequential means 40 seconds.

Rest 60% will be divided into 30 – 30% each parallel by the two processors

hence total 40 + 30 = 70 sec

If four processors then 15% each, hence total 40 + 15 = 55 sec

Option D Correct

72. f(x) = f(x − 1) + g(x)

$= f(x-1) + f(x-1) + g\left(\dfrac{x}{2}\right)$

$= 2.\, f(x-1) + f\left(\dfrac{x}{2}-1\right) + g\left(\dfrac{x}{4}\right)$

To get a lower bound for f(x) (simplifying)

f(x) > 2, f(x − 1)

f(x) > 2.2. f(x − 2)

f(x) > 2^x f(1)

f(x) = 2^x.

which shows exponential growth f(x)

option b is correct

73. Directory-based cache coherence protocols were invented as a means of dealing with cache coherence in systems containing more processors than can be accommodated on a single bus. In single bus systems, cache coherence can be ensured using a snoopy protocol in which each processor's cache monitors the traffic on the bus and takes appropriate action when it sees an update to an address matching one that it holds.

In directory based systems, the directory can be held centrally with the main memory in a multi-processor system or can be distributed among the caches as singly or doubly linked lists. This website contains models demonstrating each of these three mechanisms. For each model, students can be asked, as an exercise, to write a report explaining what protocol actions occur for each of the read and write requests that the processors make to their caches, e.g. by listing the packets which are sent around the system in response to each request and explaining the purpose of each packet.

Option C Correct

74. In cryptography, the avalanche effect is a desired effect in encryption to ensure that a person cannot easily predict a message based on the changes in the hash value through a statistical analysis.

If an input is changed slightly (for example, flipping a single bit), the output changes significantly (e.g., half the output bits flip).

So Avalanche effect is a desirable property of the cryptographic algorithm.

Option A correct.

75. The best way that I can come up with to describe the information storage capacity of a neural network is to quote the universal approximation theorem

To summarize it, say we have an arbitrary continuous function and we want to approximate the output of this function. Now say that for every input, the output of our approximation shouldn't deviate more than some given > 0. Then we can create a neural network with a single hidden layer that satisfies this constraint, no matter the continuous function, no matter how small the error tolerance. The only requirement is that the amount of nodes in the hidden layer might grow arbitrarily large if we choose the error-rate smaller and smaller.

In the network training, we design decimal weight regularization and 8-bit forward quantization to obtain the integer-oriented network representations. Moreover, we develop adaptive-bit width and non-uniform quantization strategy in the inference phase to find the neural network capacity, total valid bits. By allowing zero bit width, our adaptive-bit width quantization can execute the model reduction and valid bits finding simultaneously.

Option C Correct

76. Cloaking is a search engine optimization (SEO) technique in which the content presented to the search engine spider is different from that presented to the user's browser.

Cloaking is a search engine optimization technique in which the content or information presented to the user is different from that presented to search engine crawlers (i.e. spiders or bots) for better indexing. In other words, the web server is specially programmed to return different content to search engines than it returns to regular users, in an attempt to distort search engine rankings. The Search engine may permanently ban from our index any sites or site authors that engage in cloaking

Option A Correct

77. In computer networks, a DMZ (demilitarized zone) is a physical or logical sub-network that separates an internal local area network (LAN) from other un trusted networks, usually the Internet. External-facing servers, resources and services are located in the DMZ so they are accessible from the Internet but the rest of the internal LAN remains unreachable. This provides an additional layer of security to the LAN as it restricts the ability of hackers to directly access internal servers and data via the Internet.

A more secure approach is to use two firewalls to create a DMZ. The first firewall also called the perimeter firewall is configured to allow traffic destined to the DMZ only. The second or internal firewall only allows traffic from the DMZ to the internal network. A DMZ segments a network.

Option A Correct

78. (ECB) Electronic Code Book - symmetric encryption scheme which replaces each block of the clear text by the block of ciphertext. It is the simplest encryption scheme. The main idea is to split the clear text into blocks of N bits (depends on the size of the block of input data, encryption algorithm) and then to encrypt (decrypt) each block of clear text using the only key.

The ECB mode is rather simple in realization. It is possible to encrypt/decrypt blocks of data in parallel as there is no dependence between blocks. In case of failure of the encryption/decryption the mistake extends only within one block and doesn't influence others. Limitations of ECB encryption scheme:

If blocks of the clear text are identical the corresponding blocks of cipher text will be identical too. Otherwise if in the cipher text some blocks are identical, the corresponding blocks of the clear text are identical too. The cryptanalyst can decipher only one of these blocks to find the contents of all of them.

In case the blocks are independent it becomes possible to replace some blocks of the cipher text without knowledge of a key. The malefactor can replace part of blocks in the message with blocks intercepted during the previous message on the same key.

In case of loss or insertion at least of one bit into ciphe rtext there will be a shift of bits and borders of blocks that will lead to wrong decoding of all subsequent blocks cipher text (it can be fixed by realization of control methods of borders of cipher text blocks)

Option C Correct

79.

X → Bwd → Fwd = X → Fwd

X → Fwd → Bwd = X → Bwd

Option A Correct

80. There is some discrepancy in this question. Postorder of Tree 1 : GJIHEFDBCA . Inorder of Tree 2 : GJIHEFBDCA.

Option B Correct

PRACTICE PAPER 1

1. Which of the following IC has only one input line?
   - (a) Multiplexer
   - (b) Demultiplexer
   - (c) AND gate
   - (d) BCD to decimal decoder

2. The binary system has the radix of
   - (a) 0
   - (b) 1
   - (c) 2
   - (d) ½

3. Which of the following is simplified versions of the boolean expression $\overline{AB} + A\overline{B}C + \overline{(A + B + C)}$?
   - (a) $\overline{AB} + \overline{BC}$
   - (b) $A\overline{B} + \overline{BC}$
   - (c) $AB + BC$
   - (d) $A\overline{B} + B\overline{C}$

4. Which of the following circuit is called latch ?
   - (a) AND circuit
   - (b) NAND circuit
   - (c) Flip-flop
   - (d) ROM circuit

5. A collection of 8-bit is called
   - (a) Nibble
   - (b) Byte
   - (c) Word
   - (d) Double-word

6. Which of the following storage is volatile ?
   - (a) Semiconductor Memory
   - (b) Floppy disk
   - (c) CD-ROM
   - (d) Core memory

7. Which is a secondary memory device?
   - (a) CPU
   - (b) ALU
   - (c) Floppy disk
   - (d) Mouse

8. Number of machine cycles required for RET instruction in 8085 microprocessor is
   - (a) 1
   - (b) 2
   - (c) 3
   - (d) 5

9. Which of the following is/are correct ?
   - (a) An SQL query automatically eliminates duplicates
   - (b) An SQL query will not work if there are no indexes on the relations
   - (c) SQL permits attribute names to be repeated in the same relation
   - (d) None of these

10. A solution to the Dining Philosophers Problem which avoids deadlock is ensure that
    - (a) all philosophers pick up the left fork before the right fork
    - (b) all philosophers pick up the right fork before the left fork
    - (c) one particular philosopher picks up the left fork before the right fork, and that all other philosophers pick up the right fork before the left fork
    - (d) none of these

11. Which of the following TCP/IP protocol is used for remote terminal connection services?
    - (a) TELNET
    - (b) FTP
    - (c) RARP
    - (d) UDP

12. A network which is used for sharing data, software hardware among several users owning micro computers is called
    - (a) WAN
    - (b) MAN
    - (c) LAN
    - (d) VAN

13. What is the maximum number of dimensions an array in C may have ?
    - (a) two
    - (b) eight
    - (c) sixteen
    - (d) theoretically no limit. The only practical limits are memory size and compilers

14. What are the two types of cache that processors support?
    - (a) Internal
    - (b) Bilateral
    - (c) External
    - (d) Flash

15. The ASII code is
    - (a) numeric code
    - (b) same as BCD code
    - (c) an alphanumeric code
    - (d) seldom used

16. In a four input NAND gate, if all are inputs are 1, then output is

(a) 4   (b) 1/4

(c) 1   (d) 0

17. A monostable has

(a) single stable state

(b) two quasi stable state

(c) two stable states

(d) none of these

18. An example of non-numeric data is

(a) bank balance

(b) examination marks

(c) employee address

(d) real numbers

19. The process of putting data into a storage location is called

(a) reading   (b) writing

(c) hand shaking   (d) controlling

20. How many units in a single bus structure communicate at a time?

(a) One   (b) Two

(c) Three   (d) Four

21. How many I/O ports can be accessed by memory mapped method?

(a) 3   (b) 256

(c) 32 k   (d) 64 k

22. Let $R = (a, b, c, d, e, f)$ be a relation scheme with the following dependencies $c \rightarrow f, e \rightarrow a, ec \rightarrow d. a \rightarrow b$. Which of the following is a key for R ?

(a) CD   (b) EC

(c) AE   (d) AC

23. If an instruction takes i microseconds and a page fault takes an additional j microseconds, the effective instruction time if on the average a page fault occurs every k instruction is

(a) $i + \dfrac{j}{k}$ (b) $i + j * k$

(c) $\dfrac{i + j}{k}$ (d) $(i + j) * k$

24. Which of the following transmission systems provides the highest data rate to an individual device?

(a) Digital PBX

(b) Computer Bus

(c) LAN

(d) Voiceband modem

25. ARP (Address Resolution Protocol) is a

(a) TCP/IP protocol used to dynamically bind a high level IP address to a low level physical hardware address

(b) TCP/IP high level protocols for transferring files from one machine to another

(c) protocol used to monitor computers

(d) protocol that handles error and control messages

26. Consider the following Pascal function

function fibo (n : integer) : enteger :

begin

if (n = 0) then fibo : = 0

else if (n = 1) then fibo : = 1

else fibo : = fibo (n - 1) + fibo (n - 2)

end

If fibo (5) is the function call, fibo (1) will be used

(a) 3 times   (b) 4 times

(c) 5 times   (d) 6 times

27. The location where Input/output devices are connected to the computer is called

(a) keyboard   (b) accumulator

(c) bus   (d) port

28. The decimal number 80 can be represented in BCD code as

(a) 1000 0001   (b) 0101 0000

(c) 0010 0000   (d) 1000000

29. Minimum number of 2-input nand gates required to implement the function

$$F = (\overline{x + y})\,(z + w) \text{ is}$$

(a) 6   (b) 5

(c) 4   (d) 3

30. The output of a sequential circuit depends on

(a) present inputs only

(b) past inputs only

(c) both present and past inputs

(d) present outputs only

31. Magnetic tape can serve as

(a) Input media

(b) Output media

(c) Secondary storage media

(d) All of these

32. A complete set of programs for one specific data processing application is called a

(a) program package   (b) canned program

(c) utility program   (d) compiler

33. A beam of light used to record and retrieve data on optical disks is called
(a) polarized light
(b) unpolarized concentric light
(c) laser
(d) coloured light

34. What addressing mode is not possible in 8085?
(a) Indexed Addressing
(b) Indirect Addressing
(c) Direct Addressing
(d) Indirect register addressing

35. Which one of the following statements about normal forms is FALSE?
(a) BCNF is stricter than 3NF
(b) Lossless, dependency-preserving decomposition into 3NF is always possible
(c) Lossless, dependency-preserving decomposition into BCNF is always possible
(d) Any relation with two attributes is in BCNF

36. Time sharing systems must also provide
(a) online system
(b) off line system
(c) both (a) and (b)
(d) none of these

37. Which of the following is not an example of data communication?
(a) A teletype printing news bulletins
(b) A computer transmitting files to another computer
(c) An automatic teller machine checking account balances with the bank's computer
(d) A salesman telephoning orders to the office

38. To connect a computer with a device in the same room, we might be likely to use a
(a) coaxial cable
(b) dedicated line
(c) ground station
(d) all of these

39. One of the four instructions is not needed that is
(a) clr x
(b) inc x
(c) dec x
(d) inv x

The program
```
clr c ; clr B;
while (A not 0) do
inc ; dec A'
end ;
while (c not 0) do
inc A ; inc B ; dec C ;
end
```

(a) transfer the contents of A to B
(b) copies the contents of A to B
(c) copies the contents of A to B and C
(d) transfer the contents of A to C

40. A small dot or circle printed on top of an IC indicates
(a) V_{CC}
(b) Gnd
(c) Pin 14
(d) Pin 1

41. The 2's compliments of binary number 010111.1100 is
(a) 101001.1100
(b) 101000.0100
(c) 010111.0011
(d) 101000.0011

42. An Inverter is also called which gate?
(a) NOT
(b) OR
(c) AND
(d) NAND

43. Parrallel adders are
(a) combinational logic circuits
(b) sequential logic circuits
(c) both (a) and (b)
(d) none of these

44. Computer virus is a software program which has the essential ability to
(a) clone itself
(b) damage programs
(c) damage data
(d) hide itself

45. Which of the following coded enteries are used to control access to computer ?
(a) Code words
(b) Passwords
(c) Binary pass
(d) ASCII codes

46. A microprocessor with 12 address lines is capable of addressing
(a) 1024 locations
(b) 2048 locations
(c) 4096 locations
(d) 64 K locations

47. The ALE line of intel 8085 microprocessor is used to
(a) latch output of an I/O instruction into an external latch
(b) deactivate chip-select signal from memory devices
(c) latch 8 bits of address lines AD7-AD0 into an external latch
(d) find interrupt enable status of the TRAP interrupt

48. Which of the following is correct ?
(a) B-trees are for storing data on disk and B* trees are for main memory.
(b) Range queries are faster on B* trees.
(c) B-trees are for primary indexes and B* trees are for secondary indexes.
(d) The height of a B* tree is independent of the number of records.

49. Special software to create a job queue is called

(*a*) drive   (*b*) spooler

(*c*) interpreter   (*d*) linkage editor

50. A streaming protocol

(*a*) provides error detection

(*b*) does not provide error detection

(*c*) uses 64 byte blocks

(*d*) requires a manual setup

51. The use of telecommunications and a personal computer is (are)

(*a*) "download" free public domain programs

(*b*) send letters to be printed and delivered by the post office

(*c*) order goods at a substantial discount

(*d*) all of these

52. fortran implementation do not permit recursion because

(*a*) they use static allocation for variables

(*b*) they use dynamic allocation for variables

(*c*) stacks are not available on all machines

(*d*) it is not possible to implement recursion on all machines

53. Memory refreshing may be done

(*a*) by the CPU that contains a special regress counter only

(*b*) by an external refresh controller, only

(*c*) either by the CPU or by an external refresh controller

(*d*) none of these

54. What is the binary equivalent of decimal 269?

(*a*) 100001100   (*b*) 100001010

(*c*) 101001011   (*d*) 100001101

55. Which of the following does not represent boolean algebra operation?

(*a*) NOT   (*b*) NOR

(*c*) AND   (*d*) OR

56. A logic circuit which is used to change a BCD number into an equivalent decimal number is

(*a*) decoder   (*b*) encoder

(*c*) multiplexer   (*d*) code converter

57. Which of the following memories is an optical memory ?

(*a*) Bubble Memory

(*b*) CD-ROM

(*c*) Core memory

(*d*) Floppy disk

58. Benchmarks are

(*a*) simulator programs

(*b*) vendor's applications

(*c*) actual system programs

(*d*) representative routines for system timing

59. Which of the following statements is true about the Program Counter (PC) ?

(*a*) It is a cell in ROM.

(*b*) It is a register.

(*c*) During execution of the current instruction, its content changes.

(*d*) It counts the number of instructions executed in a program.

60. A microprocessor can be

(*a*) non programmable

(*b*) micro programmable

(*c*) macro programmable

(*d*) all of these

61. Consider the set of relations shown below and the SQL query that follows :

Students : (Roll_number, Name, Date_of _birth)

Courses : (Course_number, Course_name, Instructor)

Grades : (Roll_number, Course_number, Grade)

select distinct Name

from Students, Courses, Grades

where Students. Roll_number = Grades. Roll_number

    and   Courses. Instructor = Korth

    and   Courses. Course_number = Grades. Course_number

    and Grades.grade = A

Which of the following sets is computed by the above query ?

(*a*) Names of students who have got an A grade in all courses taught by Korth

(*b*) Names of students who have got an A grade in all courses

(*c*) Name of students who have got an A grade in at least one of the courses taught by Korth

(*d*) None of these

62. The operating system used by Macintosh computer is

(*a*) System 7.0

(*b*) AU/X

(*c*) XENIX

(*d*) Either (*a*) or (*b*)

63. Suppose the round trip propagation delay for a 10 Mbps Ethernet having 48-bit jamming signal is 46.4 ms. The minimum frame size is

(a) 94　　　　　　　　(b) 416

(c) 464　　　　　　　 (d) 512

64. Communications software package enable users to access services such as

(a) electronic mail

(b) electronic bulletin boards

(c) video channels

(d) both (a) and (b)

65. Which of the following languages is not well suited for computation ?

(a) PASCAL　　　　　 (b) FORTRAN

(c) C　　　　　　　　 (d) COBOL

66. Which logic family dissiplates the minimum power?

(a) DTL　　　　　　　(b) TTL

(c) ECL　　　　　　　(d) CMOS

67. The range of integers that can be represented by an n bit 2's complement number system is

(a) -2^{n-1} to $(2^{n-1}-1)$

(b) $-(2^{n-1}-1)$ to $(2^{n-1}-1)$

(c) -2^{n-1} to 2^{n-1}

(d) $-(2^{n-1}+1)$ to $(2^{n-1}-1)$

68. Boolean function $x'\,y' + xy + x'\,y$ is equivalent to

(a) $x' + y'$　　　　　 (b) $x + y$

(c) $x + y'$　　　　　　(d) $x' + y$

69. In which of the following adder circuits, the carry look ripple delay is eliminated?

(a) Half adder

(b) Full adder

(c) Parallel adder

(d) Carry-look-ahead adder

70. A program to detect overall system malfunction is

(a) utilities　　　　　　(b) system analysis

(c) system software　　(d) system diagnostics

71. Examples of applicaiton software are

(a) Word processing programs

(b) data management of integrated programs

(c) game programs

(d) all of these

72. Which of the following is a set of general purpose internal registers?

(a) Stack　　　　　　　(b) Scratch pad

(c) Address register　　 (d) Status register

73. DOS maintains

(a) one stack　　　　　 (b) two stacks

(c) three stacks　　　　(d) four stacks

74. A clustering index is defined on the fields which are of type

(a) non-key and ordering

(b) non-key and non-ordering

(c) key and ordering

(d) key and non ordering

75. The operating system which was originally designed by scientists and engineers for use by scientists and engineers is called

(a) XENIX　　　　　　(b) UNIX

(c) OS/2　　　　　　　(d) MS/DOS

76. Satellite in geosynchronous orbit

(a) remains in a fixed position relative to points on earth

(b) can cover about 80

(c) moves faster than the earth's rotation so that it can cover larger portion of earth

(d) remains in a fixed position so as earth rotates it can fully cover earth

77. Which of the following TCP/IP protocol is used for the file transfer with minimal capability and minimal overhead?

(a) RARP　　　　　　 (b) FTP

(c) TFTP　　　　　　　(d) TELNET

78. Which of the following is not an example of program documentation ?

(a) Source code　　　　(b) Object code

(c) Specification　　　　(d) Identifier names

79. Which logic gate has low power consumption?

(a) TTL　　　　　　　(b) CMOS

(c) DTL　　　　　　　(d) RTL

80. The number of binary relations on a set with n elements is

(a) n^2　　　　　　　(b) 2^n

(c) 2^{n^2}　　　　　　(d) None of these

ANSWERS

1. (b)	**2.** (c)	**3.** (a)	**4.** (c)	**5.** (b)	**6.** (a)	**7.** (c)	**8.** (c)	**9.** (d)	**10.** (c)
11. (a)	**12.** (c)	**13.** (d)	**14.** (a)	**15.** (c)	**16.** (d)	**17.** (a)	**18.** (c)	**19.** (b)	**20.** (b)
21. (c)	**22.** (b)	**23.** (a)	**24.** (b)	**25.** (a)	**26.** (c)	**27.** (d)	**28.** (d)	**29.** (a)	**30.** (c)
31. (d)	**32.** (a)	**33.** (c)	**34.** (a)	**35.** (c)	**36.** (a)	**37.** (d)	**38.** (a)	**39.** (a)	**40.** (d)
41. (b)	**42.** (a)	**43.** (a)	**44.** (a)	**45.** (b)	**46.** (c)	**47.** (c)	**48.** (b)	**49.** (b)	**50.** (b)
51. (d)	**52.** (a)	**53** (c)	**54.** (d)	**55.** (b)	**56.** (a)	**57.** (a)	**58.** (d)	**59.** (b)	**60.** (b)
61. (c)	**62.** (d)	**63.** (c,d)	**64.** (d)	**65.** (d)	**66.** (d)	**67.** (a)	**68.** (d)	**69.** (d)	**70.** (d)
71. (d)	**72.** (b)	**73.** (c)	**74.** (a)	**75.** (b)	**76.** (d)	**77.** (c)	**78.** (b)	**79.** (b)	**80.** (c)

1. In which of the following directories init resides in Unix ?

    (a) root

    (b) bin

    (c) etc

    (d) user

2. When a process makes a system call, its mode changes from

    (a) user to kernel

    (b) kernel to user

    (c) restricted to unrestricted

    (d) both (a) and (b)

3. Which of the following language differ the case of alphabets ?

    (a) FORTRAN

    (b) BASIC

    (c) C

    (d) Both (a) and (b)

4. The topology with highest reliablity

    (a) bus topology

    (b) star topology

    (c) ring topology

    (d) mesh topology

5. What is the general name of the device which produces hard copy graphics ?

    (a) COM

    (b) Plotter

    (c) Printer

    (d) Microfilm

6. An input device that is able to interpret pencil marks on paper media is known as

    (a) Magnetic disk

    (b) Optical Mark reader

    (c) Card puncher

    (d) Magnetic tape

7. Which of the following statement is correct ?

    (a) Bufffering is the process of temporarily storing the data to allow for small variation in devices speeds

    (b) Buffering is a method to reduce cross talks

    (c) Buffering is a method to reduce the routing overhead

    (d) Buffering is storage of data within the transmitting medium until the receiver is ready to receive

8. A central computer surrounded by one or more satellite computers is called a

    (a) bus network

    (b) ring network

    (c) star network

    (d) all of the above

9. A packet-switching network

    (a) is free

    (b) can reduce the cost of using an information utility

    (c) allows communications channels to be shared among more than one user

    (d) both (b) and (c)

10. Which layer of international standard organization's OSI model is responsible for creating and recognizing frame boundaries ?

    (a) Physical layer

    (b) Data link layer

    (c) Transport layer

    (d) Network layer

11. If digital data rate of 9600 bps is encoded using 8-level phase shift keying (PSK) method, the modulation rate is

    (a) 1200 bands

    (b) 3200 bands

    (c) 4800 bands

    (d) 9600 bands

12. Data are followed to be transmitted in only one direction in a :

    (a) Simplex channel

    (b) Dumb channel

    (c) Half-duplex channel

    (d) Full-duplex channel

13. Synchronous Protocols

    (a) transmit characters one at a time

    (b) allow faster transmission than asynchronous protocols

    (c) are generally used by Personal Computers

    (d) both (a) and (c)

14. If a special forms are needed for printing the output, the programmer specifies these through

    (a) JCL

    (b) IPL

    (c) Utility Programs

    (d) Both (b) and (c)

15. Which of the following are loaded into main memory when the computer is booted ?
- (*a*) Internal Command Instructions
- (*b*) External Command Instructions
- (*c*) Utility Programs
- (*d*) Word Processing Instructions

16. The flip-flops which operate in synchronism with external clock pulses are called
- (*a*) synchronous flip-flops
- (*b*) asynchronous flip flops
- (*c*) either (*a*) or (*b*)
- (*d*) none of these

17. A stable multivibrator are used as
- (*a*) comparator circuit
- (*b*) squaring circuit
- (*c*) frequency to voltage converter
- (*d*) voltage to frequency converter

18. A monostable has
- (*a*) single stable state
- (*b*) two quasi stable state
- (*c*) two stable states
- (*d*) none of these

19. The advantage of serial transfer compared with parallel transfer for data transmission is that
- (*a*) it is faster
- (*b*) it needs only one wire
- (*c*) BCD is compatible
- (*d*) all of these

20. Due to which of the following reasons parallel operation is preferred?
- (*a*) Circuitry is simple
- (*b*) It requires less memory
- (*c*) It is faster than series operation
- (*d*) All of these

21. In the previous problem if the computer is word addressable with the word size being 8 bytes, then the answer will be
- (*a*) 3m bits
- (*b*) 3m + n bits
- (*c*) m + n bits
- (*d*) none of these

22. The addressing mode used in an instruction of the form ADD X,Y is
- (*a*) absolute
- (*b*) immediate
- (*c*) indirect
- (*d*) index

23. Which of the following units cannot be used to measure the speed of computer ?
- (*a*) MIPS
- (*b*) MFLOPS
- (*c*) FLOPS
- (*d*) BAUD

24. A set of related programa is called
- (*a*) Script
- (*b*) Arrays
- (*c*) Stacks
- (*d*) Package

25. Program Status Word (PSW) contains various (different) status of
- (*a*) CPU
- (*b*) ALU
- (*c*) program
- (*d*) registers

26. Memory Address Register (MAR)
- (*a*) contains address of the memory locations that is to be read from or stored into
- (*b*) is a hardware device which denotes the location of the current instructions being executed
- (*c*) is a group of electrical circuit, that performs the content of instructions fetched from memory
- (*d*) none of these

27. The CPU of a computer operates at a much higher rate than peripherals. Operating speed difference between two reduced
- (*a*) by using interrupt line
- (*b*) with the help of buffer memory
- (*c*) by using matching peripherals
- (*d*) by using parallel input/output ports

28. The larger the RAM of a computer, the faster its processing speed is, since it eliminates
- (*a*) need of ROM
- (*b*) need of external memory
- (*c*) frequent disk I/Os
- (*d*) need for wider data path

29. The temporary or volatile memory of a computer is erased when the computer is turned off. Accordingly, the computer user before turning off the machine must transfer anything in the memory which is important to
- (*a*) control unit
- (*b*) ALU
- (*c*) CPU
- (*d*) permanent memory

30. The storage device which is used to compensate for the difference in rates of flow of data from one device to another is called
- (*a*) cache
- (*b*) concentrator
- (*c*) buffer
- (*d*) I/O device

31. Consider following program fragment for Intel 8085 microprocessor

```
LXI          H, 0106 H
DCR          L
LOOP :    DCX          H
JNZ                        LOOP
                HLT
```

In this program, loop will be executed

(a) 105 times

(b) 261 times

(c) 0 times

(d) forever

32. Consider the following for Intel 8085 microprocessor :

```
START :  MVI  C, FFH
             INX  B
LOOP :   ADD B
             DCR C
             JNZ LOOP
             HLT
```

How many times loop will be executed?

(a) 1   (b) 255

(c) 256   (d) Infinite

33. What are the contents of the temp location after execution of the following program for intel 8085 microprocessor ?

```
MVI  B, 00
MVI  A, 1C H
DCR  B
DAA
STA TEMP
HLT
```

(a) 12H   (b) 1 CH

(c) 22 H   (d) 82 H

34. In a microprogrammed control unit the micro-instructions Mj and the control signals (a, b, c, --) they generate are :

M_1 : a, b, e, f

M_2 : b, c, d, e

M_3 : a, c, e, g

What is the total number of maximal compatibility classes (MCCs) for the control signal?

(a) 2   (b) 3

(c) 4   (d) 5

35. A small microprocessor's micro-instructions has 6 control fields, each one triggering the following number of control lines :

Control field :	1	2	3	4	5	6
Number of conrol lines :	7	4	5	2	1	3

What is the fewest number of control bits required to describe all the control fields?

(a) 22

(b) 14

(c) 7

(d) 6

36. The **QWERTY** keyboard

(a) is the most popular keyboard

(b) is the fastest keyboard

(c) is a keyboard that is rarely used

(d) uses Dvorak layout

37. In which of the following terminals, the CPU copies the characters to be displayed to the video RAM in alternative bytes and screen is regarded as a 25×80 array of characters ?

(a) Character map terminal

(b) Bit - map terminal

(c) Rs 232 C terminal

(d) All of these

38. In which of the following terminals, the screen is regarded as an array of pixels, where each pixel is either on or off ?

(a) Character map terminal

(b) Bit - map terminal

(c) Rs 232 C terminal

(d) All of these

39. Which video terminal is generally used in engineering workstations ?

(a) Character map terminal

(b) Bit-map terminal

(c) Rs 232 C terminal

(d) All of these

40. Bit-map terminal

(a) supports displays containing multiple windows

(b) requires considerable amount of video RAM

(c) requires tremendous amount of copying and hence low performance

(d) all of these

41. A disk scheduling algorithm in an operating system causes the disk arm to move back and forth across the disk surface in order to service all requests in this path. This is a

(a) First come First served

(b) Shortest Seek Time First (SSTF)

(c) Scan

(d) Eschenbach scheme

42. A system program that sets up an executable program in main memory ready for execution is

(a) assembler (b) linker

(c) loader (d) text editor

43. A system program that combines the separately compiled modules of a program into a form suitable for execution

(a) assembler (b) linking loader

(c) cross compiler (d) load and go

44. A compiler for a high-level language that runs on one machine and produces code for a different machine is called as

(a) optimizing compiler (b) one pass compiler

(c) cross compiler (d) multipass compiler

45. An instruction in a programming language that is replaced by a sequence of instructions prior to assembly or compiling is known as

(a) procedure name (b) macro

(c) label (d) literal

46. Consider the following left-associative operators, in decreasing order of precedence :

    – subtraction (highest precedence)

    * multiplication

    $ exponentiation (lowest precedence)

What is the result of the following expression ?

    3-2 * 4 $ 1 * 2 # 3

(a) – 61 (b) 64

(c) 512 (d) 4096

47. Which of the following cannot be used as an intermediate code form ?

(a) Post fix notation (b) Three address codes

(c) Syntax trees (d) Quadruples

48. In some programming languages, an identifier is permitted to be a letter followed by any number of further letters or digits.

Given that   D = {1,2,3,4,5,6,7,8,9,0}

    and   L = {a, A,b,B,c,C,............z,Z}

Which of the following expressions below defines an identifer ?

(a) (L U D)$^+$ (b) L. (L U D)*

(c) (L.D)* (d) L. (L.D)*

49. A language L is defined by L = {xn yn | n > 1}. Which of the following definitions generates the same language as L ?

(a) E → xEy | xy (b) (xy) | (x xyy)

(c) x – y– (d) All of these

50. Which of the following strings of PASCAL language (when compiled) can definitely be said to be tokens without looking at the next input character ?

(a) = (b) case

(c) end (d) Both (b) and (c)

51. The tree shown in the figure below represents the postfix expression

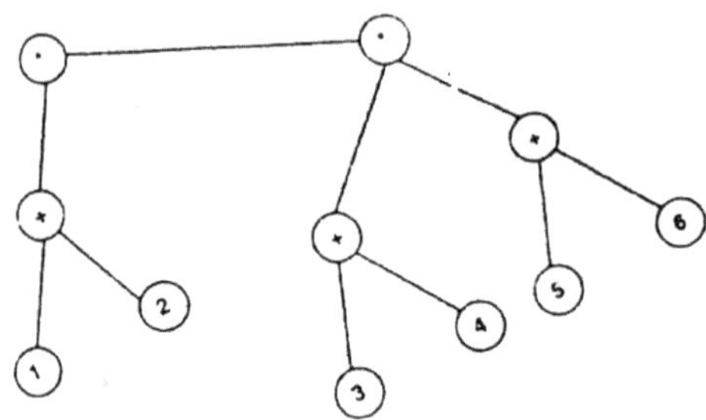

(a) 655321 + + ** + (b) 1 + 2*3 + 4*5 + 6

(c) 12 + 34 + 56 + ** (d) * + 12* + 34 + 56

52. A list of data items usually words or bytes with the accessing restriction that elements can be added or removed at one end of the list only, is called

(a) stack (b) memory

(c) linked list (d) heap

53. In what order, the elements of a pushdown stack are accessed ?

(a) First In First Out (FIFO)

(b) Last In Last Out (LILO)

(c) Last In First Out (LIFO)

(d) None of these

54. Which of the following sorting algorithms has a worst case running time of $O(n^r)$, where $1 < r < 2$?

(a) Bubble sort

(b) Insertion sort

(c) Shell sort

(d) Merge sort

55. For a linear search in an array of n elements, the time complexity for best, worst and average cases are respectively and respectively

(a) $O(n), O(1),$ and $O(n/2)$

(b) $O(1), O(n),$ and $O(n/2)$

(c) $O/1, O(n)$ and $O(n)$

(d) $O(1), O(n)$ and $\left(\dfrac{n-1}{2}\right)$

56. Which function returns the name of the day of the week from a date expression ?

(a) CDOW()   (b) CTOD()

(c) DOW()   (d) DTOC()

57. Which function is used to convert a data to a character string?

(a) DTOC()   (b) DTOW()

(c) DOW()   (d) CDOW()

58. Which function returns a number that represents the day of the week from a date expression?

(a) DTOW()   (b) CDOW()

(c) DTOC()   (d) DOW()

59. Which command shows the name, type, size and status of each active memory variable?

(a) DISPLAY STRUCTURE

(b) DISPLAY

(c) LIST

(d) DISPLAY MEMORY

60. Which command crfeates and initializes one or more memory variables?

(a) UPADATE   (b) STORE

(c) KEEP   (d) RELEASE

61. VAX architecture

(a) supports two level paging

(b) VAX is 32 bit machine

(c) logical address space of a process is divided into four equal sections each of which consists of 2^{30} bytes

(d) all of these

62. In MULTICS

(a) a single level store for data access

(b) each page in multics consists of 1 K words

(c) both (a) and (b)

(d) none of these

63. One of the main feature that distinguish microprocessors from microcomputers is

(a) words are usually larger in micro-processors

(b) words are shorter in microprocessors

(c) microprocessor does not contain I/O devices

(d) computer are not fully integrated

64. Consider a computer with three types of instructions, each with the following opcode lengths and assuming opcodes occur at the front of each machine instruction :

   6-bit opcode

   8-bit opcode

   12-bit opcode

   14-bit opcode

The number of possible commands that can be represented in the 6-bit opcode, is

(a) 32   (b) 16

(c) 8   (d) 4

65. Both silicon and gallium arsenide are used for primary storage devices. How many times gallium arsenide devices are faster than the silicon devices?

(a) 3   (b) 5

(c) 7   (d) 10

66. Consider the following program for intel 8085 microprocessor :

```
DELAY : LXI H, 0010H
LOOP  :       DCX H
              MOV A, L
              ORA A, L
              ORA H
              XRA A
        JNZ LOOP
              RET
```

How many times, loop will be executed?

(a) 16   (b) 10

(c) 1   (d) infinite

67. Which of the following keyboards is the fastest ?

(a) QWERTY   (b) Dvorak

(c) Alphanumeric   (d) Numeric

68. Which of the following grammar is LR (1)?

(a) $A \to a\,A\,a$ (b) $A \to a\,A\,a$

 $A \to b\,A\,b$ $A \to a\,A\,b$

 $A \to a$ $A \to c$

 $A \to b$

(c) $A \to A + A$ (d) both (a) and (b)

 $A \to a$

69. A language L is defined by L = {xn yn | n > 1}. Which of the following definitions generates the same language as L ?

(a) E → xEy | xy   (b) (xy) | (x xyy)

(c) x – y–   (d) All of these

70. A computer sends a message to another computer using odd parity bit with ASCII code. The message 6600 6000 is received. The message

(a) contains 1-bit error

(b) does not contain 1-bit error

(c) contains 3-bit error

(d) may or may not contain 1-bit error

71. The logic expression for output of the circuit given below is

(a) $\overline{A}\,\overline{B}C + CD$

(b) $\overline{A}\,\overline{B}\,\overline{C} + CD$

(c) $ABC + \overline{C}\,\overline{D}$

(d) $\overline{A}\,\overline{B} + \overline{C}\,\overline{D}$

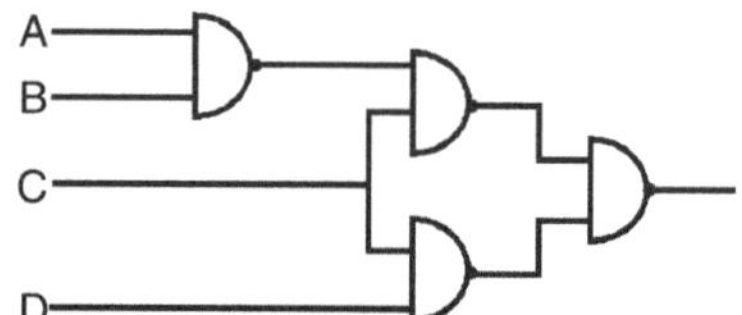

72. The wrost-case noise margin in TTL logic circuit is approximately

(a) 1 mV   (b) 400 mV

(c) 100 mV   (d) 1 V

73. How many full adders are required to construct an m-bit parallel adder ?

(a) m/2   (b) m – 1

(c) m   (d) m + 1

74. The recurrence relation

$$T(n) = m\,T\left(\frac{n}{2}\right) + an^2$$

is satisfied by

(a) $T(n) = O(n^m)$ (b) $T(n) = O(n \log m)$

(c) $T(n) = O(n \log n)$ (d) $T(n) = O(m \log n)$

75. A digital search key is implemented as a tree with n nodes each of which can contain m pointers, corresponding to the m possible symbols in each position of the key. The number of nodes that must be accessed to find a particular tree is

(a) m (b) n

(c) n^m (d) m^n

76. If a numeric field has a width of 5.2, then value of the field could be

(a) 23.10   (b) 121.8

(c) 143.87   (d) both (a) and (b)

77. A good query system

(a) can accept English language commands.

(b) allows non-programmmers to access information stored in a database

(c) can be accessed only by data processing professionals

(d) both (a) and (b)

78. Embedded pointer provides

(a) inverted index

(b) secondary access path

(c) physical record key

(d) all of these

79. Block cache and buffer cache are used

(a) to improve disk performance

(b) to handle interrupts

(c) to increase the capacity of the main memory

(d) to speed up main memory read operation

80. No preemption condition for deadlock exists when

(a) each resources is either currently assigned to exactly one process or is available

(b) process currently holding resources granted earlier can request new resources

(c) resources previously granted cannot be forcibly taken away from a process

(d) there must be circular chain of two or more processes each of which is waiting for a resource held by the next member of chain

ANSWERS

1. (c)	**2.** (d)	**3.** (c)	**4.** (d)	**5.** (b)	**6.** (b)	**7.** (a)	**8.** (c)	**9.** (d)	**10.** (b)
11. (b)	**12.** (a)	**13.** (b)	**14.** (a)	**15.** (a)	**16.** (a)	**17.** (a)	**18.** (a)	**19.** (b)	**20.** (c)
21. (d)	**22.** (a)	**23.** (d)	**24.** (d)	**25.** (a)	**26.** (a)	**27.** (b)	**28.** (c)	**29.** (d)	**30.** (c)
31. (d)	**32.** (c)	**33.** (c)	**34.** (b)	**35.** (d)	**36.** (a)	**37.** (a)	**38.** (b)	**39.** (b)	**40.** (d)
41. (c)	**42.** (c)	**43.** (b)	**44.** (c)	**45.** (b)	**46.** (d)	**47.** (d)	**48.** (b)	**49.** (a)	**50.** (a)
51. (c)	**52.** (a)	**53.** (c)	**54.** (c)	**55.** (c)	**56.** (a)	**57.** (a)	**58.** (d)	**59.** (d)	**60.** (b)
61. (b)	**62.** (a)	**63.** (c)	**64.** (b)	**65.** (b)	**66.** (c)	**67.** (b)	**68.** (b)	**69.** (a)	**70.** (b)
71. (a)	**72.** (b)	**73.** (c)	**74.** (c)	**75.** (a)	**76.** (a)	**77.** (b)	**78.** (b)	**79.** (a)	**80.** (c)

PRACTICE PAPER 3

1. Which of the following is the binary representation of the hexadecimal number 3B7F?
   - (a) 0100 1001 1110 1101
   - (b) 0110 0011 1011 1100
   - (c) 0011 1011 0111 1111
   - (d) 0010 0100 0000 1010

2. Each computer can represent a limited number of real numbers exactly in any floating-point representation. The Alpha computer represents floating-point numbers in normalized, base 2 format shown below :

S	Maintssa	Exponent

0	1	7	8	1	1

   The exponent is biased (excess- 8). What is the approximate relative error of representing the decimal value +0.4 on the Alpha Computer?
   - (a) 0.5%
   - (b) 2.2%
   - (c) 3.8%
   - (d) 5.1%

3. A computer with a 32-bit word size uses 2's complement to represent numbers. The range of integers that can be represented by this computer is
   - (a) -2^{32} to 2^{32}
   - (b) -2^{32} to 2^{31}
   - (c) -2^{31} to $2^{31}-1$
   - (d) -2^{32} to 2^{31}

4. A decimal number has 30 digits. Approximately, how many digits would the binary representation have?
   - (a) 30
   - (b) 60
   - (c) 90
   - (d) 120

5. How many possible bytes have exactly three bits on (i.e. bit = true) ?
   - (a) 8 * 7 * 6
   - (b) 8 × 7
   - (c) 8 × 3
   - (d) 8 × 7 × 3

6. For the circuit, value of input for Y = 0 is
   - (a) 11
   - (b) 10
   - (c) 01
   - (d) 00

7. Which of the following circuits can be used as parallel to serial converter?
   - (a) Multiplexer
   - (b) De-multiplexer
   - (c) Decoder
   - (d) Digital Counter

8. Which of the following ICs has only one NAND gate?
   - (a) 7447
   - (b) 7430
   - (c) 7420
   - (d) 7410

9. Which gate corresponds to the action of parallel switches?
   - (a) AND gate
   - (b) NAND gate
   - (c) OR gate
   - (d) NOR gate

10. Which logic gate is similar to the function of two series switches?
    - (a) OR
    - (b) AND
    - (c) NAND
    - (d) All of these

11. Analog methods are not used for handling extremely precise information because
    - (a) precise information always involves numbers which are inherently digital
    - (b) there are limits to how closely an analog signal can reproduce the information
    - (c) analog information never need to be precise
    - (d) they are very expensive

12. Which of the following is the first integrated logic family?
    - (a) RTL
    - (b) DTL
    - (c) TTL
    - (d) MOS

13. Resistor Ratio is used in linear ICs because
    - (a) ratios increase input resistance
    - (b) ratios increase amplifier gain
    - (c) precise resister values are not possible with IC processes
    - (d) all of these

14. The wrost-case noise margin in TTL logic circuit is approximately
    - (a) 1 mV
    - (b) 400 mV
    - (c) 100 mV
    - (d) 1 V

15. The worst-case noice margin occur with
   (a) small fanout
   (b) full fanout
   (c) no fanout
   (d) none of these

16. Which of the following systems software does the job of merging the records from two files into one?
   (a) Security Software
   (b) Utility Program
   (c) Networking Software
   (d) Documentation System

17. The Principal of Locality of Reference justifies the use of
   (a) Re enterable
   (b) Non reusable
   (c) Virtual Memory
   (d) Cache Memory

18. What is the initial value of the semaphore to allow only one of the many processes to enter their critical section
   (a) 8   (b) 1
   (c) 16   (d) 0

19. Which technique stores a program on disk and then transfers the program into main storage as and when they are needed, is known as
   (a) Spooling   (b) Swapping
   (c) Thrashing   (d) All of the above

20. A data dictionary does not provide information about:
   (a) where data is located
   (b) the size of the disk storage device
   (c) who's owner is responsible for the data
   (d) how the data is used

21. In the DBMS approach, application programs perform the
   (a) Storage function   (b) Processing functions
   (c) Access control   (d) All of the above

22. The Language uses application programs to request data from the DBMS is referred to as the
   (a) DML
   (b) DDL
   (c) Query language
   (d) Any of the above

23. The function of a database is ...
   (a) to check all input data
   (b) the check all spelling
   (c) to collect and organize input data
   (d) to output data

24. Periodically adding, changing and deleting file records is called file
   (a) Updating
   (b) Upgrading
   (c) Restructuring
   (d) History file

25. What is the language used by most of the DBMS's for helping their users to access data ?
   (a) High level language
   (b) Query language
   (c) SQL
   (d) 4 GL

26. The model for a record management system might be
   (a) handwritten list
   (b) a Rolodex Card file
   (c) a business form
   (d) All of the above

27. A record management system
   (a) can handle many files of information at a time
   (b) can be used to extract information stored in a computer file
   (c) always uses a list as its model
   (d) both (a) and (b)

28. When performing a look-up operation using a form
   (a) you enter the search value into the form
   (b) you look at each form sequentially until you see the one you want
   (c) you type the key in an entry line, and the correct form is displayed
   (d) both (b) and (c)

29. A form can be used to
   (a) modify records
   (b) delete records
   (c) format printed output
   (d) all of the above

30. In data-flow diagrams, an originator or receiver of data is usually designated by:

(*a*) a square box (*b*) a circle

(*c*) a rectangle (*d*) an arrow

31. The real "brain" of an artificial Intelligence System is referred to as :

(*a*) bubble memory

(*b*) the expert system

(*c*) natural language interfaces

(*d*) recursive technology

32. An EDP auditors must be an expert in

(*a*) accounting systems

(*b*) system analysis

(*c*) computerized business system

(*d*) computer programming

33. Which of the following is widely used in academic testing ?

(*a*) MICR (*b*) POS

(*c*) OCR (*d*) OMR

34. Data entry can be performed with all of the following except :

(*a*) OCR

(*b*) OMR

(*c*) COM

(*d*) Voice-recognition systems

35. The least expensive OCR units can read

(*a*) hand printed number

(*b*) machine printed number

(*c*) marks

(*d*) handwriting

36. What is the name of the chip which has more than one processor on it ?

(*a*) Parallel chip

(*b*) Multi-processor chip

(*c*) Transputer

(*d*) Parallel Processor

37. Character readers are those devices which read the characters printed on the source documents and then convert them directly into computer usable input. Which of the following is not a character reader ?

(*a*) OCR (*b*) MICR

(*c*) OMR (*d*) LCD

38. The monitor of a computer is connected to it by a

(*a*) cable (*b*) wire

(*c*) bus (*d*) modem

39. Which of the following is classified as an impact printer ?

(*a*) Jet printer (*b*) Daisy wheel printer

(*c*) Thermal printer (*d*) Laser printer

40. What is the name of the printer which print all the A's in a line before all the B's ?

(*a*) Thermal printer

(*b*) Electrostatic printer

(*c*) Line printer

(*d*) Ink-jet printer

41. Which of the following printers cannot print graphics?

(*a*) Ink-jet (*b*) Daisywheel

(*c*) Laser (*d*) Dot-matrix

42. Which part of the diskette should never be touched ?

(*a*) Hub (*b*) mole in the centre

(*c*) oval slot (*d*) corner

43. What is the alternative name for a diskette ?

(*a*) winchester disk

(*b*) flexible disk

(*c*) hard disk

(*d*) floppy disk

44. Which of the following performs modulation and demodulation ?

(*a*) fiber optic (*b*) satellite

(*c*) coaxial cable (*d*) modem

45. A communications device that combines transmissions from several I/O devices into one line is a :

(*a*) concentrator

(*b*) modifier

(*c*) multiplexer

(*d*) full-duplex line

46. Microprogramming is

(*a*) assembly language programming

(*b*) programming of minicomputers

(*c*) control unit programming

(*d*) macroprogramming of microcomputers

47. An example of an analog communication method is
(a) Laser beam
(b) Microwave
(c) Voice grade telephone line
(d) All of the above

48. A hard copy would be prepared on a
(a) Typewriter terminal
(b) Line printer
(c) Plotter
(d) All of the above

49. An example of digital, rather than analog communication is
(a) DDD
(b) DDS
(c) WATS
(d) DDT

50. The OCR reading unit attached to a POS terminal is called a
(a) light pen
(b) warnal
(c) cursor
(d) both (a) and (c)

51. The hexadecimal digits are 1 to 0 and A to
(a) E
(b) F
(c) G
(d) D

52. The main advantage of hexadecimal numbers is the case of conversion from hexadecimal to ...... and vice versa.
(a) decimal
(b) binary
(c) ASCII
(d) BCD

53. A gate is a logic circuit with one or more input signals but how many output signals?
(a) Two
(b) Double
(c) One
(d) More

54. An Inverter is also called which gate?
(a) NOT
(b) OR
(c) AND
(d) NAND

55. Which of the following memory has greater density of storage cells in the same chip area?
(a) Stable MOS RAM
(b) Dynamic MOS RAM
(c) Core memory
(d) All of these

56. Bipolar RAM usually makes use of
(a) TTL high speed circuit
(b) DTL circuit
(c) RTL high speed circuit
(d) none of these

57. The schmitt trigger may be used to
(a) change voltage to corresponding frequency
(b) change frequency to voltage
(c) square slowly varying input
(d) none of these

58. Popular application of flip-flop are
(a) counters
(b) shift registers
(c) transfer register
(d) all of these

59. The heart of any computer is the
(a) CPU
(b) Memory
(c) I/O Unit
(d) Disks

60. A computer consists of
(a) a central processing unit
(b) a memory
(c) input and output units
(d) all of these

61. The hardware in which data may be stored for a computer system is called
(a) register
(b) memory
(c) chip
(d) peripheral

62. Which is the computer memory that does not forget?
(a) RAM
(b) ROM
(c) DRAM
(d) SRAM

63. How many modes of operation are there in 8255 PPI?
(a) 1
(b) 2
(c) 3
(d) 4

64. The RST 5.5 Interrupt Service routine starts from location
(a) 0020 H
(b) 0024 H
(c) 0028 H
(d) 002C H

65. Advantage of magnetic input media is
(a) high speed
(b) flexibility in accessing data
(c) low cost
(d) all of these

66. Which of the following is not one of the three primary functions that on-line direct access system can serve?
(a) Inquiry
(b) Back-up
(c) Update
(d) Programming

67. Compiler is a program that

(a) places programs into memory and prepares them for execution

(b) automates the translation of assembly language into machine language

(c) accepts a program written in a high level language and produces an object program

(d) appears to execute a source program as if it were machine language

68. Loader is a program that

(a) places programs into memory and prepares them for execution

(b) automates the translation of assembly language into machine language

(c) accepts a program written in a high level language and produces an object program

(d) appears to execute a source program as if it were machine language

69. A programming language is to be designed to run on a machine that does not have a big memory. The language should

(a) prefer a 2 pass compiler to a 1 pass compiler

(b) prefer an interpreter to a compiler

(c) not support recursion

(d) all of these

70. The number of edges in a regular graph of degree d and n vertices is

(a) maximum of n, d (b) $n + d$

(c) nd (d) $nd/2$

71. Which of the following sets of component (s) is/are sufficient to implement any arbitrary boolean function ?

(a) XOR gates, NOT gates

(b) 2 to 1 multiplexors

(c) AND gates, XOR gates

(d) Three-input gates that output $(A . B) + C$ for the inputs A. B. and C.

72. The dynamic race hazard problem occurs in

(a) combination circuits only

(b) sequential circuits only

(c) both (a) and (b)

(d) none of these

73. The word processing task associated with changing the appearance of document is

(a) writing   (b) formatting

(c) editing   (d) storing

74. Which of the following coded enteries are used to control access to computer ?

(a) Code words   (b) Passwords

(c) Binary pass   (d) ASCII codes

75. The CPU after receiving an interrupt from an I/O device

(a) hands over control of address bus and data bus to the interrupting device

(b) halts for a predetermined time

(c) branches off to the interrupt service routine immediately

(d) branches off to the interrupt service routine after completion of the current instruction

76. Microprogram is

(a) name of source program in micro computers

(b) set of instructions indicating the primitive operations in a system

(c) primitive form of macros used in assembly language programming

(d) program of very small size

77. Device independence

(a) allows the computer to run without I/O devices

(b) allows programs to be written much more easily

(c) makes all devices look the same to the operating system

(d) allows tape drives to be substituted for disk drives

78. Multiple repeaters in communication satellites are called

(a) detector

(b) modulator

(c) transponders

(d) stations

79. Baseband is

(a) transmission of signals without modulation

(b) a signal all of whose energy is contained within a finite frequency range

(c) simultaneous transmission of data to a number of stations

(d) all of these

80. Binding can't be done

(a) when separately compiled modules are being linked together

(b) during loading

(c) while writing a program

(d) both (b) and (c) above

ANSWERS

1. (b)	**2.** (b)	**3.** (c)	**4.** (c)	**5.** (b)	**6.** (a)	**7.** (a)	**8.** (b)	**9.** (c)	**10.** (b)
11. (b)	**12.** (a)	**13.** (c)	**14.** (b)	**15.** (b)	**16.** (b)	**17.** (d)	**18.** (b)	**19.** (b)	**20.** (b)
21. (b)	**22.** (a)	**23.** (c)	**24.** (a)	**25.** (b)	**26.** (d)	**27.** (b)	**28.** (a)	**29.** (d)	**30.** (b)
31. (b)	**32.** (c)	**33.** (d)	**34.** (c)	**35.** (c)	**36.** (c)	**37.** (d)	**38.** (a)	**39.** (b)	**40.** (c)
41. (b)	**42.** (c)	**43.** (d)	**44.** (d)	**45.** (c)	**46.** (c)	**47.** (d)	**48.** (d)	**49.** (b)	**50.** (b)
51. (b)	**52.** (b)	**53.** (c)	**54.** (a)	**55.** (a)	**56.** (a)	**57.** (c)	**58.** (d)	**59.** (a)	**60.** (d)
61. (b)	**62.** (b)	**63.** (c)	**64.** (d)	**65.** (d)	**66.** (d)	**67.** (c)	**68.** (a)	**69.** (d)	**70.** (d)
71. (b,c)	**72.** (d)	**73.** (b)	**74.** (b)	**75.** (d)	**76.** (b)	**77.** (b)	**78.** (c)	**79.** (a)	**80.** (d)

Printed by Libri Plureos GmbH in Hamburg,
Germany